The Green PC

The GREEN PC

Practical Choices That Make a Difference

Revised & Expanded

2nd Edition

Steven Anzovin

Windcrest®/McGraw-Hill

New York San Francisco Washington, D.C. Auckland Bogotá Caracas Lisbon London Madrid Mexico City Milan Montreal New Delhi San Juan Singapore Sydney Tokyo Toronto

Printed in Canada

Printed by Webcom Ltd., on 100% recycled and recycleable paper, containing 75% postconsumer waste. The paper exceeds both Canadian ECP (Environmental Choice Program) and American EPA (Environmental Protection Agency) standards for recycled fiber content. The ink is water- and vegetable-based, and the printing process uses nonheat-set presses, which release less volatile organic compounds into the atmosphere than conventional printing presses.

Published by Windcrest, an imprint of McGraw-Hill, Inc.
The name "Windcrest" is a registered trademark of McGraw-Hill, Inc.

pbk 1 2 3 4 5 6 7 8 9 0 WEB/WEB 9 9 8 7 6 5 4

Library of Congress Cataloging-in-Publication Data

Anzovin, Steven.
The green PC : practical choices that make a difference / by Steven Anzovin.—2nd ed.
p. cm.
Includes index.
ISBN 0-07-003007-3
1. Microcomputers. 2. Microcomputers—Environmental aspects--Citizen participation. I. Title.
QA76.5.A55 1994 94-15519
004.16—dc20 CIP

Acquisitions editor: Jennifer Holt DiGiovanna
Editorial team: Robert E. Ostrander, Executive Editor
Sally Anne Glover, Book Editor
Production team: Katherine G. Brown, Director
Ollie Harmon, Coding
Wanda S. Ditch, Desktop Operator
Nadine McFarland, Quality Control
Jodi L. Tyler, Indexer
Design team: Jaclyn J. Boone, Designer
Brian Allison, Associate Designer
Cover design by Lori E. Schlosser
Cover photograph © Charles Campbell/Westlight
Back cover copy by Cathy Mentzer

WK2
0030073

To Rafael, Miriam, Hannah, and the world they will inherit.

"Turn it over and over because everything is in it.
And reflect upon it and grow old and worn in it and do not leave it,
For you have no better lot than that."

Ethics of the Fathers

Contents

Acknowledgments

Many people contributed their time, effort, and knowledge to help make the first and second editions of this book possible: Diane Kopperman Podell, B. Davis Schwartz Library, C.W. Post University, who provided fast, fast, fast research assistance; Linda Latham and Brian J. Johnson, Global Change Division, Office of Air and Radiation, Environmental Protection Agency, for information on Energy Star; Ted Smith, founder of the Silicon Valley Toxics Coalition, for invaluable background material on pollution in the computer industry; Alex Randall of the East-West Educational Development Foundation; nomadic technologist Steven Roberts; Phil Blaisdell, environmental research specialist at PC Connection-MacConnection; Jim Davis, senior technical staff, IBM, Boca Raton, for his history of Energy Star and the PS/2 E; Royce Green, whose analysis of CRT power use was helpful, as was Ian Gilman's information on telecommuting; RobertR71, for his informative harangues on computer longevity; and Dan Lombardo, for his unflagging enthusiasm for this project.

For their help on various aspects of this book, I also want to thank: Rob Beal, Green Seal, Washington, D.C.; John Young, Worldwatch Institute; Jan Gable, Computer and Business Equipment Manufacturing Association (CBMA); Amy Perry, Massachusetts

Recycling Initiative Campaign; Mark Fournier and Dick Nathorst, Physical Plant, University of Massachusetts, Amherst; Robert G. Chaplick, Wheaton, Maryland; Bruce Marchesani, Lyndhurst, New Jersey; Willow Ann Solow, National Association for Humane and Environmental Education; Prof. Armand Gilinsky, California State University, Hayward; Sue Hugus, Massachusetts Library Association; Doug Seale, Boston Computer Society Environmental SIG; Don Lesser and Sandy Wise at the Pioneer Valley Personal Computer Users' Group.

Netters who offered ideas or comments include: RandyD15, SprtanBndo, Fredri5331, Eucephalus, RightWing4, Lizard NYC, Ozone1, Toner King, ELBB, MacMan24, BrianTTS (Brian Lowry), Rluhn (aka PCW Luhn), GStiek, RobertR71, MikeM61443, and John Moulder; also Don Rittner, head of America Online's Environmental forum.

People in the computer and environmental remediation industries who also contributed: Judy Tarabini and Kathy Kruse, Adobe Systems; Marianne L. Lettieri, Apple Computer, Inc.; Jeff Donn, Associated Press; Bill Franklin III, B&B Electronics; Dave Rohr, Brant Publications; David Stephenson, Brodeur and Partners; Jan Gable, Computer Business Equipment Manufacturers Association (CBEMA); Jill Sporleder, Public Relations, and Dayle Smitt, environmental research specialist, Dialog Information Services; Jeff Gelder and P.J. Grimes, Earthbeat; Rachel Hassard and Nicole Noland, Electronic Arts; Peter M. Smeets, French International Inc.; Brian Doyle, IBM Corp.; Ken Bissell, Lexmark Corp.; Ray Emery, David Purvis, and Anne Rupley, Microsoft Corporation; Christine O'Connell, MicroTech; Linda Pendergast, Miller Communications; Michelle C. Hartzell, NoRad Corp.; Norm England, Portable Rechargeable Battery Association (PRBA); the staff of Real Goods, Ukiah, California; and Kip Walls, Toshiba America Information Systems.

My thanks to these organizations: The American Paper Institute; the Association for Information and Image Management; BIS Strategic Decisions, Norwell, Massachusetts; the Council on Office Products Energy Efficiency (COPEE); Datek Information Services, Waltham, Massachusetts; EDI, Spread the Word!, Dallas, Texas; the Electric Power Research Institute (EPRI); the Energy Information

Administration, U.S. Department of Energy; the Global Action and Information Network; LINK Resources, New York; Mail Boxes, Etc.; New England Anti-Vivisection Society; the Society for Plastics Industry/Partnership for Plastics Progress.

And, most importantly, my thanks to Janet Podell for her editing genius, diligent fact-checking, wise advice, and loving support. This book could never have been completed without her help.

Introduction
to the second edition

Since the publication of *The Green PC: Making Choices That Make a Difference* less than two years ago, green computing has become a familiar computer-industry buzzword. All the major computer magazines, and even a few environmental periodicals, have published at least one article on the subject. New publications, on paper and online, are springing up to cover this expanding field. Dozens of computer companies are scrambling to develop and market green products, from Energy-Star-compliant PCs to screen-saver software that flashes ecologically correct messages. The first computer trade show devoted exclusively to green computing products and services is scheduled for fall 1994.

The green computing movement now has a life and a momentum of its own. To continue its usefulness, the second edition of *The Green PC* has been updated to incorporate the latest research, user tips, and business resources.

In addition to the minor revisions that can be found on nearly every page of this book, several chapters have been substantially revised. Chapter 3 covers PC energy consumption in greater depth, with new statistics that reflect the great amount of research in this area since the first edition. The new chapter 4 has much more on Energy Star, including a list of companies with Energy-Star-compliant products. Chapter 5 has new material on universal digital documents, as well as e-journals, CD-ROM publishing, and electronic publishing in general. Recycling PCs is covered in more depth in chapter 6. Chapter 9 features a more balanced discussion of EMF pollution, incorporating the most recently published research. Chapter 12 includes a greatly expanded list of green bulletin boards, online forums, and research databases, including new EPA contact information.

I hope that the second edition of *The Green PC* continues to be a useful tool for anyone who is looking for real-world, money-saving ways to reduce the environmental impact of computing. Please e-mail me with your comments and suggestions for making future editions even more useful. My e-mail address is: ANZOVIN@aol.com

About this book

Each chapter in *The Green PC* provides in-depth coverage of a particular area of green computing. Included are up-to-date descriptions of products and addresses of organizations and businesses that can help you attain your environmental goals. End-of-chapter checklists detail specific green-computing practices you can adopt. Many of these come from suggestions posted on electronic bulletin boards and online services by computer users like yourself.

Chapter 1 describes the environmental impact of personal computing on the world and provides a definition of green computing. Chapter 2 shows how to choose new green hardware and how to save plastic and money by squeezing more performance from your present hardware setup. Power computing with less electrical power is the subject of chapter 3. Energy Star, the U.S. government's power-efficient computing initiative, is the subject of chapter 4.

Chapter 5 covers ways to eliminate the paper blizzard by tapping into the power of networks, e-mail, fax, OCR, digital documents, and paperless computing systems. Chapter 6 provides dozens of tips on how to recycle paper, floppy disks, ribbons, toner cartridges, and other computer consumables, as well as how to recycle, sell, and donate PCs and software.

Telecommuting is one of the growing trends in the workplace. Chapter 7 has valuable information on the environmental benefits of telecommuting and how to get your organization to start a telecommuting program. You, the computer user, are the part of the environment most immediately and most strongly affected by your PC. Chapter 8 covers the basics of designing a comfortable, productive, and healthy workstation. Chapter 9 describes workplace computing hazards and pollutants, both chemical and electronic. Chapter 10 discusses pollution problems in the computer industry and what some firms are doing to clean up their acts.

Chapter 11 reviews PC games and simulations that educate about environmental problems. Chapter 12 lists online resources, databases, news services, and CD-ROMs essential for the work of PC environmentalists. Chapter 13 covers finding green computer vendors and services and becoming a green computing consumer. The last chapter suggests how to use your PC as a tool of environmental advocacy.

Revised introduction to the first edition

There are about 140 million personal computers in the world today, and the people who use them are among the most highly educated on earth. They have an active interest in world problems, including the progressive deterioration of the earth's environment. Often, computer users who support environmental action at home, in their communities, and at work treat computing as a benign technology that has little or no impact on the environment. Some wasted printer paper here, a toner cartridge thrown away there, a few extra kilowatt-hours on your electric bill. All pretty innocent.

But multiply those few pages, toner cartridges, and watts by 140 million, and the impact suddenly becomes much larger. In fact, computers contribute to processes that increase atmospheric pollution, destroy the ozone layer, pour toxic chemicals into the water, and create millions of tons of toxic solid waste that cannot be recycled. And, because the number of computers in the world doubles every few years, that impact is growing exponentially.

The computer industry and computer users in general have recently started worrying about the environmental impact of computing. This change of mind has been spurred not only by concern for the earth, but also by such immediate economic problems as high power expenses related to computers; the high cost of paper and other computer consumables; rising health costs due in part to unhealthy, uncomfortable computer workstations; and the pollution and solid-waste problems caused by the manufacture and disposal of computer equipment.

This same idea has been attracting the growing numbers of individual PC users who want to minimize the damage that computers cause to the environment. But that's hard to do without access to practical information. And until now, very little material has been available to help PC users evaluate the possibilities and decide what they can reasonably do.

The Green PC: Making Choices that Make a Difference presents a wide range of possible actions. Many of them are matters of conservation, requiring a simple change of habit. They are easy to implement, easy to follow, and immediately effective. Others require a degree of technical know-how or a substantial commitment of time or money. The idea is to take what you can use from this book and consult its recommendations whenever you have an opportunity to make a decision. *The Green PC* will show you how to:

- Squeeze more from your existing hardware.
- Reduce your use of electricity.
- Create a (virtually) paperless office.
- Recycle consumables, PCs, and peripherals.
- Purchase used equipment.
- Design a more healthful computing environment.
- Reduce computer-generated pollutants and hazards in the workplace.

- Find software that conserves resources, time, and power.
- Tap into online sources of environmental information.
- Use modems, networks, and telecommuting to save gas and lessen air pollution.
- Use your computer as a tool of environmental advocacy.

I hope that *The Green PC* will stimulate new ideas on conserving energy and supplies at your workplace and help businesses meet their environmental goals. But this book is aimed at all computer users, not just those in organizations. Even if you use your computer at home for little more than playing games, you can adopt simple green-computing habits that will help to keep your planet healthy and your wallet a little fuller.

Can green computing really make a difference? Yes. Everything you do makes a difference in the long run. As the sages say, "In accord with the effort is the reward." This book can help you get started.

1

PCs & the earth

CHAPTER 1

DAY IN AND DAY OUT, millions of computers whir away, digesting the world's data streams and turning them into information. Every day, thousands of new computers come online, feeding on infinite oceans of data.

According to recent estimates by the U.S. government, Dataquest, and other statistics providers, there are about 140 million personal computers in the world today. That's about 1 PC for every 40 human beings on earth. A decade ago, there was about 1 PC for every 800 people. Ten years before that, the ratio of PCs to human beings was perhaps 1 to 100 million. Fifty years ago, computers didn't even exist.

And ten years from now? If things continue as they're going, half the people on earth will own or have daily access to a PC, and computer networks will have spread to every corner of the globe. Soon after, computers will outnumber us. In fact, they'll become the most numerous human-made devices on earth, embedded in almost every gadget and machine we make, dominating all other industries: transportation, telecommunications, manufacturing, health care. Computers will drive our technical, social, and popular culture like no innovation since the discovery of fire. Much of our effort and ingenuity, and many of the resources that we derive from the earth, will be directed to keeping PCs fed, fit, and functioning. If you doubt this, just consider that the computer and electronics sector is already the biggest single industry in the U.S. economy, according to a 1992 report by the research group Cahners Economics.

That future will be on us quickly enough, whether we're ready for it or not. We aren't ready now; but we can be.

What PCs are doing to the earth

To take responsibility for our use of computers, we have to know how PCs affect the earth. Many people think that the environmental impact of personal computers is negligible. PCs don't spew pollutants into the air like cars or send toxic waste into rivers like manufacturing plants. But that view of computing is shortsighted. After all, no PC is an island. Without constantly drawing on the earth's resources, computers can do nothing. PC electronics consume electrical power; disk drives need floppy disks; printers need paper, ribbons, and other supplies; the telephone net has to be running and accessible for network access, and so on. And you have to sit there in front of the computer, often for many hours a day.

Let's take a closer look at the environmental resources that PCs command. For the purposes of the following discussion, I'm defining a PC in terms of what is on most desks today: a 486-class or mid-range Macintosh central processing unit (CPU) with a hard drive and a floppy drive, one expansion card, a 14-inch color monitor (CRT), and a personal laser printer.

A mountain of computers

The typical desktop PC weighs about 80 pounds. (Keep in mind this is an average; the mostly metal Macintosh with a 16-inch monitor and laser printer on my desk tips the scales at a portly 107 pounds, and a typical notebook PC plus portable inkjet printer weighs in at about 12 pounds.) Of that total, about 35 pounds are various plastics, 25 pounds are metals, and about 20 pounds are glass, ceramics, and assorted other materials. These proportions vary among makes and models of PCs.

Sooner rather than later, all current PCs will have outlived their usefulness and will be discarded. Worldwide, they'll make nearly 10 billion pounds of solid waste—the weight of a good-sized meteor. Studies confirm that computers pose an increasing solid-waste disposal problem. "Environmental Consciousness: A Strategic Competitiveness Issue for the Electronics and Computer Industry," a report that included an evaluation of PC solid waste, was published in March 1993 by the U.S. Department of Energy and the Microelectronics and Computer Technology Corporation. Author Robert Ferrone, a consultant for Digital Equipment Corporations's Environmental Division, and his colleagues calculated that an estimated 150 million PCs will require disposal by the year 2005. They will make a mighty mountain of electronic waste one acre in area and 3.5 miles high (or fill a hole 3.5 miles deep). The disposal cost will be more than one billion dollars.

The volume of PC waste is one problem; the toxicity of it is another. The entire "life-cycle pollution" of every PC—the solid waste and pollution created as a by-product of mining the raw materials, manufacturing it, marketing and distributing it, using it, and disposing of it—involves scores of toxic and hazardous substances. Manufacturing a PC alone can require 100 different toxic substances, some of which end up in the finished product. (For more on toxins in the computer industry, see chapter 10.)

Although some parts of a PC can be and often are recycled, eventually all will end up in landfills. The metal parts will oxidize over decades, the glass will crumble into sand over centuries, and the plastic parts will last essentially unchanged for millennia. Some components, such as batteries and monitors, contain toxic materials that can leach into the soil.

If PCs are incinerated rather than buried, their plastics and other materials will add tons of toxic materials to the atmosphere. The ash that remains after incineration might contain toxic waste, and it still has to be dumped in a landfill. By the way, it's consumers, not PC manufacturers, who pay for PCs' life-cycle pollution through taxes and municipal landfill fees.

PCs have a shorter useful life than many other types of machinery. Many owners, anxious to keep up with the latest advances in hardware, discard their PCs after every major computing innovation. Most PCs purchased today are replacements for older models. Those obsolete PCs enter the solid waste stream in distinct waves every three years or so, and the interval between waves is shortening. Computers introduced only two years ago, like those based on 80386 and 68030 chips, are now seen as pitifully inadequate. Manufacturers add to the problem by pushing consumers to replace their machines whenever a new generation of CPU emerges, but so far computer companies have taken little responsibility for the waste problem that results.

A flood of power

According to the U.S. Environmental Protection Agency, a typical PC (that's CPU, color CRT, and laser printer combined), consumes 235 watts of power during normal operation. A PC operating for the typical 8-hour workday, 240 workdays per year, consumes 451 kilowatt-hours (kWh) of electricity annually. (A *kilowatt-hour* is a measure of electricity use equal to the amount of energy consumed by a 100-watt bulb operating for ten hours.) However, again according to studies by the EPA, about 40% of PCs are in operation 24 hours per day, 365 days per year. Each of those PCs consumes 2059 kWh per year. Taken together, the world's PCs will consume about 153 billion kWh this year, with the energy consumed increasing as the number of PCs increase. That doesn't include the energy it takes to manufacture, deliver, and recycle or dispose of the PCs.

To provide that amount of electrical power will require the burning of almost 77 million tons of coal this year (burning one pound of coal yields one kilowatt-hour of energy), or some 4.2 billion gallons of fuel oil (burning a gallon of oil yields 36.6 kilowatt-hours of electricity at current levels of combustion efficiency). It would take a flotilla of 420 oil tankers, each carrying 10 million gallons, to transport all that oil.

The combustion of 4.2 billion gallons of fuel oil releases some 164 million tons of carbon dioxide into the atmosphere every year; converting fuel oil to electricity releases approximately 2.14 pounds of carbon dioxide for every kilowatt-hour generated. That's more than ¾ of 1% of the annual 20 billion tons of CO_2 emissions worldwide from all industrial, resource management, and agricultural activity. Not quite at the level of emissions from automobiles, but not bad for an invention that didn't exist 20 years ago. And that percentage is growing. If things go on as they have, it will double within ten years.

Scientists who subscribe to the idea that the earth's atmosphere is gradually rising in temperature due to human activity (the theory of global warming) point to increasing levels of carbon dioxide as the factor most responsible. In addition, burning coal releases sulfur dioxides, the main cause of acid rain. If the electricity needed for computers were to be generated by nuclear power, many tons of radioactive material would be added to the world's nuclear waste disposal problem. In short, there is no way to power the world's PCs without adding significantly to the world's pollution problems.

In the U.S. today, it costs about seven cents on the average to generate one kWh, according to the U.S. Department of Energy's Energy Information Center. Using that figure as a basis, the annual cost to generate all the power to run all the PCs in the world is almost $11 billion. As a point of comparison, that's more money than the gross national product of most African nations. It's also far more than the United States spends each year on alternative energy research.

Computers now use about 50% of the energy consumed by office equipment. That percentage will rise in the future as computers continue to replace older types of office machinery. (For more details on PCs and power, see chapters 3 and 4.)

180 million trees a year

Paper is the major PC "consumable." (A *consumable*, in computer jargon, is any product that's consumed in the process of computing. Pizza, cheese puffs, and Jolt cola aren't included.) No one knows exactly how many pieces of paper are fed into computer printers every year, but it's possible to make some guesses.

According to a 1992 report of the Association for Information and Image Management, about one trillion sheets of paper are used by American business each year. Today, nearly every piece of paper is run through a computer-controlled printer of some kind. The U.S. accounts for 35% of the world computer market, according to a 1993 International Data Corporation report. So, even if we assume that Americans use 50% of the world's business paper, that means that about 2 trillion sheets of computer paper are used for business worldwide each year, or about 4 billion 500-sheet reams.

A ream of letter-sized paper weighs about 5 pounds, so those 4 billion reams of letter-sized paper weigh about 10 million tons. Paper manufacturers estimate that it takes about 18 trees to make 1 ton of paper. Therefore, 180 million trees, or more than 4,000 square miles of forest (an area about the size of Jamaica), must be cut down each year to feed the world's computer printers. Not all of this forest is replanted and managed; unplanted areas erode and become useless for forestry or agriculture.

Paper manufacturing is among the most wasteful and polluting of industries. Each year, the paper-making process consumes millions of kilowatt-hours of energy. Making a ton of paper requires 7,000 gallons of water, which when discharged contains dioxin and other hazardous chemicals. It also adds 60 pounds of air pollutants to the atmosphere. All told, about 600 million pounds of pollutants are discharged annually into the air just for the paper used by computers, or roughly 20 pounds every second.

Discarded paper composes nearly half of the solid waste stream in the United States. Some papers can take decades to decompose. The EPA estimates that half the landfills in the United States will have to be closed by 1997, and they will have been filled mainly with discarded paper. (Conserving and recycling paper are covered in chapters 5 and 6.)

Floppies outnumber us

PCs might eat a lot of paper, but that isn't their only source of nourishment. The list of PC support and waste products is long—from the cardboard boxes, polystyrene foam inserts, and bags in which the machines are packed, to the manuals, software documentation, and warranty cards that many of us never even read. Let's take a close look at the most inconsequential-seeming consumable—the blank floppy disk.

All PCs use floppy disks, and all floppy disks need stick-on paper labels; the old 5.25-inch flexible variety also require plastic or paper sleeves. (For now, we won't factor in the sealed disk envelope, manuals, warranty cards, quick-start cards, catalogs, plastic inserts, cardboard boxes, and shrink-wrap packed with commercial software programs.) If you assume that every PC on earth is equipped with just 50 floppy disks, including applications disks and backups, that makes 6.5 billion floppy disks and 6.5 billion little paper labels waiting to be discarded. That's more floppy disks than there are people in the world. If three floppy disks weigh about an ounce, then the weight of all those floppy disks is 135 million pounds.

And that's just the floppy disks that people actually own. In 1990, disk makers sold one billion floppies, and you can assume that at least the same number are on dealers' shelves and in warehouses worldwide waiting to be sold today. Blank disks are packaged ten to a box in about one square foot of cardboard and 0.5 square feet of plastic shrink-wrap. Also included in the box is a 0.3 square-foot sheet of labels on nonrecyclable waxed paper, and a disk sleeve for each disk at 0.1 square-feet each. One hundred million boxes of blank disks waiting to be sold are composed of:

- 21 million pounds of disks.
- 2.8 square miles of polyethylene or Tyvek™ disk sleeves.
- 3.6 square miles of cardboard.
- 1.3 square miles of shrink-wrap.
- 1 square mile of disk labels.

That's about enough packaging material to cover the typical suburban town. The labels alone would paper over New York's financial district. And, of course, disk makers usually put other things in the box, anything from discount coupons to scratch-off sweepstakes entry cards.

All of the packaging is discarded soon after purchase. The disks themselves can be used many times, of course, and most people do reuse them. But sooner or later they develop disk errors and become useless. Dead floppies can't be recycled, so they all end up in landfills, where they'll last for centuries. (See chapter 6 for hints on floppy conservation.)

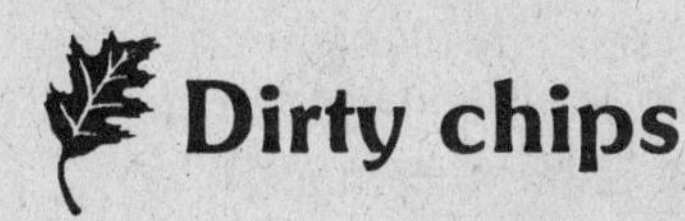

Dirty chips

You've seen that the world's computers do indeed have an impact on the earth, and one that's growing every year. But what about the computer manufacturing industry itself? Most of us have an image of computers being manufactured in dust-free labs and spotless robot factories, all located in beautiful industrial parks. The reality, however, isn't so pristine.

According to a 1992 report by the Silicon Valley Toxics Coalition, the microchip manufacturing process involves many substances that are toxic—most of them organic solvents and gases that are difficult to handle and dispose of safely. The accidental release of just one cylinder of arsine gas, a common dopant used in the manufacture of semiconductors, could kill hundreds of people over an area of several square blocks.

Since 1981, more than 100 known toxic chemicals have been spilled in and around Silicon Valley, center of the U.S. semiconductor industry. Today the Valley area has the highest density of Federal Superfund sites of any county in the United States. Well-known polluters include IBM, Hewlett-Packard, Intel, and the U.S. Navy.

Worker health in the industry is also a problem. So-called "clean rooms" are kept dust-free to produce flawless microchips, but they can also be contaminated with toxic solvent vapors that are hazardous to the workers. Workers are routinely exposed to small amounts of hazardous chemicals, many of which are classified as carcinogens (cancer-causing agents) or teratogens (reproductive toxins) by the Environmental Protection Agency.

An internal study conducted by Digital Equipment Corporation in 1986 found that the miscarriage rate among female employees who worked with solvents and other chemicals was double that of female clerical employees. Overall, the electronics manufacturing industry has a worker illness rate three times that of other manufacturing industries.

Such problems aren't confined to Silicon Valley. There are dozens of electronics industry centers in the United States. Mexico, Ireland, Malaysia, Taiwan, Korea, Singapore, and Japan all have thriving semiconductor industries. Many U.S. firms have moved their electronics manufacturing operations to developing countries where wages are low and pollution laws don't exist or enforcement is lax. (See chapter 10 for more details on the computer industry's efforts to clean up.)

The unhealthy PC

Your PC can also have a direct effect on you. Computing isn't as safe for users as it might appear. Only in the past few years have experts acknowledged that computing might actually be a health hazard.

A computer can't adapt itself to you, so you must adapt yourself to it. You wear out your eyes staring at a poorly lit screen, and you strain your neck and back working in a fixed, unnatural position for long hours. Your forearms, wrists, and hands might suffer from new types of strain injuries that are very difficult to treat and can eventually render you unable to work. Many employers and insurers, mindful of lost profits if the scope of computer-related strain injuries were more widely known, deny the very existence of the problem. All the while, PCs emit electromagnetic radiation whose long-term health effects aren't yet understood.

Potentially, the health problems associated with PCs could affect each owner of one of the world's 140 million PCs—that is, one person out of every 40 people in the world. (Chapter 8 looks at the problem of PCs and health and offers some simple solutions; chapter 9 discusses PCs and electromagnetic pollution.)

Green computing

So the effect of personal computers on the earth isn't negligible after all. PCs are fueled by immense quantities of fuel and fed by millions of trees. They generate millions of tons of waste. The electronics manufacturing industry is a heavy polluter, and even you, the individual computer user, can be exposed to PC-related health risks. No, the PC isn't yet as big an environmental problem as the car. But the number of PCs in the world is growing rapidly. Computer chips already outnumber cars.

Radical environmentalists claim that the computer is a symbol of what's wrong with our technology, our society, and our attitude towards the earth, just as much as the gas-burning car and nuclear power plant. It's hypocritical, they argue, to claim that computers can be used in an environmentally responsible way; no product of high technology can possibly be harmless, and all should be eliminated. So the best thing you could do for the earth is toss your computer into the recycling bin, along with your car, your refrigerator, your television set, and your microwave oven.

This radical environmentalist position might, in theory, be best for the earth, but it isn't one that's likely to be heeded by many people today. Most of us will never give up our PCs, much less the rest of modern civilization. Computers are integral to our work, vital to managing our complex society, and just too much fun to forego. Like the automobile and the refrigerator, the PC is an empowering invention, one that gives us new freedoms that, once tasted, are difficult to live without. For good or ill, PCs are here to stay.

For most people, there's no going back to a pretechnological existence. That doesn't mean that we bear no responsibility for the way we use (and are used by) technology, especially computers. At the beginning of the automotive era, few people had the foresight to plan for what the widespread use of cars would do to our world. The result is that cars have profoundly reshaped our society, not necessarily for the better, and they have changed the face of the earth, definitely for the worse. We can learn from that experience and plan now to control the environmental effects of the widespread use of computers.

And there are good reasons to set computers apart from other products of high technology. Unlike cars and nuclear power plants, computers can emulate and replace a wide range of other technologies at less cost to the environment. For example, working at home and sending computer files by modem to your office is more environmentally benign (as well as more healthy and more satisfying) than commuting to work three hours a day by car (a topic discussed in chapter 7).

Computers can also be used to solve environmental problems. To take one example, environmental researchers can use PCs to model the spread of toxic wastes in a river and thus anticipate, cope with, and reduce environmental hazards. And students can be taught about environmental problems with computer simulations that provide an unequalled view of the ecological "big picture" (as explained in chapter 12).

Used responsibly and creatively, PCs could help preserve the global environment, not despoil it. But first we need to change the way we think about computers by weighing the environmental consequences of every computing choice we make. That is, we need to do not only productive computing, but also "green computing."

The concept of green computing can be reduced to three simple principles:

- Use computing resources efficiently.
- Reduce computing waste.
- Use PCs to communicate and educate about the environment.

If these three ideas are applied to every area of PC use, they can't help but make a major difference to our computing habits and to the earth.

Going green

The effort to reduce the environmental harm of computing has to start with each of us. That doesn't mean you have to completely change the way you use your PC, much less your way of life. All that's needed is to make a succession of small adjustments to your computing habits. Start small; small changes quickly add up.

Here's an example. Begin by shutting off your computer during your lunch hour. If every computer user in the world shut off his or her PC for just one additional hour a day, it would save 216 million gallons of fuel oil or more than 7.9 billion pounds of coal, and it would keep as much as 17 billion pounds of additional carbon dioxide out of the atmosphere.

Green computing can also save money. That same hour per day costs nothing to implement and, at seven cents per kilowatt-hour, would save four dollars in electricity per PC per year. Okay, that's not even a decent business lunch, but a large corporation with 1,000 PCs would save $4,000. City, state, and federal agencies, with their hundreds of thousands of PCs, would save tens of thousands of your tax dollars in unnecessary electrical bills. Imagine the savings if each PC user conserved not just one hour of power per day, but 17 hours per day—lunch hour and all night—for the expenditure of nothing but the effort to flick a switch a few more times.

Short-term monetary gain shouldn't be the only reason to take on green computing, however. Some green PC choices, such as using only 100% recycled paper stock, might initially cost money. Consider the overall cost, not just to you or your organization, but to society and the environment as a whole.

Hard choices

Environmental issues are complex, especially as they apply to high technology such as PCs. With little collective experience in green computing to guide us, we're still feeling out the answers to difficult questions. In deciding what course of action is best for the environment, you'll often have to weigh contradictory benefits, and occasionally there will be no right decision. Here's an example of the kinds of real choices you might have to make:

Every week, you want to distribute a 10,000-word report to 100 business associates around the world. You can print 100 copies of the 40-page report and mail it to the 100 coworkers, or you can send it instantly through the global computer network via electronic mail. From the strictly environmental point of view, the e-mail method is more environmentally benign. Every week, it saves 4,000 sheets of paper, 100 envelopes, 100 stamps, 100 mailing labels, and all the resources needed to get those envelopes to their destinations. But there's a health cost. Extensive use of e-mail requires your coworkers to work in front of their PCs more than before, risking strain and stress disorders and exposing themselves to unknown radiation hazards from their PC monitors. So which do you choose: environmental benefit or human health?

One answer is to choose both: send documents by e-mail and other paperless technologies to save paper, but also install low-emission, high-resolution computer monitors and ergonomic workstation furniture for coworkers to preserve their health. But this course entails new environmental consequences and new decisions. For one thing, you'll have to purchase new computer hardware manufactured by industries that are notable polluters. And what will you do with the old monitors and furniture? How will you dispose of the packaging of the new monitors, which includes polystyrene foam?

There are no easy answers. It is tempting to ignore the whole issue of environmental responsibility as just too difficult or expensive. That simply puts off problems until they are much harder to solve. Inaction is much worse than having to deal with new problems. Conversely, trying to solve all possible problems can result in complete paralysis and despair. Take the time to educate yourself in the wider implications of the problem at hand. Think through your proenvironment actions as far as possible, looking at long-range effects, not just the immediate ones. Thorough analysis takes time, but in the long run it saves time, resources, and money.

Make a start now with the simplest and easiest measures, keeping in mind that no one solution can solve all problems. And stay flexible. Change your green computing strategies as new information about the environment becomes known and as your own needs change.

Once you've begun, take on more as your commitment increases and as you see for yourself the economic and environmental benefits of green computing. This book will give you the tools and information you need to begin.

Choices that make a difference

Here are ten basic green-PC principles to guide your decisions:

- ❐ Consider the environmental cost of any computing choice.
- ❐ Reduce PC-related waste.
- ❐ Repair and reuse PC hardware.
- ❐ Conserve power.
- ❐ Use as little paper as possible.
- ❐ Recycle consumables.
- ❐ Create a healthful computing workplace.
- ❐ Don't drive. Telecommute.
- ❐ Support green businesses and organizations.
- ❐ Spread green information through the global net.

Green-PC resources

A basic understanding of environmental issues will help you make intelligent computing choices. The following books contain a high concentration of green information:
The 1994 Information Please Environmental Almanac
Compiled by World Resources Institute
Houghton Mifflin Co.
2 Park St.
Boston, MA 02108
An overview of the global ecosystem and detailed statistics on every state in the United States and every country in the world.

1994 Earth Journal Environmental Almanac and Resource Directory
Compiled by the Editors of *Buzzworm Magazine*
Buzzworm Books

2305 Canyon Blvd., Suite 206
Boulder, CO 80302
303-442-1969
A compendium of essays, statistics, sources, tips, and factoids.

The report "Environmental Consciousness: A Strategic Competitiveness Issue for the Electronics and Computer Industry," is available from:
MCTC
Attention: Information Center
3500 West Balcones Center Drive
Austin, TX 78759-6509
512-338-3526

The following organizations are working to redefine and humanize the evolution of computers and other high technologies:
Campaign for Responsible Technology
c/o Ted Smith
760 North First St.
San Jose, CA 95112
408-287-6707
Dedicated to extending democracy into the design and development of new technologies.

Computer Professionals for Social Responsibility
P.O. Box 717
Palo Alto, CA 94301
415-322-3778
An industry group working for responsible business practices by computer companies, free access to electronic information, and other issues.

Electronic Frontier Foundation
155 2nd St.
Cambridge, MA 02141
617-864-0665
Also on America OnLine, the Well, and other online services. Focuses on freedom-of-information issues. It also maintains forums on most online information services.

Green Seal
1250 23rd Street NW
Suite 275
Washington, D.C. 20037
202-331-7337, fax 202-331-7533
Contact: Robb Beal, Program Manager
A national environmental labeling organization that is currently developing environmental guidelines for computers and seeks your comments.

LOKA Institute
c/o Richard Sclove
P.O. Box 355
Amherst, MA 01004
413-253-2828
Works to promote humanity in high technology.

Union of Concerned Scientists
26 Church St.
Cambridge, MA 02238
617-547-5552, fax 627-864-9405
Focuses on advanced technology issues, especially arms control and energy.

The first green-PC special interest group (SIG) was founded by the Boston Computer Society in 1991. Contact:
Doug Seale, Director
BCS Environmental Group
617-782-2347
or
The Boston Computer Society
One Kendall Square
Cambridge MA 02139
617-252-0600

This newsletter contains both editorial content on green computing and a catalog of green computing products.

Environmental Business Machines Newsletter & Catalogue
Geosoft: The Company
PO Box 643
Bellows Falls, VT 05101
603-756-4245

"Global Network: Computers in a Sustainable Society," by John E. Young (World Watch Paper 115), a report on the environmental impact of computers and networking, is available from:
Worldwatch Institute
1776 Massachusetts Ave, NW
Washington, DC 20036

50 simple ways to save your hardware

CHAPTER 2

HALF OF THE 30 million-or-more computers shipped in 1992 were replacement PCs. Most of the 15 million machines that were replaced had plenty of computing life left in them and were working reasonably well for their owners. Now they've headed right into the waste stream, along with all their packaging. That's 900 million pounds of functioning PCs that had to be warehoused, recycled, stripped, or dumped in a landfill. Meanwhile, the PCs that replaced them are adding yet more packaging to the waste stream, and they will likely be replaced themselves in three years.

The main reason most people give for buying a replacement PC is that the old one wasn't fast enough to do their work. But that isn't all that's going on. Intense pressure is applied by PC manufacturers and operating system developers to buy hot new machines and chuck out the despised old ones. Modern consumer culture, epitomized by the instant obsolescence that prevails in the computer industry, has conditioned us to think that it's necessary to have the latest and greatest product.

"There must be something wrong with you if you're still using that old clunker," or so the PC ads, following their models in the automobile industry, would like you to think. Similar arguments are aimed at businesses. "Your competitors are using our newer, faster PCs/peripherals/software to eat your business alive. You'd better trade up before it's too late." But the manufacturers and developers take no responsibility for dealing with all the hardware they render suddenly obsolete, though it would make good business sense for them to do so. (See chapter 6 for what to do with your used PC, and see chapter 13 for suggestions on how to be a green-PC consumer.)

Ask yourself whether you really need a new computer. Sure, it would be great to have the latest desktop turbo screamer. And for the few whose work involves computationally intense tasks like searching million-record databases, designing jet engine parts, or rendering elaborate computer graphics for TV and movies, owning the most advanced PC available is well justified. However, most of us do little more than word processing and spreadsheet or database work, which the older generation of machines performed quite well.

Nonetheless, it's hard not to be envious of those happy few with faster, sexier machines. The trick to living happily with your PC is not to compare it with the latest supercomputer. Someone will always have a faster machine than you will, anyway. Instead of comparing your PC to someone else's, measure your computer against the work you do. Your PC might not look slick, but if it still does the job, albeit a little slowly, then you'd be better off taking the $2,000 to $4,000 a fast new machine would cost and putting it into something that will really do some good, both for you and the earth. There are many no-cost and low-cost things you can do to make working with your current PC more productive while adhering to the green principles outlined in chapter 1.

The 50 simple tips in this chapter have as much to do with old-time thrift and "making do" as they do with '90s environmentalism. It makes good, practical sense, as well as good, green sense, to make the most of the computing resources you have before you spend your or your organization's money on new hardware. These tips can be summarized as follows:

- Save waste and resources by maintaining your existing hardware with regular maintenance, cleaning, and checkups.
- Use inexpensive commercial or public-domain software tools to squeeze more performance from your present setup.
- Upgrade only the hardware that really needs upgrading.

Regular maintenance

Don't buy a whole new computer. Save plastic, metal, and packaging by getting your current hardware to do more for you. The first step is to make sure your PC is in good shape.

1 Clean your machine

Dust is a deadly enemy of any PC. Chances are good that the innards of your PC are coated by gray fuzz that's drawn in by your computer's cooling fan. The dust acts as an insulating blanket, keeping in the heat generated by chips on the PC's printer circuit boards. Sooner or later, the chips will overheat and fail.

You'll know it's getting too dusty in there when you start smelling hot electronics or if your floppy disks don't work right. Don't wait until then. A clean machine lasts longer and works better. Any PC service center will be happy to clean your machine, usually for about $25 or so.

If you feel confident about poking around inside your PC, you can also do it yourself. First unplug the PC, then pop off the top and touch the power supply (the big silver metal box usually located toward a back corner of the PC) to release any static electricity in your body. For complete safety, you can wear a grounding strap that connects your wrist to grounded metal outside the PC; a metal lamp works fine. (Wrist grounding straps and other aids for cleaning electronics are available at Radio Shack or your local electronics supply store.) Now pull out any expansion cards and SIMM memory chips standing upright in their slots, and gently dust them with a soft camera-lens brush. Or use one of the small battery-powered vacuums made for cleaning electronic components. Also clean the *system board*, the green board at the bottom of the PC that contains the main chips and slots, using care not to damage any of the chips or wires. Also dust and wipe the casing.

2 Scrub the connections

Dirt or oxidation on printed circuit board connectors can also cause erratic PC performance. While you're dusting out your PC (see the previous tip), take an ordinary, clean pencil eraser and carefully scrub off any oxidation or gunk on the connectors. Clean the slots with a foam swab that's wet with isopropyl alcohol.

3 Clean or replace filters

Some components, such as external hard drives and laser printers, might have filters that need periodic cleaning. A clogged filter reduces the amount of air that's drawn in by the fan to cool the unit, so it runs hotter, possibly shortening its life. Also, some laser printers use filters to catch ozone emissions from the printing process. If the filter is no longer effective, then that ozone is wafting out into the air, where it contributes to indoor pollution. (See more on ozone pollution in chapter 8.) Follow the manufacturer's recommendations for cleaning or replacement.

4 Keep components covered
The easiest way to keep unwanted dust, dirt, and liquids from your PC is to protect it with dust covers. Most commercially available covers are vinyl or nylon, but you can find cotton canvas covers for about $15 or so. Or make your own out of scrap fabric; pillowcases work pretty well.

5 Use a power strip
You'll benefit two ways from plugging all your components into a multioutlet power strip and turning them on and off from there. You'll make it easy and convenient to turn on your hardware, and you'll save energy by turning off all components at once when your work is done. Power strips range from $8 to $40; the higher-priced models include some form of surge suppression (see the following tip).

6 Suppress power spikes
Sudden spikes and surges of ac electricity can fry your PC. Spikes and surges can be caused by electrical storms, heavy electrical machinery operating on the same line, or even routine generator switching at the power utility. A surge-suppressing power strip provides extra protection against chip-frying power spikes and surges. It costs $25 to $40. For even more protection, consider an uninterruptible power supply, which switches your system over to batteries in the event of a heavy surge, brownout, or blackout. These can cost anywhere from $100 to $1,000s.

7 Keep it cool
High ambient temperatures are bad for PCs; overheated chips can melt or pop out of their sockets, bringing your work to a sudden and expensive halt. Keep your PC cool by working in the cool part of the day, turning it off when the temperature gets too high, and keeping the unit out of direct sunlight. Use air conditioning if you must, but try other methods of cooling first. (See more about the energy aspects of air conditioning your PC in chapter 3.)

8 Run diagnostics
Just as doctors recommend that you get regular medical checkups as you get older, so older PCs need regular checkups, too. Most PCs are shipped with custom diagnostic programs that check out basic

components like the microprocessor, random access memory (RAM), ports, disk controllers, disk speed, bad hard disk sectors, and so on. Run a diagnostic occasionally to make sure everything is working as it should, and definitely run one if you're having problems that seem to be hardware related, like difficulty booting from the hard disk or less memory available than you think you should have.

Commercial programs run even more tests and give more detailed reports on your PC's health. Such reports can help you decide what components need to be replaced or upgraded. Many shareware or public-domain, general-purpose PC diagnostic programs, such as Infosys, Test Drive, and Burn-In, are available from commercial online services, user groups, and software catalogs. They cost a few dollars.

Display tips

Computer displays, especially color displays, typically represent 20% or more of the cost of the entire PC. A large-screen color display can cost more than the PC. Here are some simple tips on protecting your monitor investment.

9 Clean your screen

A monitor screen attracts dust and grime like a magnet. Save wear and tear on your eyes by cleaning the screen often with a soft cloth sprayed with a citrus or vinegar-based glass cleaner. Because it could run down inside the casing, don't spray cleaner directly on the screen. Antiglare coatings can be fragile; follow the manufacturer's recommendations for cleaning.

10 Keep it cool

Monitors produce plenty of heat, so make sure there are a few inches of ventilation space all around the unit, especially on top. Don't put papers or books up there if you want your screen to last.

11 Reduce interference

Audio speakers and fluorescent lights can interfere with monitor performance, so keep them at least two feet away, preferably three or four feet. Don't put two monitors closer than two feet apart, as

Macintosh users are often tempted to do. Close monitors distort each other's picture.

12 Degauss

During long work sessions, demagnetize the screen by hitting the degauss button on the back of the unit, if your monitor has one. (Some displays do this automatically every time the unit is turned on.) Degaussing will improve monitor colors and linearity.

13 Turn down the brightness

The layer of phosphors on the inside of your monitor's screen wears out over time and loses its brightness. The more they're illuminated, the faster they fade, resulting in a dim screen. Extend the life of your phosphors by lowering the brightness of the screen. Even better, see the following tip.

14 Use a screen saver

Screen savers put colorful graphics on your monitor when you aren't working with the PC. By using a predominantly dark pattern, you can prolong the life of your screen's phosphors. For the ultimate in screen saving, however, turn off your monitor when you're not using it. Chapters 3 and 4 have more on monitor power-saving.

15 Fine-tune your monitor

Display tune-up programs help you get the most from your monitor. One category of program runs a series of tests to adjust focus, convergence, linearity, color balance, and other aspects of monitor performance. Another type of utility increases the readability of the screen by enlarging fonts, changing screen colors, providing virtual pan and zoom, and so on. See the Green-PC resources section of this chapter for a list of display utilities.

Keyboard suggestions

No keyboard is perfect for every typist, and no keyboard lasts forever. But there are a few things you can do to make yours last longer and suit you better.

16 Skin your keyboard

Keyboards take more abuse than any other part of your PC, especially if there are kids or coffee-drinkers around. Protect your keyboard by covering it with an inexpensive plastic skin over the keys. You can still type with the skin on, and it keeps out paper clips and peanut butter. See the Green-PC resources section of this chapter for a list of keyboard-cover vendors.

17 Don't unplug it

Some keyboards draw power from your PC. Unplugging them while the computer is on can damage chips on the keyboard itself or fry the keyboard controller on the PC's system board. Macintosh keyboards connected to the ADB port are especially prone to this: you can kill the keyboard and the ADB controller chip just by pulling out the connector while the Mac is on. It's an expensive repair.

18 Remap the keys

If the keys on your keyboard aren't where you want them to be, there's still hope. A variety of commercial and shareware programs can assign values to keys other than the standard values (a process called keyboard remapping). For example, you can switch the Alt and Control keys, make a typical IBM-compatible keyboard emulate a VT100 terminal keyboard, or assign the tilde key to type a thousand characters of boilerplate text.

Remapping the keyboard can make it unnecessary to buy a new keyboard with a different arrangement of keys, and it can significantly speed up typing as well. Remapping programs can be turned off when you want to return to the standard configuration. Remapping utilities are available through software catalogs for less than $20, or they can be downloaded from commercial online services such as CompuServe.

19 Increase speed with macros

Another way to increase your PC's speed through the keyboard is with a macro program. Like remapping utilities, they allow you to assign any value or combination of values to any key on the keyboard, so that, for example, you can type your name and address just by hitting the F10 key. Macro programs do more, however; they can record a series of actions such as making menu choices, moving the mouse, entering text, and drawing graphics, then macros replay the actions in sequence at a single keystroke.

If your work involves repetitive series of actions (and whose doesn't?), then a macro program is a must. It can do more to speed your work than adding a new microprocessor and a faster hard disk. Macro software ranges in price from $100 or so for a commercial application to $10 or less for a public-domain program. Many commercial word-processing programs also contain macro utilities.

20 Shrink your keyboard

If you do need to purchase a new keyboard, you can even save plastic. The Datalux Corporation makes a compact keyboard that uses only half the materials in the standard 101-key version and occupies only 40% of the space. It costs about $150. See the Green-PC resources section for contact information.

Getting your hard disk in shape

Sooner or later, you'll fill up your hard disk and start thinking about getting a bigger one. Hard drives aren't that expensive anymore, but before you shell out for another piece of hardware, look for no-cost or low-cost green-PC solutions. A really thorough cleaning of your disk might reveal capacity that you didn't suspect was there. Even if your disk is nearing capacity, file compression software can come to your aid, making room where there was none before. Adding a disk cache can speed disk operations and make your old disk work like a brand-new speedster. Other programs can help you increase the performance of your disk operating system.

21 Delete unnecessary DOS files

Periodically comb through your hard disk for unnecessary files. Check your root directory to find outdated DOS files. The installation routines for commercial DOS software can litter your disk with extra copies of AUTOEXEC.BAT and CONFIG.SYS files, usually labeled with an .OLD or .BAK extension. These can safely be deleted as long as you're sure you won't need to switch back to a previous configuration at some point. There are many DOS commands you'll probably never use either; you'll find them in your DOS directory. Ruthlessly eliminate them.

22 Tune your disk

To free up yet more DOS disk space, run CHKDSK/F periodically to find differences between your file allocation table (FAT) and the actual files on your disk. This procedure locates areas on the hard disk that aren't claimed by any file, but that the FAT doesn't recognize. Delete the resulting .CHK files to open up the previously unavailable space.

23 Upgrade your version of DOS

It's usually (though not always) worthwhile to upgrade to the latest version of DOS. You'll gain a little speed, modestly improve the performance of your machine, and perhaps be able to remove utility programs that occupy space on your disk. For example, MS-DOS 5.0 fixed many problems with earlier versions and added capabilities, like an undelete feature and access to memory above 640K, that previously could be found only in third-party software. On the other hand, MS-DOS 6.0 was widely viewed as a dangerous upgrade; it's built-in disk compression trashed many a hard disk. The universal rule is to never upgrade to any software version that ends with 0—at least until other early upgraders have discovered all the problems.

There are also many operating system alternatives to DOS. Most of them work even better and faster than MS-DOS and cost about the same, around $100 on the street.

24 Evaluate your need for Windows

Windows 3.1 and later versions take up immense quantities of disk space—10 to 12MB or more, not counting all the utility programs you need just to make Windows work right. Most popular Windows applications, like AmiPro and Word for Windows, occupy up to 10MB more. That's a sizable chunk of the hard disk on the vast majority of PCs, which are equipped with hard drives under 80MB in size.

Is the functionality improvement to be gained from Windows really worth losing half your hard drive? This is an even more crucial issue for users of notebooks, whose machines often have drives less than 40MB. Windows also doesn't work well on slower machines (low-end 386s) and in 2MB of RAM. And you have to buy all new applications to run with Windows. Think of the trees and petroleum being consumed to package all those new Windows applications and ship them to you.

Unfortunately, DOS is a dying operating system, and developers are no longer releasing new DOS versions of major business software. But, for plain-vanilla computing (word processing, spreadsheet, and database programs) on PC-compatible machines, DOS is still the greenest choice.

25 Delete unnecessary Windows files

If you're already running Windows, you can save up to 1MB or so of disk space by using the File Manager or the DOS DEL command to delete wallpaper files (.BMP), unwanted Windows game files, game help files, unnecessary screen-saver modules, and unnecessary printer drivers. Take a look at your Windows applications, too. Erase Paintbrush, Recorder, Notepad, Clock, and other Windows utilities you don't use. Get rid of tutorial files, help files (.HLP), example files, sample forms, and clip art (extensions .BMP, .TIF, or .WMF). Delete files in Microsoft applications with the extension .CBT (for computer-based training); these are tutorial files.

26 Delete unnecessary Mac files

The Macintosh's System 7.0 might be a much better user interface than Windows, but it's hardly less bloated. Get rid of those System 7 files you don't need. If you use Type 1 Postscript fonts, delete all the TrueType fonts in your Extensions folder. Get rid of unnecessary desk accessories, notably Easy Access and the Puzzle. Delete useless aliases and help files. Keep only one copy of TeachText on your disk. If you have no need for networking, delete the file-sharing files in the Extensions folder and the Apple Menu folder. Ditch printer drivers for printers you don't have. Keep the number of fonts in your System to a minimum; unless desktop publishing is your business, you won't use most of those fancy fonts you've collected anyway. If you have the font utility Adobe Type Manager, you need only two sizes for any font.

27 Defragment your disk

Once you've thrown away all the files you can, it's time to defragment your disk to improve its speed. As your hard disk fills up, files get spread all over your disk as the drive writes files to any available empty sector. This happens quickly if you move many large files on and off your disk every day. Retrieving these widely scattered files takes more time and slows down hard-disk performance. Instead of getting a faster hard disk, periodically use a defragmenting utility (there's one in most PC utility collections) to recombine files and speed file-access times. Not only will your hard disk do its job faster every day, but you'll also save more time when you back up your disk. Backing up a file in contiguous sectors takes less time than backing up a file spread all over the disk.

28 Squeeze your files

Even after you've cleared out every unwanted file, chances are you'll still have too little disk space. One inexpensive solution is to use a compression utility to shrink your files. These programs let you squeeze up to double the number of files onto your hard disk, so you can put off buying a larger one. You can go for a file squeezer that works only on demand and only on files you choose, or you can choose a program that works in the background to compress all your files while you work on something else.

The consensus on background compression programs is that they yield real space savings, but you take a slight risk using them. They have been known to trash disks and destroy files. If that makes you nervous, stick with an on-demand file squeezer like PKZIP or StuffIt. Commercial compression utilities run about $50 to $75. Some popular file compression programs are listed in the Green-PC resources section.

29 Archive, archive, archive

If your hard disk is like mine, there are hundreds of files on it that you'll never refer to again. Take an hour to trim the fat from your disk and archive the files onto floppies. Use an on-demand file compression program to get the most backup into the fewest floppies.

30 Add a disk cache

A *cache* is an area of memory devoted specifically to storing data read off the hard disk, such as files and data frequently needed by your current application. Access to RAM is faster than access to disk, so your work goes faster every time your PC reads the cache instead of the disk. Most newer PCs come with a cache, but older ones probably do not have one.

You can get a cache in two ways: with a cache-equipped hard disk controller, and with disk-caching software. Cache-equipped disk controllers have extra memory for the cache onboard and are the ultimate hard-disk accelerators, but they tend to be expensive—$200 to $1,000, depending on features. This is the solution when you already have a sizable investment in large hard disks and need every possible bit of speed.

If you can't afford a caching hard-disk controller, turn to disk-caching software. Disk-caching programs, often packaged with other utilities at around $100 for the set, are excellent investments in hard-disk performance—if you have extra memory to support them. You'll still clock speed improvements of up to 90% in some operations. See the Green-PC resources section.

Getting more from your printer

If treated with respect, printers can live a long, long time. These tips will help you get the most from your current printer, as well as improve your printed output and give you more time to compute.

31 Keep printers clean

A clean printer runs smoothly and prints better copy. Periodically swab off the head of impact printers with a foam swab dipped in isopropyl alcohol. Also, gently wipe dust out of the printer's innards and remove any paper debris from around the tractor-feed wheels. Clean a laser printer's toner cartridge area with a damp cloth. Check the printer's operation manual for other recommended cleaning procedures.

32 Use the right laser paper

Use paper recommended specifically for laser printers. (There's a wide selection of laser paper with recycled content; see chapter 6.) Never put plain acetate or nonlaser labels in the printer; they'll melt all over the fuser. Print paper on the side recommended by the manufacturer; the paper's natural curl will match the curve of the printer drum and reduce the likelihood of paper jams. (You can print on both sides with reasonable success if you take a little extra time. To minimize jams, first print on the wrong side. Then press the printed pages flat under a weight and print on the correct side.)

33 Use a type manager

Type managers are programs that improve the look of fonts on the screen and in printed output, even dot-matrix output. The best known is Adobe Type Manager, available for popular DOS applications, Windows, and System 7. Both Windows and System 7 also come with their own system-level type manager, called TrueType. While type managers do slow down your computer somewhat, they're well worth it if you want clear fonts on screen and great-looking fonts from impact printers.

34 Spool your print jobs

One way to speed up your work without new hardware is to use a print spooler. These invaluable utilities store up print jobs in a special area on disk and give you back control of your PC. Then the spooler prints the job while you work, or at a time set by you. No more having to take a coffee break while you print. A spooler alone can increase your PC productivity by 10% or more, depending on how much printing you do. (Windows comes with its own print spooler, as does the Mac's System 7.) For suggestions on doing less printing, see chapter 5.

35 Add a print buffer

Software spoolers require space on your hard disk and tend to slow down your work if you try to print while running another program. A hardware printer buffer can address these problems. Buffers are little more than a box with extra memory that sits between your PC and your printer. A buffer intercepts print jobs as they are sent to the printer from your PC and stores them in its own memory. Then the buffer spools out the job to the printer, leaving your PC free to do other things. Hardware printer buffers are justified only if you do a lot of continuous printing and need maximum access to and speed from your PC.

36 Rev up your printer

There's not much you can do to improve impact printer performance, short of adding a spooler and a type management program (see the previous tips). Laser printers are always happy to get more RAM and more fonts. More memory means you can print bigger pages and more graphics. While printer memory is usually expensive, font cards come pretty cheap—under $150.

Printer accelerators for laser printers, hardware you install in the printer to speed its performance, can speed up the rasterizing (that is, the processing of fonts and graphics) of complex print jobs so the printer runs at or near its rated pages per minute. Printer resolution enhancement boards, which can also be installed inside the laser printer, can turn a standard 300 dots-per-inch machine into a 600 or 800 dpi imagesetter. Most hardware solutions to printer speed and resolution cost thousands of dollars, however, and are justified only if you already have a large investment in an expensive printer.

37 Share a printer

One printer can make do for many PC users, even if they aren't on a network. A simple parallel or serial A/B switchbox is the usual answer for hooking up two, four, or even six PCs to one printer. Connect each PC to one side of the switchbox, plug the printer into the other, and you can print from any PC by simply flicking a selection switch. Simple A/B switches generally cost less than $30. More sophisticated versions can let up to a dozen users share a laser and incorporate software that spools the print job at each PC until the printer is free.

Macintoshes in a DOS environment often have a problem because they can't interface with PC-compatible printers. Rather than getting a printer just for the Mac, try an inexpensive solution like GDT Softwork's PowerPrint, which includes printer-driver software and a special cable that can be configured for different PC-compatible printers. PowerPrint lets Macs access a wider range of printers such as Canon BubbleJets and LaserBeams, Epson FX and LQ series printers, Hewlett-Packard DeskJets, LaserJets and ThinkJets, NEC Pinwriters, and Toshiba P series printers. See the Green-PC resources section.

Upgrading your PC

Suppose you've done your best with these suggestions and you conclude that you really do need new hardware. Stop—there are still some alternatives left. Don't buy an entirely new machine until you've investigated performing a facelift on your current one. Many kinds of hardware upgrades short of total PC replacement are better for the environment and will likely save you money.

How do you decide what parts of your PC to upgrade? It depends on the kind of work you do. If you want to speed up work that requires intensive calculations, you should upgrade your CPU, add an accelerator board, or install a math coprocessing chip. If the programs you use constantly read from or write to your hard disk, as many databases do, then get a faster hard disk, or buy enough RAM to create a RAM disk or a disk cache (see the discussion of disk caches in tip number 30). If you work with color graphics, get a graphics accelerator. Get an entirely new PC only if you need to upgrade several components at once.

You can replace almost every component of a modern PC yourself, if you're patient, careful, and have a few common tools like a narrow screwdriver and needlenose pliers. Before you open the top of your PC for any do-it-yourself upgrades, however, make sure you have everything you need, and ground yourself with a grounding wrist strap as described in tip number 1. Or you can take your PC down to a local computer service center and have the installation done there.

38 Choose internal components

Some components, such as hard disks and modems, come in both internal (fits inside the PC) and external (sits next to the PC) designs. All else being equal, internal designs are greener than external ones. External components need their own power supplies, casings, and fans, and thus use up more materials and resources. They are usually less power-efficient, as well, and they take up room on your desk that you probably can't spare. The only times you should choose an external component is when you plan to use it with more than one

PC, or when you want to keep it when you trade-in your old PC for a new one.

39 Add a new CPU

Many leading PC manufacturers now design their machines so they can be easily upgraded by replacing the old central processor with a new one. Prices for CPU upgrades vary greatly from manufacturer to manufacturer. There's no doubt that popping in a new chip is far easier on the environment than buying a new machine and trashing your old one. But don't expect a new CPU to speed up everything in your PC. You'll probably also want to investigate upgrades for your hard drive, RAM, and display.

40 Speed up with an accelerator

If you can't just pop in a chip, you can still upgrade your PC's microprocessor with an accelerator board. Various types of boards are available, but the most popular can be plugged into a slot in your PC, with only a small amount of rewiring on the system board required. Some Mac accelerators just plug into a NuBus slot and immediately take over for the older processor. Accelerators are expensive and are worth installing only if you need to at least double your processor speed; other measures, like installing a cache or adding RAM, might do just as much to speed your work. Even so, accelerators are a good alternative to buying an entirely new PC. As with CPU upgrades, accelerators vary greatly in price.

41 Add a math coprocessor

Computer-aided design, engineering applications, spreadsheets, and statistics programs can take advantage of a *math coprocessor* (also called an FPU, for floating-point unit), a number-crunching chip that speeds certain types of math calculations. PCs built around Intel's 80486DX chip (or its clones) and the Pentium, as well as most versions of Motorola's 68040, have a math coprocessor built in. But SX versions of Intel's 386 and 486, and "lite" versions of Motorola chips, have been dumbed down by disabling the math coprocessor.

Many PCs have an empty socket on the system board for a math chip, so installation is usually simple. Costs for math chips have been falling for some time, and you can buy many models for less than $100.

42 Upgrade your hard disk

You'll probably see a greater overall speed increase by installing a faster, bigger hard drive than by upgrading your processor. It's likely to be cheaper, too. A fast internal 300MB drive costs less than $300 today. Think of all the time you'll save by not waiting for a sluggish drive to retrieve your data. If you are handy, you can install a standard hard disk into a PC drive bay yourself, but hard disks that fit into a slot in your PC are even easier to install and don't cost a lot more.

43 Infinite storage

Even a new hard disk fills up too soon, especially if you're using huge Windows or System 7 applications. Consider removable hard disk storage instead. Removable drives offer between 45 and 660MB of storage on each removable cartridge, depending on the technology used, and some offer access times nearly as fast as a hard disk. When one cartridge is full, just pop in another. You never need to run out of storage. This is a much greener and more cost-efficient solution than buying one hard drive after another.

44 Add RAM

Adding random-access memory (RAM) to your PC is another inexpensive performance booster. Additional memory gives your programs more room to work in; you can even work with several programs at once under multitasking operating systems like Windows, DESQView, and System 7. Older PCs often have no built-in provision for adding RAM, so you'll need to buy a RAM expansion card for an empty slot. That will cost you around $100. For older machines, you'll need memory-management software to break the DOS 640K RAM barrier—another $75 or so. Newer PCs, whether Macs or IBM-compatible, usually come equipped with empty slots on the system board that you can fill with single inline memory modules (SIMMS). With 1MB SIMMs going for less than $40, more RAM is a bargain you shouldn't pass up.

45 Install a RAM disk

Putting your data on a RAM disk, the memory equivalent of a hard disk, speeds most operations considerably because access to RAM is far faster than access to disk. You'll probably need to add more memory (see the previous tip) and purchase a memory-management program. Remember that a RAM disk, like regular RAM, doesn't store information when the PC is turned off, so always be careful to back it up to the hard disk before you leave the machine.

46 Upgrade your graphics

Color displays aren't essential to most computer work. Witness the success of the Macintosh, which for years was available only with a black-and-white display. But you might feel you need a color monitor anyway. Getting SuperVGA for your older PC can be as simple as popping in a new color graphics adapter board and hooking it up to a color monitor. The least expensive SuperVGA graphics adapters cost less than $100 today. Bear in mind that color monitors use more power than monochrome displays (see chapters 3 and 4). If you already own a VGA monitor, it might have SuperVGA capability built in, so all you'll need is a new graphics card.

47 Make your graphics fly

If your screen still seems to poke along even after you've upgraded your microprocessor, you might need a graphics accelerator. These expansion boards speed graphics calculations such as line draw, area fill, and bit-block transfers, improving display speed for color graphics and Windows up to ten times over standard VGA. Many of the newest graphics adapters, both for DOS and Macintosh PCs, have acceleration built right into the board.

48 Choose an upgradeable PC

In the end, you might decide that buying a new PC is a necessity. A good strategy to put off the inevitable obsolescence of your new machine is to choose one with upgradeability built in. Most major manufacturers, including Compaq, Dell, and AST, now offer PCs with removable system boards that can be replaced when you want to upgrade to a faster processor.

So the PC you're buying today can eventually get a complete upgrade—a faster CPU, more memory, a faster bus, a new BIOS—and serve you for a lot longer. Two things to keep in mind: make sure the manufacturer doesn't charge an arm and a leg for the upgrade—it shouldn't cost more than about half the price of an entirely new PC—and choose an upgrade design that's easy to install and set up.

49 Compute small

In computing, smaller is greener, so choose new hardware that's small. Small-format hard drives use less material than bigger ones while providing the same or better performance. Perfectly functional high-speed modems can be made as small as a pack of gum. Small desktop PCs with four slots or less require less plastic in their construction and still provide the expansion capabilities most users need.

A notebook PC is more material-efficient than a desktop PC, and it takes up less space. (Notebooks use less energy, too; see chapter 3.) If you need only one computer, a notebook is the greener choice. Even greener are lightweight subnotebooks and the new personal digital assistants (PDAs). (Notebooks and other portables do have some environmental drawbacks, notably their use of batteries containing toxic metals. See chapters 3 and 6 for more.)

50 Share seldom-used peripherals

Do you really need to purchase your own color scanner, video digitizer, color printer, or other exotic device? Most of these peripherals come in handy for the occasional job but are rarely used otherwise. Find a like-minded person or group and share the purchase. Better yet, rent the equipment.

Choices that make a difference

- ❒ Conserve resources and prevent waste by maintaining your existing hardware.
- ❒ Keep equipment clean.
- ❒ Take care of your monitor.
- ❒ Tune and prune your hard disk.
- ❒ Use inexpensive software tools to squeeze more performance from your printer.
- ❒ Upgrade only the hardware that needs upgrading.
- ❒ Buy internal modems, hard drives, and other components instead of external ones.

- ❒ Choose small components over large ones.
- ❒ Share seldom-used peripherals with another person, or rent them.

Green-PC resources

Software Labs publishes a shareware/public-domain software catalog with many PC diagnostic programs and other low-cost utilities for improving hardware performance:
The Software Labs
3767 Overland Ave., #112-115
Los Angeles, CA 90034
800-359-9998

Commercial PC diagnostic programs include:
Micro-Scope
PostProbe
Micro 2000, Inc.
1100 E. Broadway, Suite 301
Glendale, CA 91205
800-864-8008

QAPlus, QAPlus/WIN
DiagSoft, Inc.
5615 Scotts Valley Dr., Suite 140
Scotts Valley, CA 95066
800-DIAGSOFT, 408-438-8247
For DOS and Windows
Reviews hardware configurations, does performance benchmarks, and diagnoses problems; it also includes LAN support.

Snooper
Maxa
800-788-6292
For Macintosh
A complete diagnostics program, including system tests, benchmarks, audio, SCSI, and other port tests.

Protective keyboard skins are made by several manufacturers, including:
Merritt Computer Products
5565 Red Bird Center Dr., Suite 150
Dallas, TX 75237
214-339-0753, fax 214-339-1313

These programs will help you maximize your existing monitor investment:
Display Mate Utilities
Sonera Technologies
P.O. Box 565
Four Robin Rd.
Rumson, NJ 07760
800-932-6323, 908-747-6886, fax 908-747-4523
For DOS and Windows
Includes an extensive set of test patterns and monitor diagnostic tests.

These programs provide general-purpose and on-the-fly compression:
PKZIP
PKLITE
PKWARE, Inc.
9025 N. Deerwood Dr.
Brown Deer, WI 53223
414-354-8699, fax 414-354-8559
For DOS
General-purpose compression and decompression; PKLITE compresses .EXE and .COM files down to 40% of their original size.

Stacker
Stac Electronics
5993 Avenida Encinas
Carlsbad, CA 92008
800-522-7822, 619-431-7474
For DOS
Stacker provides on-the-fly general-purpose compression and decompression.

StuffIt Classic (shareware)
StuffIt Deluxe
StuffIt Lite
Aladdin Systems
165 Westridge Dr.
Watsonville, CA 95076
408-761-6200
For Macintosh
General-purpose compression and decompression; the standard for Macs.

PC-Kwik Power Pak includes five programs for speeding your PC, including a disk cache, print spooler, and easy command-line editor:
PC-Kwik Power Pak
PC-Kwik
15100 S.W. Koll Pkwy., Suite P
Beaverton, OR 97006
800-288-5945

Invaluable printing utilities include:
Adobe Type Manager
Adobe Systems
1585 Charleston Rd.
P.O. Box 7900
Mountain View, CA 94039
800-833-6687
For selected DOS programs, Windows, and Macintosh:

The industry-standard type-management program:
PrintCache
LaserTools Corp.
800-767-8005, 510-420-8777
For Windows
A print spooler with many advanced printing features.

SuperPrint
Zenographics
4 Executive Circle, Suite 200
Irvine, CA 92714
800-366-7494, 714-851-6352
For DOS
Another advanced spooler.

Network up to 12 HP Laserjet printers without a network. Contact:
ASP Computer Products
160 San Gabriel Dr.
Sunnyvale, CA 94086
408-746-2965, fax 408-746-2803

PowerPrint is a collection of software printer drivers along with a cable that enables the Apple Macintosh to print to more than 950 printers.
PowerPrint
GDT Softworks
4664 Lougheed Hwy., Suite 188
Burnaby, Canada BC V5C 6B7
800-663-6222, fax 604-291-9689

The Jameco catalog contains lots of switchboxes, cables, chips, system boards, expansion boards, power supplies, computer casings, tools, and other stuff for the do-it-yourself hardware hacker. It also maintains its own technical-information bulletin board system (BBS).
Jameco
1355 Shoreway Rd.
Belmont, CA 94002
800-831-4242, fax 800-237-6948, BBS 415-637-9025

A truly compact "space saver" keyboard is available from:
Datalux Corp.
155 Aviation Dr,
Winchester, VA 22602
800-DATALUX, fax 703-663-1682

Power computing with less power

CHAPTER 3

WHAT'S THE LARGEST single source of air pollution from the burning of fossil fuels? Not cars or factories. It's the generation of electricity from power plants that burn oil, coal, and natural gas. According to the EPA, 35% of all U.S. carbon dioxide emissions come from electricity generation, as do 75% of U.S. emissions of sulfur dioxide and 38% of nitrogen oxides. Fully one-quarter of that electricity is consumed in offices and other commercial buildings where computers are used.

In the past, electric utilities met our growing need for power by building more generating capacity. Today, with the cost of new construction skyrocketing, utilities have turned to energy conservation as the best way to meet the demand for more and more electricity. It's cheaper for utilities to promote energy efficiency than to build new capacity, and it's cheaper for you as an energy consumer to be energy efficient, too.

Energy conservation is probably the easiest way to help the environment and save money at the same time. Every little bit of electricity not used saves generating capacity, reduces carbon-dioxide emissions, relieves the demand for foreign oil and nuclear power, and keeps change in your pocket. If even the utility companies are anxious to promote energy conservation, you know there must be something to it. And it's something we all can do.

There are even more benefits. Every taxpayer in the United States finances a huge national debt that's partly the result of U.S. dependence on foreign oil and the need to maintain a military force capable of defending our access to it. We also underwrite (through federal tax shelters, subsidies, and environmental cleanups) the oil, gas, coal, and nuclear industries that have the least to gain from conservation. Consider the dollars you save by using less energy as a payment on the national debt.

Every kilowatt-hour (the standard measure of energy consumption) saved through conservation prevents two pounds of carbon dioxide from reaching the atmosphere. Climatologists who subscribe to the theory of global warming believe that a reduction in CO_2 emissions might help slow the process. Consider that an investment in the lives of your children.

What power costs

Electric power costs money and uses resources. PCs and their electronic servants eat power, accounting for as much as 5% of commercial electricity consumption, according to the EPA. By the year 2000, computers will be consuming closer to 10%. But how much does that cost the individual PC user? That depends on your actual use.

Many electrical devices state their electrical requirements and average consumption somewhere on the unit. However, this information is only a general guide to the actual electricity a device uses. Most of the time, devices are operating at less than their rated wattage, except for color monitors, which use close to the rated wattage at all times. Some devices, like laser printers, faxes, and hard drives, surge to or beyond rated wattage when active, but draw less power when idle. So, for example, the more you actually print with your laser, the more power it uses, but it still draws some power even when it's doing nothing at all.

The EPA has come up with some estimates for PC power use. According to the EPA's Global Change Division, Office of Air and Radiation, the typical CPU, monitor, and laser printer combination consumes 235 watts. If you leave your setup on all the time, as many people do, powering it for a year at seven cents per kilowatt-hour costs you $144. (See chapter 1 for more on kilowatt-hours and energy use.)

Of course, most people have additional electrical and electronic devices in their offices. The typical energy consumption of PCs and other standard office equipment is shown in Table 3-1. The figures are composite estimates drawn from studies by several electrical power research groups; real power consumption in your office could be higher or lower, depending on what hardware you have and your patterns of usage. Multiply the total energy consumption shown in this table by the number of PCs and other devices in your organization and you'll begin to get a feel for how much power your computer equipment is using and how much it costs. If you run your equipment all the time, you use a lot more juice—about $925 in electricity per year.

Table 3-1

Average Energy Used by a PC Office Operating 9 hours per day, 240 Days/Year

Electrical device	Kilowatt hours per year	$/year ($0.07/kWh)
PC	300	$ 21
Laser printer	260	18
Impact printer	100	7
Modem	22	2
Fax machine	150	11
Copier	1500	105
Two 100W incandescent lights	430	30
Two overhead 40W fluorescent lights	175	12
Answering machine	40	3
Total	2977	$209

Source: EPA; American Council for an Energy-Efficient Economy; US Dept. of Energy.

If you were able, through conservation, to save just one kilowatt-hour per workday—if, for example, you turned off your PC, laser printer, and lights during your lunch hour and breaks—you'd save $17 a year. Corporations with thousands of PCs can realize savings sufficient to fund new R&D efforts and pay an additional dividend to shareholders. Keep in mind also that the cost of electricity isn't fixed. It fluctuates at the whim of the market. The less power you use, the less your energy bill affects your business.

The indirect economics of energy conservation are even more significant. Manufacturers agree that turning off PCs and most other electronic devices when they aren't being used extends their useful life. This is especially true for the cathode ray tube (CRT)—the heart of most computer monitors. The phosphor coating on the inside of the CRT decreases in sensitivity with every hour it's illuminated.

Reducing electricity use can also ease the burden on office building power systems, which often break down under the simultaneous demands of high-powered servers, large-screen monitors, laser printers, high-speed copiers, and the air conditioning required to cool them, piled on top of other building power requirements. No-cost power conservation compares very favorably with the high cost of replacing the electrical infrastructure of a building or living with data-destroying brownouts. The cost of air conditioning modern office electronics is also a significant factor; see later in this chapter for more.

Conserving PC power

Your PC workplace, with its many electricity-eating devices, is an excellent place to begin a no-cost or low-cost conservation program. To get started, you don't have to spend a dime. All you have to do is change a few wasteful habits.

Powering down

According to the EPA, about 40% of PCs are left running all night and on weekends. The single best way to conserve electricity, combat global warming, and save money is so obvious that hardly anybody does it: turn off your computer, monitor, printer, and modem when you're not using them.

A reasonable number of daily on-off cycles (about four) doesn't shorten the life of your computer, as many people once thought. On the contrary, today's PCs and peripherals are generally so well made that they continue to operate far past the point of technological obsolescence, no matter how often you turn them on and off. The mean time to failure (MTTF) for computer switches and power supplies is typically around 50,000 cycles and 25,000 to 50,000 cycles for other components.

In 1993 a Dataquest report for the EPA found that the heat generated by the electronics inside a PC has a larger (and more negative) impact on the life cycle of a computer than does turning it off and on. The report concluded that the two factors most affecting the useful life of a computer are heat and the number of hours of operation. In short, the fewer hours a PC operates, the longer it will last.

Another 1993 report, this one by the Swiss Federal Institute of Technology, came to this conclusion about monitors: "Switching on and off the monitor 5 times or more a day increases the frequency of faults in the power transistors in the control and deflection assembly only after the monitor has been used 20–30 years. After 20,000 cycles [17 to 19 years, assuming a 230–240 day workyear], the cathode starts to weaken. The other components are not impaired by constant switching. Based on the parameters measured and known from the technical literature, the critical operating times can be determined when wear caused by the switching cycles shortens the life cycle. For monitors, this critical operating time is about 16 minutes. This means that switching off the monitor is worthwhile for breaks lasting more than 16 minutes."

If you cycle the switch just 4 times a day—on at the beginning of the workday, on/off for two breaks and your lunch hour, and off at the end of the day—it will be a long time before you wear out any parts in your PC from power cycling, even if you wanted to keep it that long. In fact, if you really want to extend the life of your computer, make sure to turn it off and unplug it when the workplace gets hot, when an electrical storm threatens to spike the power supply, or when the local electricity supply fluctuates, like that moment around 9:30 in the morning when many local utilities switch capacitors at their main generating plants. Any of these events can fry your power supply and system board, a much more likely cause of PC failure than power cycling.

This is not to say that your PC might not be brought down by other factors, too. Some manufacturers ship poorly designed products that won't last long under any circumstances. For example, the original Macintosh 512K and the Macintosh Plus suffered from unpublicized design flaws in their power supplies and built-in monitors that caused many of them to burn out within months. Poor environmental conditions can cause computers and peripherals to die before their time. The dusty, hot environment of the typical home office is not conducive to long computer life. Some residents of an office can even commit computer homicide. I recently spent $300 to replace parts of the system board of one of my PCs when a mouse crawled inside and was electrocuted.

Some engineers have also argued that PCs, like all other electrical and electronic devices, draw more power in their first few seconds of operation than after they've been running a while, so frequent on/off cycles actually use more power than leaving the PC on all the time. That might be true if you were switching the PC on and off every five minutes. But no one actually works like that, and that is not what I am advocating here. (Even Energy Star computers, which could be set to automatically power down after five minutes of nonuse, simply go into a lower-power "sleep state. " It requires only a little more juice, not a huge surge, to wake them up again. See chapter 4 for more on Energy Star.) You will save plenty of power just by turning the machine on and off four times a day as previously described.

Laser printers, which really do gulp a lot of power at start-up, should not be cycled on and off too frequently, but it is an expensive folly to leave them on all the time just to avoid the power surge at start-up.

Turn off peripherals If you can't bring yourself to turn off the computer every time you get up from your desk, or if the PC is connected to a network or is being used as a fax machine, at least turn off the monitor, printer, and desk lights. They use more watts than the CPU itself.

How much can a company save by simply turning off monitors? The experience of Royce Green, the issue coordinator for the Dallas branch of the Sierra Club, sheds some light on the issue. Green works at an auto-parts firm that uses 150 IBM workstations with InfoWindow displays. One day Green's supervisor noticed that he was the only worker to turn off his monitor whenever he left his desk. Nearly all the other monitors were left on all the time. The supervisor asked Green to prove that conserving monitor power outweighed possible damage caused by switching the monitor on and off more frequently. After gathering data from IBM and the local electrical utility company, Green was able to show that turning off all the company's monitors overnight and on weekends would save more than $17,000 per year in electricity.

Screen savers, by the way, do nothing to reduce monitor power usage, though they might extend the life of the display screen by preventing phosphor burn-in. In fact, screen savers that burden the

CPU by making it calculate animations of flying toasters, Klingon warbirds, and the like, actually cause your PC to use a little more electricity than it would otherwise.

Use a switch box To make it easier to turn off your components, plug them all into a switch box. This can be an inexpensive, ten-dollar strip outlet with an on-off switch, or better yet a "power commander" with a master on-off switch as well as individual switches for each device.

The main advantage is that when you turn off the master switch, all your components will power down simultaneously, eliminating the possibility that you'll leave one or more components running all night or all weekend. And you can control distant devices right from your chair, so you aren't tempted to leave the laser printer on because "it's way over there."

Try timers It's like pulling nails to get some people to turn off their PCs, especially in a corporate setting where clerical workers feel little responsibility to the company. Managers can put timers on each PC power line or on a dedicated circuit to power down all computers and peripherals at the end of the day. Just make sure that all work is saved to the PC or the network server before a timer shuts down the power. It's a good idea to set an alarm on each PC to go off five minutes before power-down.

Increasingly, businesses need PCs to be on after-hours to do timed backups or to receive fax/modem transmissions. There are several PC-specific devices that turn on your computer at preset times, then turn it off when the task is done. Some will even boot up the computer when a modem transmission is received, and shut it down when the transmission is completed. Better yet, invest in Energy Star computers, which power down all by themselves, or use one of the energy-saving devices described at the end of chapter 4.

Unplug everything See all those little green and red lights that continue to glow when you turn off the main lights in your office? Many devices in your office can continue to draw power even when they're switched off. These can include your monitor, fax machine, telephone, strip outlets, surge protector, and power commander. To conserve every last bit of juice, unplug everything in your office when you leave. This is easier if you have a master switch box or power commander, so all you have to do is pull its plug from the wall.

Keep it clean Clean computers use less power and last longer. Regularly dust out the innards of your PC, following the directions in chapter 2. So you don't have to turn up the brightness (which uses more watts), clean your monitor screen with vinegar- or citrus-based glass cleaner (it's amazing how many people use dusty, grimy monitors).

Low-power computer designs

The trend toward power efficiency took another jump forward when the EPA announced the Energy Star Computer Program in 1992. Energy Star sets out specifications for computers and other peripherals that will automatically enter a low-power state when the unit is inactive. Energy Star and other aspects of low-power computer designs are covered in detail in chapter 4. You don't have to purchase a new Energy Star PC to practice low-power computing, however. You can save by choosing today's power-efficient hardware and peripherals.

Choose a low-power PC Some PCs use more power than others. There are natural variations among computers from different manufacturers, of course, but you can make choices that will reduce your power consumption even without much comparison shopping. One general principle is to buy a slimline computer with a small power supply and only one or two expansion slots. These consume less power than watt-hungry towers with eight slots and 300-watt power supplies.

Today's notebook computers are more energy-efficient than desktop models, even those desktop that conform to Energy Star (see chapter 4). The newest notebooks draw as little as 3.3 watts of power in idle mode, compared to the approximately 160 watts consumed by their desktop siblings (CPU plus monitor). On top of their naturally low power drain, notebooks incorporate power-saving circuitry and system software that puts the computer into a "sleep" mode when it hasn't been used for a set time. Clever power-saving features can keep the notebook asleep for hours, days, or even years, drawing just enough battery power to keep it ready to awaken on your command. In fact, many new notebook computers are never really "off" at all.

Such features are now becoming standardized. Intel and Microsoft have issued a specification called Advanced Power Management (APM) that monitors system activity on any Intel-compatible notebook and cuts battery power automatically to idle hardware. The two developers claim that APM can double the amount of computing you can do on a battery charge.

Two microprocessors currently dominate the low-power-consumption notebook market: Intel's 386SL and i486SL, plus clones of those designs from IBM, Advanced Micro Designs (AMD), and Cyrix. The SL processors not only draw less power than earlier designs—as little as 2.7 volts, half the 5.5 volts consumed by standard desktop microprocessors—but they're also designed from the ground up to work hand-in-hand with the APM specification and with third-party power-management software.

With an SL-equipped notebook, expect to get up to twice as much on-the-go computing out of standard batteries between charges and to use less ac when the computer is plugged into an outlet. In addition, your batteries won't need to be charged as often. Interestingly, the faster (and somewhat pricier) i486SL design saves even more power than the older 386SL. The i486SL can whip through your work quicker and thus spends more time in sleep mode (theoretically, at least).

Choosing a notebook based on one of these chips—or one powered by the new PowerPC 603 chip that will appear in Apple and IBM computers in 1994 or 1995—will ensure that you get the most on-the-go computing per erg consumed. A new generation of power-miser chips will consume even less battery power. One of them, the Advanced RISC Machines ARM 610 processor, was chosen by Apple for its personal digital assistant, the Newton. The Newton can get up to 100 hours of operation on one battery charge.

Consider using a good notebook as your primary and only computer; it will save power costs and desk space. Notebooks are becoming more powerful, with faster CPUs and bigger hard disks squeezed into ever-smaller packages, and they're also becoming more comfortable to use. The color screens in today's notebooks are more readable and more suitable for high-demand graphical user interfaces, keyboards are becoming more ergonomic, and many notebooks now incorporate pointing devices conveniently built right into the keyboard.

Most notebooks now allow you to hook up a standard CRT display for improved viewing. This combination might be the best power-saver of all. A 1993 *PC Week* comparison review touted the notebook/CRT combination as more power efficient than the new crop of Energy Star PCs, and more convenient as well. (See chapter 4 for more on Energy Star.)

Choose power-efficient peripherals You can save power by choosing the right peripherals, too. Peripherals such as hard drives and fax modems designed to fit on an expansion card and draw power from your PC are more power efficient than external models with their own power supplies. Small-format hard disk drives are more power efficient than large-format models because it takes less energy to spin them. A 3.5-inch 80MB hard disk uses only 25% of the power of a 5.25-inch 80MB disk. The tiny 2-inch disks in laptops and notebooks are even more energy-efficient. And the new 1-inch micro hard disks and 2.5-inch removable media drives use very little juice.

Monochrome monitors use less power than color monitors, and small-screen monitors use less than large-screen ones. No matter what PC and monitor manufacturers and designers of graphical user interfaces tell you, most computing work doesn't require color. (Any old-timer Macintosh user can confirm this.) Keep in mind that the monitor is one part of your computing setup that draws close to its rated wattage at all times.

Laser printers (and their techno-cousins, plain-paper copiers and plain-paper fax machines) are mighty power hogs. The hot-fusing process used by lasers to develop, transfer, and bond toner to paper requires large amounts of energy.

Networked offices can all share one big laser printer, which is power- and hardware efficient, as well as economical. Individual users don't have that option. If you use a printer mainly for correspondence and other small print jobs, consider an inkjet printer rather than a laser. Inkjets use up to 99% less power in active mode and are much cheaper to buy and operate as well. The ink-smearing problems that bedeviled the first generation of inkjet printers has been solved, and most inkjets now can print satisfactorily on plain paper.

Another relatively new printing technology called electron-beam printing equals laser printing in quality, is more power-efficient, requires fewer working parts in the printer, and costs less per page. Currently, electron-beam printers are available only in heavy-duty models for high-volume printing.

Buy the latest Here's a case where it's difficult to make the green computing choice that's best for the environment. Older peripherals tend to be energy eaters compared to new equipment. Modern microprocessors, circuit boards, hard drives, and laptops can do more computing with less juice than the components in that old clunker XT you might be using now. But, as the last chapter suggests, it's also good green computing practice to make do with the hardware you have, to reduce the amount of life-cycle pollution and solid waste that discarded PCs create. Which course should you choose?

Considering how many hours a day you use your PC might help you decide. If you use it only occasionally and for short periods, then the solid waste/life-cycle pollution argument wins over the energy-conservation argument, and you should stick with the hardware you have, upgrading it as long as possible. But if you use your older PC constantly, then energy conservation and increased performance might well outweigh the waste consideration. You should buy the fastest new Energy Star PC you can afford.

Use electronic communications Printing, especially laser printing, uses more power than telecommunications—that is, communication by modem, fax modem, and electronic mail. Conserve paper as well as power by using your modem instead of your laser whenever possible. See chapter 5 for more on the "paperlite office," chapter 12 for environmental online services, and chapter 14 for more on using electronic mail in environmental advocacy. Chapter 8 discusses the health problems of spending more time in front of your PC, which you'll do if you use telecommunications extensively.

Solar-powered PCs

For the ultimate in green-PC power, generate your own juice from the sun's rays. Solar panels are now available that can recharge the batteries of a notebook PC or supply enough converted ac power to run the biggest desktop powerhouse you can find.

The electricity you get from the power grid (that is, over the power lines) is alternating current, or ac. Off-grid power sources like solar panels put out direct current (dc). The two electricity types are incompatible, so devices designed to use one type can't use the other without a special mediating device called an inverter (described later).

Don't try to power notebook computers directly from the sun; use solar power to charge the batteries instead. The battery recharger/ac adapter units of some notebook PCs can be hooked up directly to an external dc source like a solar panel, and some can't. If you're lucky, your notebook manufacturer offers a 12-volt dc charger that allows you to run your notebook's recharger off a car cigarette lighter. Hook the dc charger to a solar panel (many solar units are designed to output 12-volt dc and even have a car-cigarette-lighter receptacle) and use the sun to recharge your batteries.

You'll want at least two batteries, one in the notebook and one recharging from the solar recharger outside or near the window. With enough spare batteries and a run of sunny weather, you might not have to hook up to the grid for a long, long time.

Desktop PCs run on ac only, but with some ingenuity you can run them off the sun. Here's where you'll need the inverter, a handy device that converts low-voltage dc into standard 110- to 120-volt ac. Pocket-sized inverters, which cost around $150, can be packed into your briefcase and carried anywhere. Make sure that the inverter outputs precisely regulated ac power, or your computer might not operate correctly; PCs can be very sensitive to fluctuations in power.

The inverter works not just with solar power, but with any 12-volt dc power source, like a car battery or generator. Obviously, any off-the-grid source you tap into must output steady, dependable power.

Solar solutions If all this seems too complicated to pull together on your own, check out the off-the-shelf solar solutions that are just coming to market. The solar rechargers sold by The Complete Portable will charge virtually any portable computer battery (as well as batteries used by mobile phones) because the voltage automatically adjusts to that required by the battery. CreateCo's Sunpak line includes three battery rechargers based on thin-film amorphous silicon technology for Macintosh PowerBooks and Apple's Newton PDA. The solar panels are sewn into a carrying case for the Newton or built into a flexible panel that will fit inside most PowerBook carrying cases or briefcases. The panels are state-of-the-art, thin film, flexible solar panels. In full sunlight, they can safely run the computers at a rate that is equal to the ac wall adapters that come with the computers. The panels are equipped with diodes and resistors that regulate the amount of power being sent to the computers and prevent battery drain or battery overload. In less than full sunlight, the panels can recharge Newton or PowerBook batteries.

Similar devices to run notebooks off solar-generated ac or to recharge batteries with solar panels can be easily assembled out of components sold by Real Goods, the alternative power specialists. In fact, Real Goods reports that the number of people who ask them questions about how to run PCs off the sun's energy is increasing all the time. See the Green-PC resources section for vendors of solar power and inverter equipment.

Conserving power in the PC office

Once you've minimized your PC's power consumption, you can turn to the other major electricity eaters in your office—lights and air conditioning.

Green lighting tips

Computing in the dark might be okay for hackers, but most people need plenty of light for computing. You might spend minutes every day fiddling with your lights to get them just right, but you probably don't think much about their energy consumption. Desk lamps and overhead lights use two to ten times the power of your PC. Here are some tips for getting the most light for the least power:

Turn off the lights This is the easiest way to save lighting energy. Plug your desk lights into your PC's power commander so they'll power down when you shut off the computer.

Use free sunlight If there are windows in your workplace, keep the curtains open. A 3-foot-by-5-foot office window in direct sunlight lets in more light than 100 60-watt incandescent bulbs. To avoid glare from windows, keep computers out of direct sunlight, tilt monitors away from the window, and if necessary put a polarizing or filtering plastic screen over the windowpane. (These are available from photo supply stores for a few dollars.) Think of it as sunglasses for your window. Plain white paper taped over the lower part of the window makes a cheap and serviceable substitute, though it reduces window light by about half.

Use the next lowest wattage Replace higher-wattage bulbs with the next lowest wattage. Change 100-watt bulbs to 95-watt, or 75-watt to 60. The lower-wattage bulbs use less power and give off less heat, and you probably won't even notice the slight reduction in illumination.

Put brighter bulbs in fewer fixtures One high-wattage bulb is more energy efficient than two lower-wattage bulbs that provide the same light. Reduce lighting in overhead fixtures by replacing one bulb out of every three with a burned-out bulb (for safety). If necessary, make up the difference in illumination by using brighter bulbs.

Concentrate lighting where it's needed Desk lamps apply light directly to the areas you need to use. And, unlike overhead lights that are shared by many workers, you can turn off desk lights whenever you don't need them. A good rule of thumb is to light your PC work area three times brighter than the ambient room lighting. Reduce unnecessary overhead lighting in little-used areas—but not to the point of reducing safety.

Choose energy-efficient lighting Most offices already use energy-efficient fluorescent overhead lighting, but there are still plenty of standard incandescent bulbs in desk lights. Every one of them should be changed to a more efficient type of light. In the past few years, new types of lighting have come on the market that are significantly less power-hungry than incandescents. According to the EPA, if everyone in the United States switched to energy-efficient lighting, 202 million tons of carbon dioxide, 1.3 million tons of sulfur dioxide, and 600,000 tons of nitrogen oxides would be kept out of the atmosphere.

Halogen lights are two to three times as efficient as incandescent lights: you can use a 20-watt halogen where you once had a 60-watt incandescent. They also last four times longer and give off an intense, warm glow that's close to that of natural sunlight. Because they are very compact and light, halogen lamps are ideal for desk lamps. New halogen bulbs don't require expensive imported fixtures, but can screw into any standard lamp socket. The bulbs themselves are two to four times as expensive as incandescent bulbs of similar light output.

Even more energy-efficient than halogens are the new compact fluorescent lights (CFLs), which are among the greenest lights you can buy. They're long-lasting, economical, and much smaller than the familiar strip fluorescent bulbs. Like the latest halogens, they can screw into any standard lamp socket. The ballast, a special power unit required by all fluorescents, is incorporated right into the bulb. Most current models don't contain the radioactive trace elements used in the first generation of CFLs. They make excellent energy-saving replacements for incandescents in most situations. Read on for a detailed discussion of CFLs.

Are CFLs for you?

Compact fluorescent lights operate on the same principle as standard tube fluorescents. The inside of the glass bulb is coated with a fluorescing powder, and the bulb is filled with a gas that emits ultraviolet radiation when an electric current is applied to it. Flick the switch, and the powder glows as the UV hits it. This process is more efficient than the one used in incandescent lights, in which electricity running through a metal filament heats the filament until it glows. Fluorescent lights also emit more light per watt than incandescent lights. A 15-watt CFL emits about the same light as a 75-watt incandescent bulb because it converts electricity to illumination with five times the efficiency.

The savings to be gained with CFLs don't stop there. Fluorescent bulbs last much longer—ten to thirteen times longer. You won't have to replace the average CFL for three to four years. They also give off little heat, keeping the workplace cooler in warm weather and reducing the need for air conditioning. It has been estimated that 30% to 50% of the energy consumed by air conditioning in a large office building goes to remove heat produced by the lighting; much of that could be saved by switching to cool fluorescents.

Amory Lovins, director of the Rocky Mountain Institute, an environmental think tank, figures that over its lifetime a single CFL will keep as much as a ton of carbon dioxide and twenty pounds of acid-rain-causing sulfur dioxides out of the atmosphere. It will also keep ten to thirteen times its weight in glass, metal, and packaging out of our landfills. And, over its lifetime, it will save $30 to $50 on electric bills.

Green lights Recognizing the advantages of energy-efficient CFLs, in 1991 the EPA launched a voluntary program dubbed Green Lights to encourage energy conservation among large businesses and institutions by switching to energy-efficient lighting, mostly CFLs. So far, about 600 companies, including such industrial giants as IBM and Mobil, are participating, benefiting both from the EPA's technical assistance and the good publicity that energy efficiency generates. If you belong to a large organization considering a switch to energy-efficient lighting, contact the Green Lights program at the address in the Green-PC resources section.

CFL drawbacks Even CFLs aren't perfect. Among the drawbacks are the following:

- CFLs are somewhat larger than incandescent bulbs, so they might be too long or too wide to fit in the lamps in your office. If that's the case, you might still be able to use CFLs by installing special adapters available from most places that sell the bulbs.
- Some people complain about the perceptible, irritating 60-cycles-per-second flicker and hum associated with older types of CFLs. Your best bet is to choose a CFL with an *electronic ballast*. This is a chip in the base of the CFL that operates the bulb at a flicker-free 20,000 cycles per second. Electronically ballasted CFLs contain no radioactive elements, either. And they're completely silent. They cost about the same as older CFLs.
- CFLs cost much more than incandescent bulbs—up to 20 times more. You'll make the money back in energy savings and reduced need for bulb replacement, but the initial expense of switching from incandescent to fluorescent lighting can be high. Contact your local electric utility and ask whether they have a CFL replacement program that will pay you a rebate or give you a discount on the purchase of CFLs. CFLs can be purchased through such a program for as little as $5 or $6—a discount of up to 80% off the retail price.
- CFLs do contain trace amounts of mercury vapor to aid in current induction, as do all other fluorescent lights. Dead CFLs should be treated as hazardous waste and disposed of through the appropriate municipal program.
- CFLs are too complex in construction to be recyclable through most current municipal recycling programs. That should change as recycling becomes more sophisticated and CFLs become more common.

- So-called "full-spectrum" CFLs—bulbs that claim to reproduce a light like the sun's—don't last as long and aren't usually worth the extra expense.
- Install high-priced CFLs only in often-used lamps. They aren't economical in seldom-used lighting.

To AC or not to AC

After lighting, the biggest power consumer in the PC office is air conditioning. (It would be the biggest consumer by far if your PC needed air conditioning all year, the way mainframes still do.) You'd be surprised at the number of full-load air-conditioning hours (hours when your air conditioner is working at peak power draw) that your office might require, even if you live in a cool northern state like Vermont or Massachusetts. Table 3-2 lists a range of values for some larger U.S. cities, based on degree-day tabulations from the National Climatic Data Center. Keep in mind that each full-load hour might cost your office anywhere from about 15 cents (for a home office with one 1500-watt window unit) to thousands of dollars (for a large office building with central air). PCs and their peripherals add to the problem because nearly 100% of the energy they consume is given off as heat. An office with many computers, laser printers, and other office equipment is much hotter in summer; that makes air conditioners work all the harder and adds to the total number of full-load hours. True, computers help keep offices warmer in winter, but that's only an advantage if winters are cold in your area. Plus, because air conditioning systems are relatively less efficient than heating systems, it costs more to cool an office than to heat it.

Besides the cost of air conditioning, there are environmental considerations. The standard green line about air conditioning is that the earth would be better off without it, so don't use it. Air conditioning uses plenty of power—between two and six kWh per window unit every hot day—with all the pollution problems and energy costs that entails. But that's not the worst of it.

Table 3-2

Air Conditioning Full-Load Hours of Operation —Selected U.S. Cities

City	Full-load Hours
Albuquerque, NM	800–2200
Atlantic City, NJ	500–800
Boston, MA	400–1200
Burlington, VT	200–600
Charlotte, NC	700–1100
Chicago, IL	500–1000
Cleveland, OH	400–800
Columbia, SC	1200–1400
Corpus Christi, TX	2000–2500
Dallas, TX	1200–1600
Denver, CO	400–800
Detroit, MI	700–1000
Honolulu, HI	1500–3500
Indianapolis, IN	600–1600
Little Rock, AR	1400–2400
New Orleans, LA	1400–2800
New York, NY	500–1000
Oklahoma City, OK	1100–2000
Pittsburgh, PA	900–1200
Rapid City, SD	800–1000
St. Petersburg, FL	1500–2700
San Diego, CA	800–1700
Seattle, WA	400–1200
Washington, DC	700–1200

Nearly all air conditioners today use the ozone-damaging coolant chemicals called chlorofluorocarbons (CFCs) or hydrochlorofluorocarbons (HCFCs). CFCs, and to a lesser extent HCFCs, are strongly implicated in the destruction of the ozone layer. Normally, the coolant is sealed inside the air-conditioning unit, where it can't get away. But sooner or later—sooner, if the unit is used regularly—leaks appear and the coolant evaporates into the atmosphere, where it eventually reacts with and destroys thousands of ozone molecules in the upper atmosphere. These are the molecules that shield the earth from most of the sun's intense ultraviolet radiation.

There has been some recent progress in designing air-conditioning units that don't require CFCs or HCFCs, but they aren't yet commercially available. Until then, it's true that not purchasing or using air conditioning is the best thing you can do for the ozone layer.

AC reality check However, in the real world, PCs in hotter climates probably need air conditioning. Most computers and other forms of electronic equipment are rated for operation at ambient temperatures up to 104 degrees Fahrenheit and relative humidity of up to 95%, with the exception of laser printers, which don't work well in high humidity. In most parts of the United States, your computing environment, even without air conditioning, is probably within those limits.

But those limits are set by the manufacturers after testing their products under ideal conditions, with filtered power, constant temperatures, clean, dust-free PCs, and no unusual stresses. In the dusty, variable conditions that are more likely to prevail in your workplace, a power spike at temperatures as low as 85 degrees Fahrenheit can cause your PC to fail—maybe for good. Air conditioning will help prevent that. AC lowers the humidity too, which is good for laser printers.

So how do you balance the environmental and economic costs of air conditioning with its computer-related advantages? First, explore these AC alternatives:

Install a fan Fans are less expensive to buy and run, and they use far less energy. Window fans can pull in cool air at night that will keep a room comfortable for much of the day.

Change your computing habits If possible, do your computing during the cooler parts of the day and at night. Move your computer to a cooler location—to a workplace without south-facing windows, for example. At all costs, keep your PC out of direct sun.

Compute in someone else's cool Take your notebook PC on the bus to the local library and do your computing in air-conditioned comfort there. At least you're not adding to the problem.

Getting the most from air conditioning

Let's say you decide that you must have air conditioning. It's just too hot where you work, or your office is air conditioned already. At least you can maximize the benefits of air conditioning and minimize the costs. Air conditioning in large office buildings probably has already been tuned by maintenance staff to minimize energy consumption. If you suspect it hasn't, or if you're using a window unit for your home office, take the following measures:

Select an efficient system Window air-conditioning units are assigned an Energy Efficiency Rating (EER) number that appears on the unit's Energy Guide label, which is mandated by the Federal Trade Commission. The higher the number, the more efficient the unit. Central air-conditioning systems don't have a federal rating, but you can ask the manufacturer for an estimate of a year's air-conditioning energy expense in your area.

Maintain the system Regularly clean the filters and condenser coils. This will help the unit run with maximum efficiency and keep it free of pollutants, molds, and bacteria. Also, have it checked for coolant leaks. With regular maintenance, it's possible to keep air-conditioning coolant in the system and out of the atmosphere.

Raise the thermostat Set the air-conditioning thermostat to 78 degrees Fahrenheit. That's cool enough to ensure safe operation of PCs. If we all set our air conditioning thermostats just one degree higher, says the EPA, we'd save the equivalent of 35,000 barrels of oil every day.

Reduce heat Reduce or eliminate sources of heat that make air conditioners work harder. Shade the outside condenser part of window air-conditioning units. Don't put window and portable units in direct sun. Switch to low-heat fluorescent lighting. Put tinted films on windows, or install awnings. Turn off your heat-producing computer equipment when you leave.

Choices that make a difference

- ❐ Turn off your PC and lights when you're not there.
- ❐ Choose low-power computer designs.
- ❐ Let timers control electrical devices for you.
- ❐ Keep equipment clean and well-maintained.
- ❐ Use appropriate lighting.
- ❐ Put brighter bulbs in fewer fixtures.
- ❐ Replace incandescent bulbs with fluorescents.
- ❐ Don't use air conditioning if you can avoid it.
- ❐ Raise air-conditioning thermostats and reduce air-conditioning use.
- ❐ Keep air conditioners clean and leak-free.

Green-PC resources

Information about the EPA's Green Lights Program is available from:
EPA Green Lights Program, 6202J
401 M St., SW
Washington, DC 20460
Green Lights hotline: 202-775-6650

The following organizations can supply information on energy conservation:
Alliance to Save Energy
1725 K St., NW, Suite 509
Washington, DC 20006
202-857-0666

Conservation and Renewable Energy Inquiry and Referral Service (CAREIRS).
U.S. Dept. of Energy
P.O. Box 8900
Silver Spring, MD 20907
800-523-2929

Energy Conservation Coalition
6930 Carroll Ave., Suite 600
Takoma Park, MD 20921
301-891-1104

National Appropriate Technology Assistance Service
U.S. Dept. of Energy
P.O. Box 2525
Butte, MT 59702
800-428-2525

This organization holds seminars and educational programs on saving energy in buildings:
American Council for an Energy Efficient Economy (ACEEE)
2140 Shattuck Ave.
Berkeley, CA 94704
510-549-9914

These companies make intelligent switchboxes that can turn a PC on and off when you aren't there:
Sequence Electronics
150 Rosamond St.
Carleton Place, Ontario
Canada K7C 1V2
613-257-4773, fax 613-257-1840

Server Technology
408-988-0142

Sophisticated Circuits
800-827-4669

S&K makes a line of lightweight external batteries for Powerbook and Duo notebook computers that last up to 7 times as long as internal batteries. Contact:
S&K Manufacturing Inc.
215 S. Market St.
Oskaloosa, Iowa 52577.
515-673-6930, 800-952-8972, fax 515-673-8602

Solar battery chargers and other alternative power equipment for portable PCs are available from:
The Complete Portable
505 Shawn Lane
Prospect Heights, IL 60070
800-328-4827 ext. 3317, 708-577-6342, fax 708-577-6551

Keep It Simple Software/CreatCo
32 S. Ewing, Suite #211
Helena, MT 59601
406-442-3559, fax 406-442-1316

Real Goods carries a large selection of CFLs and other interesting power-saving products:
Real Goods Trading Company
966 Mazzoni St.
Ukiah, CA 95482
800-762-7325

Portable inverters are available from:
Trace Engineering
5916-195th, NE
Arlington, VA 98223
206-435-8826, fax 206-435-2229

Use your Macintosh to monitor energy use and other environmental factors with this complete package of remote controller, sensors, and software.
EnviroMac
Remote Measurement Systems Inc.
206-328-2255

4

Energy Star PCs

CHAPTER 4

JUST FOUR DECADES AGO, massive amounts of electrical power were required to energize the vacuum tubes in the world's few electronic computers. Today, computing power has increased 10,000-fold, and computer prices have fallen by a factor of 1,000. Yet, on the average, today's PCs use 10,000 times less electricity than their antediluvian ancestors.

This trend toward power efficiency in computers is taking another jump forward. In mid-1992 the EPA announced a new initiative, called Energy Star, to encourage manufacturers to design lower-power PCs. The Energy Star program has as its goal the development of computers and other peripherals that will automatically enter a low-power state (often called a sleep mode) when the unit is inactive. This low-power state is defined as 30 watts or less of power draw. When activity resumes (that is, when the keyboard or mouse is used), the PC will snap back into full wakefulness. All notebook computers already do this in order to conserve scarce battery power, but not desktop units, which still make up the vast majority of PCs.

According to the EPA, by the year 2000 these new computers could save some 25 billion kilowatt-hours of power, enough electricity to power Vermont and New Hampshire each year. That's equal to the output of ten coal-fired power plants. In terms of its environmental benefit, says the EPA, the Energy Star program will prevent yearly emissions of 20 million tons of carbon dioxide, the gas chiefly responsible for global warming, as well as 140,000 tons of sulfur dioxides and 75,000 tons of nitrogen oxides, the pollutants most responsible for acid rain. Energy Star will also save computer users up to $1 billion in annual electricity bills—even more if they use Energy Star versions of other energy-hungry devices like laser printers and copiers.

By November 1993, more than 200 PC and peripheral manufacturers, including major players like IBM, Apple, and Compaq, had signed on to the Energy Star program. Products with the Energy Star logo began appearing on the market in the summer of 1993 after the program's official launch at the White House by Vice President Albert Gore.

Manufacturers are scrambling to bring Energy Star products to market for two reasons: they can be cheaper to manufacture than less-energy-efficient designs, and, as of October 1993, the U.S. government is purchasing only Energy-Star-compliant PCs. Corporate marketers have not lost sight of the fact that the federal government is the single biggest buyer of PCs on the planet. It already owns 1.4 million PCs and expects to buy $4 billion in computer equipment in the near future. Some state and municipal governments, which buy yet more billions of dollars of computer hardware, are already following suit. Suffolk County on Long Island is one municipality that has made a public commitment to the program. Canada has adopted a similar standard. The state of California is likely to sign on by the time you read this.

Most electric utility companies have endorsed the standard as well. Like energy-efficient lighting and other conservation measures, Energy Star PCs benefit the electric companies by reducing the growth of electricity consumption. That helps utilities make do with existing capacity rather than forcing them to build expensive new power plants. Expect to see electric companies promote Energy Star to their large corporate customers. Soon you might even be able to buy an Energy Star PC at a discount through your electric company, just as many utilities now sell compact fluorescent light bulbs (see chapter 3 for more on CFL).

Why IBM turned green

Few companies have environmental benefits in mind when they set out to design a ground-breaking new product. But, just as bees in search of nectar pollinate the flowers they depend on, companies can sometimes do environmental good while pursuing purely economic ends. An excellent case in point is the design evolution behind IBM's PS/2 E, the first Energy Star personal computer.

Jim Davis is product manager for the PS/2 E and one of a small group of IBM engineers who define new technologies for IBM's personal computers. "In the fall of 1991," Davis told me recently, "I was asked to look at low-power technology, which was evolving very quickly in portable PCs, to see how it could be leveraged into the rest of our product line, especially our desktop computers."

"The original thinking was that low-power technology would generate less heat, leading to a number of important benefits," Davis continued. "The enclosure could be smaller, and thus cheaper to build. Everything would be less thermally stressed, which meant we could dispense with a fan, another cost saving. The lower heat would yield longer lifetimes for many of the components inside the box. Basically we were looking at low-power technology to derive a marketing benefit that would be easy for our customers to understand: a better warranty."

Meanwhile, the EPA, pleased with the success of its "Green Lights" lighting energy-saving program (see chapter 3 for more on Green Lights), contacted IBM's government programs office in Washington and asked Big Blue to help design an industrywide voluntary energy-saving program for PCs. Davis was assigned in January 1992 to help draft the original specifications for what would become the EPA's "Energy Star" program.

Davis, the EPA, the Computer Business Equipment Manufacturers Association (CBEMA), and other advisory groups came up with a model specification that just about everyone in the industry could meet without undue hardship. The system unit (the CPU) when not active would consume no more than 30 watts of power. The monitor would also consume no more than 30 watts.

Because energy-saving technology was already well-developed for portable computers, the model specification proved to be relatively easy to achieve even in desktop computers. Nonetheless, it was really a quantum step forward in reducing PC energy consumption. Davis measured a typical IBM desktop model and found it consumed close to 250–300 watts every hour it was on. Industry-standard power supplies were so inefficient that they consumed twice as much power as was actually required to run the computer.

Davis noted that it was especially important to have maximum voluntary involvement from all PC manufacturers, including the clone makers. "We were looking for total industry buy-in at the time the specification was announced. We set 30 watts as the limit because, although IBM could do better, many clone makers could not. We wanted even the smallest members of the industry to be able to make a compliant product."

Another important piece fell into place when President Clinton signed an executive order on Earth Day 1993 requiring the U.S. to buy Energy-Star-compliant computers. "That woke up corporate America," said Davis. "When Vice President Gore appeared with 22 different Energy Star manufacturers in June 1993, it was clear that this was the coming thing to all corporate buyers. They said to themselves, 'If the government is requiring that on their quote, we will, too.' If Gore had unveiled only two or three computers—meaning that we had made the specification too difficult to achieve—we would not have been successful at all."

It was easy enough for manufacturers to build stripped-down computers that were Energy Star compliant, but that's not what Davis wanted to do. He was determined to build a world-class energy-efficient computer that would, as he put it, "push desktop computing to a new paradigm." He got the green light from IBM in May 1992, with the proviso that he had to show a finished product at Comdex, the world's largest computer exhibition, in November of that year. That wasn't long to design, manufacture, and debug a radical new computer.

Davis pulled together a "virtual" development team of five designers from around the world: Japan, Scotland, Boca Raton, and Lexington, Kentucky. Over PROFS, IBM's proprietary network, Davis and his coworkers shared everything from rough concepts to blueprints to bills of materials. "The epitome of the virtual design approach is that my team only met physically on November 14, late in the evening the night before the show. They literally showed up with boxes from Scotland and Japan and Lexington and assembled the whole computer for the first time in my hotel room that night. The only tool we used was a Swiss Army knife. Plainly, we had succeeded in creating a machine that was easily assembled, reducing the cost of manufacturing and servicing and disassembly for recycling."

"Even we didn't think the product would turn out to be as successful as it was. At Comdex, we won *Byte Magazine's* best system of show. The *Byte* folks said to us that they were skeptical that energy efficiency was important to users, but they thought we had really redefined the desktop parameter, that we had brought to the marketplace what customers had been demanding all along: a small computer that didn't take up much space, was quiet (because there was no fan), used plug-and-play PC cards (formerly called PCMCIA), had a high-quality flat-panel display, and, least important, was energy-efficient, used recyclable plastics, and so on."

Davis's mandate now is to make the qualities and specifications of the PS/2 E pervasive throughout IBM's product line. Does he consider himself an environmentalist? "I certainly am not an environmental activist. I did this strictly for the technical challenge." His thinking has evolved, however. "I've become more aware of environmental issues," he noted with a laugh. "It's a little strange for a hardcore engineer like myself."

Energy Star specifications

The technical specifications for Energy Star compliance (which still are pretty much as Davis drafted them) are relatively simple. For computers or monitors, the unit must enter a low-power (sleep) state of equal to or less than 30 watts of power draw when the unit is inactive. With software, the user of the computer can set the number of minutes before the unit enters the low-power state.

Energy Star printers For printers, the specification is a little more complex. Energy Star sets a range of low-power states and maximum idle times according to the printer speed. Printer speed is a fair measure of the amount of power the printer requires. Also, high-speed printers are likely to be hooked up to a network and therefore are more often in use, so it is counterproductive for them to go into a low-power state every few minutes. Table 4-1 lists the Energy Star specifications for printers.

Energy Star Specifications for Printers in Low-power State Table 4-1

Printer speed (pages per minute)	Default time to low-power state	Max power (watts)
1–7	15	30
8–14	30	30
15 & above & color laser	60	45

Source: EPA

Energy Star monitors Most Energy Star PCs ship with compatible Energy Star monitors that enter a low-power, 30-watt or under state at the same time as the PC itself. There are Energy Star monitors in every category, including big-screen (21-inch) 24-bit color monitors for high-end graphics work. Sony, NEC, Apple, Nanao, and other well-known manufacturers have several Energy Star monitors on the market right now. (Most also meet the MPR 2 radiation emissions standard; see chapter 9 for more.)

If you are buying a monitor and graphics card separately from your Energy Star PC, you must be sure that they all work together. You can't just assume that they do because manufacturers might use any of a number of incompatible technologies to comply with the Energy Star specification. Ask the various manufacturers if their products will work with the others you are considering.

At the time of writing, the best approach is to make sure that your entire system conforms to the Video Electronics Standards Association (VESA)'s Display Power Management System (DPMS) protocol. A DPMS-compliant monitor will, theoretically, work with any other PC or card that is also DPMS compliant. DPMS offers the additional advantage of allowing three different power-saving modes:

- Standby, with modest energy savings but fast recovery.
- Suspend, with average power-savings and a longer power-up time.
- Off, which saves the most power but requires the monitor to warm up from a cold start.

How much energy does Energy Star save? The EPA figures that the typical PC (computer, monitor, laser printer) uses 235 watts. At seven cents per kWh (the 1993 U.S. average, according to the U.S. Energy Information Center), a PC that is on all the time consumes $144 in electricity each year. A typical Energy Star computer left on all the time will consume $74 in electricity, a savings of $70, or close to 50%. But if you turn off your Energy Star computer at night and on weekends, the annual electrical cost will be just $25, a savings of $119 over the full cost of running an ordinary PC day and night for a year.

Figuring the actual savings from your Energy Star PC depends on several factors:

- The actual power draw of the PC in both full operation and sleep mode.
- The number of hours the PC operates in each mode.
- The actual energy cost in your area.

Calculate your yearly electricity costs for an Energy Star PC by using this method:

$$(F + S) \times T \times .001 \times \$R = \$E$$

1. Find the watts consumed by your PC and monitor at full power and multiply that by the number of hours per day they run at full power. We'll call this value "F."
2. Find the watts consumed by your PC and monitor in sleep mode and multiply that by the number of hours per day they are asleep. We'll call this value "S." Add F and S.
3. Multiply the hours per day of operation times the days per year of operation. We'll call this "T." Multiply (F + S) by T.
4. Multiply by .001 to convert to kilowatt-hours, then by the average rate cost per kWh in your area, which we'll call "$R".
5. The result, "$E," is the electricity cost per year to run your Energy Star PC.

If you work this out for different Energy Star PCs, you'll find that energy savings can vary considerably between machines. According to the American Council for Energy Efficient Office Equipment, an

Energy Star PC that consumes 25 watts at full power and 5 watts in sleep mode, and is in sleep mode 70 percent of the time, will use only a tenth of the electricity consumed by another Energy Star PC that uses 160 watts at full power, 25 watts in sleep mode, and is asleep only 30 percent of the time.

A January 1994 review in *Computer Shopper* magazine showed that 5 early Energy Star models consumed from 25 to 33 watts in sleep mode. Their monitors ranged from 0 to 25.2 watts of electricity consumption in sleep mode. Total system draw in sleep mode ranged from 25.3 to 58.0 watts.

Another consideration: many models ship in an Energy-Star-compliant configuration, but when fully loaded with expansion cards they guzzle more than the Energy Star power limit. Buy the most efficient unit possible if you plan to stuff it full of expansion cards.

Maximize your energy savings by:

- Choosing the most energy-efficient Energy Star computer.
- Making sure your power management software is on and operational.
- Setting your PC to enter sleep mode within a few minutes of becoming idle; the more time it spends asleep, the more electricity you will save;
- Turning the computer completely off when you end work for the day.

Other Energy Star savings There are other, indirect ways that Energy Star PCs can save you money and electricity. Because Energy Star PCs use about one-quarter the electricity used by conventional PCs, they are well suited to buildings with older, light-duty wiring. The cost of rewiring a building for conventional computers can run into the hundreds of thousands of dollars.

By switching to Energy Star, companies that require uninterruptible power supplies (UPSs) for mission-critical work can make do with fewer or lighter-duty, less expensive units. Given that the cost of a UPS ranges from $0.50 to $3 per watt, providing protected power for a 30-watt Energy Star PC could cost $300 less than protecting a standard 130-watt desktop.

Energy Star PC performance The EPA claims that consumers can get all the benefits of Energy Star without sacrificing computing performance. But is that actually true? Recent comparative reviews in computer magazines suggest that early Energy Star models are not yet at the cutting edge of performance or price, but they soon will be.

The first crop of Energy Star desktops falls somewhat short in overall speed. The main reason is that the hard disk, monitor, and other components take a little time to come up to full operation from low-power sleep mode. You might feel impatient as the machine gets up to speed. One work-around for this is to reactivate your PC, then do another small office task. When you turn back to your PC, it will be ready for you.

Energy Star PCs might also be limited to slower processors. For example, no current Energy Star design can be built around Intel's powerful but power-hungry Pentium chip. Not all high-speed chips are power-hungry, however; Energy Star and notebook systems built around Intel's energy-efficient 735 and 815 chips and the Motorola/IBM PowerPC 603 chip should appear in late 1994.

The first Energy Star models were priced somewhat higher than similar, noncompliant models. That came as no surprise to those who know that the cost of developing any new technology is borne mainly by consumers who purchase early. Prices came down for green PCs as the market for them expanded, so that by mid 1994, a green PC cost no more than a compliant PC.

Inside an Energy Star PC

IBM's Energy-Star-compliant PS/2 E is one of the most power-efficient desktop computers you can buy. Its other green attributes make it a good example of where environmentally responsible PC design is going. Let's take a closer look at some of the features of this state-of-the-art green computer, many of which follow from its low-power design.

Low power Awake and fully loaded with 4 PC Card expansion cards, the PS/2 E draws 24 watts, 6 watts less than the Energy Star maximum for sleep mode. The PC Card slots, which accept expansion cards about the size of a thick credit card, draw a maximum of 3.3 watts when occupied, as opposed to 5 or more watts for standard plug-in expansion board slots.

Quiet operation The PS/2 E runs so cool that it needs no internal fan. Operation is nearly silent (10 dB at the operator's ears) except during hard-disk access, when there is a slight whir.

Small size The system unit (CPU) of the PS/2 E is the size of a small pizza box, 12 inches by 12 inches and less than 3 inches high. (In fact, it's so small that it even surprises IBM service representatives. One rep I talked to who was unfamiliar with the product assumed it was an external hard disk drive.) The system unit fits easily inside a desk drawer or can be hung on the wall. The unit's small size is due mainly to the fact that it does not have to be big enough to accommodate standard plug-in expansion boards, a fan, and a large power supply. Instead, the PS/2 E accepts 4 smaller PC Cards.

Light weight The PS/2 E is also light. It weighs just a little over ten pounds as shipped, not much more than a notebook PC. Moving it around is easy. The reason it is so light is that it has a small power supply, no fan, and is made mostly of plastics, not metals.

Energy-saving displays The PS/2 E is shipped with either a low-power CRT that conforms to Energy Star and Swedish MPR 2 specifications, or an innovative TFT (thin-film transistor) flat panel display that uses only 37 watts in full operation and 17 watts in sleep mode. The 10.4-inch TFT display can be hung on the wall.

Easy disassembly The case snaps together without screws or clips. In fact, snap fittings are used throughout to make the unit easy to disassemble and reuse or recycle. There are only seven metal screws, as opposed to 40 or more in the typical desktop PC. Even the green plastic strips on the case can be snapped off.

Uses recycled materials A single resin, PC/ABS, is used for the case. Twenty-five percent of the plastic is a mix of postindustrial and postconsumer recycled material. All plastic parts are coded for recycling. The internal stainless metal shield contains 35% recycled content. The electro-galvanized subpackage for the system board contains 60% recycled content. (There's more on the use of recycled materials in computers in chapter 6.)

Responsible packaging The PS/2 E is shipped in unbleached cardboard boxes that contain 10 to 30% recycled material and are 100% recyclable. The inner foam packing contains 25% postconsumer recycled content. (See chapter 6 for more on green-PC packaging.)

The Energy Star program

The Energy Star program is a voluntary partnership between the EPA and computer, monitor, and printer manufacturers. Many companies have said that they will convert their entire lines to Energy Star compliance. There are two main enticements to do this: compliance opens the door to the huge federal government computer market, which is required to buy Energy Star products, and manufacturing compliant products can often be less expensive than making traditional PCs (for example, a fan might not be necessary to cool the enclosure of a compliant PC).

The EPA offers technical assistance to companies and formal recognition of their compliant products. Perhaps more importantly, the EPA acts as an adviser to federal, state, and local government and agencies planning to buy Energy-Star-compliant products. The EPA does not endorse any particular product, but it does supply lists of compliant products that are used by the government and other purchasers.

For manufacturers, the EPA has set up several levels of Energy Star participation: one for primary manufacturers of PC, printer, and monitor manufacturers, and an "ally" program for chip and circuit board manufacturers, power-supply makers, software developers, and manufacturers of other components. The ally agreement does not contain individual product specifications, so ally products are not necessarily compliant with the program.

The Energy Star logo The Energy Star logo—the word "energy" and a star under an arc representing the world—is only authorized for use on products that meet the precise Energy Star specifications. Be cautious, however, because an informal perusal of energy-saving products currently on the market indicates that even Energy Star allies are using the logo on their packaging and products. Such products might be worthwhile, but they might not meet Energy Star specifications. If you are in doubt and need to verify the status of a product for government or corporate purchase, call the EPA hotline for the latest listing of compliant products. (See the Green-PC Resources at the end of this chapter for EPA contact information.)

Industry participation

Following is a list of companies manufacturing Energy Star compliant computers, monitors, or printers as of November 1993:

Acer/Acros
ADI
Advanced Intelligence
ALR
American Megatrends
Apple
AST research
Austin Computer
Avnet Computer
Brother
C-Tech
Canon
Capetronic
Compaq
CSS Labs
CTX International
Cyberstar
Daewoo Telecom
Data General
Dell
DEC
DTK
Duracom Computer Systems
DynaColor
Everex Systems
Gateway 2000
GoldStar
Hewlett-Packard
Hyundai Electronics
IBM
ICL
IDP
IDEK/Liyama N.A.
Insight Distribution
IPC
Kyocera
Lexmark
MAG Innovision
Mecer
Memorex Telex
Mitsubishi
Mustek
Nanao USA
NCR
NEC
Nissei Sangyo America
Olivetti
Optiquest
Packard Bell
Panasonic
PC&C
Progen
QHT Systems
Qume Peripherals
Relisys
Samsung
Samtron Displays
Shuttle Computer
Siemens Nixdorf
Sony
Star Micronics
Summagraphics
Sun Microsystems
SunPICS
Tandberg Data Display

Tatung
Tatung of America
Taxan
TECO
Tektronix
Texas Instruments
Tulip Computers International
United Solutions
USA Teknik
ViewSonic
Wyle Laboratories
Zenith Data Systems

Companies that are participating in the program, but which have not yet announced compliant products as of November 1993, include:

ACMA
ACTech
Action Electronics
Advanced Digital Systems
Alaris
Alps ElectricAMAX
Ambra Computer
Applied Digital Data Systems
ATC
ACC
APF
Apricot
Area Electronics Systems
Bankers Systems
Bull Italia
CFC Technology Services
Cheer Electronics
CHEM
Commax Technologies
Compal Electronics
Compaq (has not yet announced a compliant printer)
CompuAdd
Compudyne
Computer Sales Professional
CompuTrend Systems/Premio
Comtech Micro System
DataExpert
Dataproducts
DEC (has not yet announced a compliant printer)
DDI
Desktop Displays
Destiny
DFI
Display Technologies
Dimension Computer Systems
EFA
EKM Computer
Elonex
EMPaC International
EPS Technologies
Epson
Ergo Computing
Flytech Technology
Fountain Technology
Fujitsu
GCC Technologies
GCH Systems
General Parametrics
Genicom
HIQ Computer Systems
Hitachi America
HSI
IDEA
Infotel/Midwest Micro
Intergraph
International Data Systems
Intra Electronics USA
J-Mark Computer
Key Power
Keydata International
KFC
Kodak
Leading Edge
LION America
Lite-On Technology
Metrovision Microsystems
Micron Computer
Micronics
Mitac
Mitsuba
Modular
NAI
National Advantages
National Microcomputers
NCD
NEC (has not yet announced a compliant printer)
NETIS Technology
Nokia
Ocean Information Systems

Office Automated Technology
Okidata
PC Pros
Perpetual Technologies
Philips
PSI
Quantex Microsystems
H&S Computers & Enhancements
Radius
Republic Technology
Royal Computer Sampo Technology
Sceptre Technologies
Samsung (has not yet announced a compliant printer)
Sharp Electronics
Sigma Designs
Silicon Graphics
SKV International/ Computermill
Smith Corona
SuperMac Technology
Swan Technologies
Tagram
Tandy
Tangent Computer
TeamMax
Toshiba
Total Control Products
TriGem
Tri-Star Computer
TS Micro
TWC
Unisys
Unitron
USFO Technology
USIT
Viglen
Vision Computer Technologies
Vtech Computers
Western Imaging
Wyse Technology
XCV
Xerox
Young Microsystems
Z&M Advanced Technology
Zenon
Zeos

Together, these companies make up more than 70% of the U.S. computer market and more than 90% of the U.S. printer market.

Companies participating as Energy Star Allies (manufacturing peripherals, software, power supplies, low-power chips, and other components) as of November 1993 include:

Advanced Digital Systems
Advanced Micro Devices
AFEQT
Anigma
AnteChron Research
Artec Innovations
Arvee Systems
Asian Computer
Astec
ATMEL
Award Software
Axelen
B&B Electronics
BCM
CAREO
Cartaco
Chips and Technologies
Cirrus Logic
Computer Resources
Conner Peripherals
Connectix
CreSonic
Cyrix
Databook
DELTEC
Diablo Scientific Labs
DIA Semicon Systems
Diamond Computer Systems
DINEXCOM
DynaComp
EFA
EFAR
Elitegroup
Ergonomics
Exide Electronics
Free Computer Technology

Glitch Master
Golden Power Systems
Hampton Technology
Harmony
Harmony Power
Hibernation Software
HIPRO
Image Plus
Infomatic Power Systems
Intel
J-Mark Computer
Jabil Circuit
Lattice
LION America
Lite-On, Inc.
LLR Technologies
Market Central
Maxtor
Metasoft
Michi Tech System
Micro Energetics
Microsoft
Microtest
Minta Technologies
North American Power Supplies
OPTI
Palo Alto Digital Systems
PAUKU P&C
Phoenix Technologies
PicoPower Technology
Powercard
PSC
Pulizzi Engineering, Inc.
Seagate Technology
Sejin America
Squence Electronics
Smart Industries
Symphony Laboratories
SystemSoft
T&T Computer
TAKEN
Tamarack
TEKRAM
Texas Instruments
TMP
Topower
Tripp Lite
Unipower
United Solutions
USAR Systems
U.S. Power & Technology
VLSI Technology
Wave Energy
Western Digital
Zytec

Energy Star alternatives

Can't afford a new Energy Star PC, or want to keep the one you have? Can't remember to turn off that pesky, energy-guzzling monitor on your own? You can still save quite a bit of juice, and a fair amount of bread, with some low-cost energy-saving devices that provide much of the benefit of Energy Star at far less cost.

Several manufacturers now make inexpensive external devices that automatically turn off your monitor and other peripherals for you. B&B Electronics' Green Keeper, a box that plugs into the keyboard port of any PC, is one. Like a screen saver, the Green Keeper software (which is provided in Windows and DOS versions) watches for keyboard or mouse input and, if nothing has happened for a while, completely shuts off the monitor and any other peripherals that are plugged into Green Keeper's AC outlet. Resuming work brings the monitor back to life. There's no effect on the CPU because only peripherals are powered down; the unit just won't work if you try to plug your PC into it. Depending on usage, monitor power draw, and the cost of electricity in your area, Green Keeper can pay for itself in less than a year. You can save more by using Green Keeper to power down other devices at the same time, like a printer or lights. The unit costs $50–$60 on the street, as do some other products of this type. (One advantage of Green Keeper is that the manufacturer, B&B Electronics, ships it in a box made of recycled materials and includes documentation on a recycled disk.)

When shopping for one of these energy-savers, choose one that provides software operation (some units only have timer switches on the box, which are less flexible than software and aren't sensitive to mouse movement). Also choose an energy saver that will plug into your PC (PS/2s and some older PCs use nonstandard keyboard connectors).

While an energy saver can potentially save you more energy than an Energy Star monitor (because it turns the monitor entirely off instead of sending it into a sleep mode), you will have to wait for the monitor to power up from a cold start every time you resume work. That typically takes 5 to 10 seconds.

Choices that make a difference

- ❒ Purchase low-power Energy Star PCs.
- ❒ Adopt Energy Star computers throughout your organization.
- ❒ Become an Energy Star developer or ally.
- ❒ Use energy-saving devices like Green Keeper.

Green-PC resources

To learn more about the EPA Energy Star Computers Program, contact:
Environmental Protection Agency
Global Change Division, 6202J
Office of Air and Radiation
401 M St., SW
Washington, DC 20460
Attn: Linda Latham
202-233-9114

You can request a basic Energy Star information packet from:
EPA Energy Star Fax Line 202-233-9659
EPA Energy Star Hotline 202-775-6650

If you are a manufacturer, you can order a customized agreement to join one or more of the Energy Star programs by requesting a form through the Energy Star Fax Line, filling it out, and then faxing it to: 202-775-6680.

More information on the IBM PS/2 E can be obtained by contacting:
IBM PC Direct
Bldg 203, 3039 Cornwallis Rd
Research Triangle Park, NC 27709
800-426-2968, fax 800-426-4182

The following devices turn off monitors and other peripherals when your PC is not being used:
Green Keeper
B&B Electronics
815-434-0846, fax 815-434-7094
Has the best combination of hardware, software, and price.

EcoLite
ProGen Technology
800-PROGEN-8, 714-549-5818

Monitor Miser
Inversion Development Corp.
415-940-7805, fax 415-940-7849

PC Ener-G Saver
PC Green Technologies
800-984-7336

5

Paperlite computing

CHAPTER 5

BY NOW, EVERYONE KNOWS that the digital office wastes more paper than the old analog office ever did. The so-called "paperless office," which has been predicted for two decades, has never materialized and is even something of a joke. Offices buy oceans of paper for printing all kinds of computer-generated documents that were never needed before—newsletters, reports, cover sheets, memos to everyone in the organization, and on and on. The PC makes it so effortless to spit out endless paper publications that few of us stop to think about what happens to them all.

And it's a sure bet that only a tiny fraction of paper communications are effective. Millions of memos and reports are read once—if at all—and then trashed, adding to the 40% of our landfills composed of paper waste. How many memos have you thrown away unread? How many times have you printed a document over again just to correct a minor typo or layout problem? You'd never have done that if you had to rekey the document on a typewriter or, the ultimate horror, rewrite it by hand.

The good news is that the technology to kick our paper habit is finally at hand. We just have to use it. Paper isn't really required to communicate effectively using your PC. In fact, you don't even need a printer. Instead, you can tame the "paper tiger" by tapping into the power of networks, e-mail, fax modems, integrated paperless office systems, and universal digital documents. Even if you can't eliminate the use of paper, you can reduce it significantly with what might be called "paperlite computing."

The real cost of paper

Paper has always been an inexpensive, portable medium of communication, which is the key to its 3,000-year success. Today an individual sheet of paper is cheaper than ever, but we use more paper than ever. The result is that paper is becoming too expensive—both to businesses and to the planet.

What does paper really cost? You have to consider not just what you pay at the stationery store for a ream of white bond, but the larger, less obvious life-cycle costs of manufacturing, distributing, and discarding paper. Some of these costs are covered by the money you pay for the paper; the rest you pay indirectly through taxes and reduced quality of life. Here are the major costs of paper:

- ➢ The number of trees that have to be cut.
- ➢ Costs for replanting trees or dealing with the effects of deforestation.
- ➢ The cost of transporting wood to the paper mill.
- ➢ The amount of energy used to create the paper.
- ➢ The environmental cost of generating that energy at the power plant.
- ➢ The amount of water used at the mill, and the cost of cleaning it.
- ➢ The life-cycle environmental cost of manufacturing the chemicals used at the mill.
- ➢ The cost of removing mill waste and pollution from the local environment.
- ➢ The labor of all the workers involved in all stages of paper manufacturing.
- ➢ The health costs incurred by workers and local residents.
- ➢ The cost of packaging, warehousing, and distributing the paper.
- ➢ The gas you consume going to and from the stationery store.
- ➢ The electricity used to print on the paper.
- ➢ The cost of disposing of or recycling the paper waste.

Multiply this total cost by the 2 trillions or so sheets of paper used worldwide every year, and you can see that it represents a significant drain on world resources.

The argument that paper is a renewable resource is partly true because it's made from living trees that can be replanted. However, new trees take decades to grow, and mature forests, with all their varied flora and fauna, require centuries to develop. Recent studies have shown that timber companies and governmental forest services rarely replant the same number of trees that have been cut, resulting in a worldwide net loss of forest every year.

Practical benefits of the paperlite office

The cost of paper seems especially high when you realize that digital forms of communication can take the place of paper at less cost to the environment, and to your organization's bottom line. The financial benefits of paperlite computing include:

Saving paper Take a look at the money you spend each year on paper used exclusively for in-house publications. That money does little or nothing to build your organization, and it does harm to the earth. The same money invested in paperlite computing can yield savings every year thereafter.

Making full use of your PC investment The EPA estimates that PCs are idle for up to 40% of the workday. You have a significant amount of computer time, therefore, to create and distribute electronic correspondence and organize electronic documents. Using paperlite computing can help you take full advantage of the power inherent in PCs, and it also makes sure you get the maximum return for your PC investment.

Saving space in the office Paper storage takes up a significant portion of the cubic footage of every office. We buy filing cabinets and other furniture that do nothing but store paper. Paperlite storage is far more efficient. One high-density 3.5-inch floppy disk can hold the equivalent of 750 sheets or about a 5-inch-high stack of typed pages. A 100MB hard disk that fits comfortably inside your computer can hold the entire contents of a 4-drawer filing cabinet crammed with letters and memos. One CD-ROM can hold the information equivalent of an entire roomful of books. The space you save by not using paper could make it possible to move to a smaller, less expensive office. You can also get rid of those old-fashioned desks with poor ergonomics that were constructed around paper-based work operations.

Saving filing labor One source estimates that it costs $25,000 to fill a standard filing cabinet (including paper and labor costs, most of them associated with computers), and more than $2,000 a year to maintain it. And you'll still lose track of more than 3% of your documents and spend an average of $120 to locate each one. Electronic archiving systems, by contrast, take up little space, require much less labor to handle, and are easier to duplicate and transport.

Speeding up communications Digital communications are far quicker than sending a letter. You can choose the time and date of transmission and reception and know immediately if the message got there.

Getting information fast Access to documents in digital storage is fast and clean. And documents aren't in a fixed order, as they are in a filing cabinet. A good paperlite filing system allows you to search, sort, and examine your documents in new ways, extracting useful information that wasn't apparent before. That can be a valuable strategic asset.

Drawbacks of paperlite computing

There are some environmental negatives to the paperlite office. These include higher energy consumption and possible health problems from increased computer use.

More power needed Your office might consume more electricity after switching to paperlite computing. This is because computers, fax modems, and other equipment will be on longer to handle the additional tasks of electronic communications and document handling. How much more energy you'll consume depends on several factors. If your office adds many PCs to create a new network for e-mail and document storage, then electrical consumption will increase significantly, adding atmospheric pollution and draining your finances at the same time. (See chapters 3 and 4 for more on how to save power when computing.)

However, if you're already running a network of PCs all day long, adding additional paperlite systems will make better use of energy you're consuming anyway. Even if your office does end up using more computer-related energy than before, you still might be able to save energy in other areas. For example, you'll save electricity (and rent) if you can move to a smaller office with less storage space. Paper manufacturing, distributing, and printing is an energy-intensive process. In the big picture, the energy savings from reducing paper use eventually offsets the increased energy consumption of running more computers.

Increased health risks If all your documents appear on the screen, you'll have to spend more time in front of the computer to read them. More time in front of a PC can affect your health. It can lead to various stress and strain disorders, vision problems, and possibly even illnesses resulting from low-frequency radiation.

If your organization is planning to adopt a paperlite computing system, make sure that the health of workers is protected. Install ergonomic workstations and displays that can be read without eyestrain. Take measures to reduce radiation emissions from monitors and PCs. All this will add to the total cost of installing paperlite systems, but it will save your business money in reduced health costs and increased productivity. These topics are covered in more detail in chapters 8 and 9.

Conserving PC paper

The best way to reduce the mountain of PC paper is, of course, to use as little as possible. But kicking the paper habit isn't easy. Most of us could use paper a lot more efficiently. Here are some tips for reducing paper use by squeezing the most printed information onto the least amount of paper. These ideas are suitable for letters, memos, reports, press releases, and other daily corporate communications.

Use smaller type A smaller type size in a more compact font—for example, 10-point Times Roman instead of 12-point Courier—lets you fit more words on a line. Ten-point type is quite readable; you read type much smaller than that every day in the newspaper. Decreasing the leading (the blank space between lines of type) lets you fit more lines on a page. Condensed fonts, like Helvetica Narrow, squeeze even more type into a small space. But don't make print so small that people have trouble reading it. Get a second opinion if necessary.

Leave narrow margins No law says that left and right margins must be wider than one-half inch.

Reformat Minor reformatting or editing can often keep the last line or two of your documents from spilling onto a new page.

No extra spaces Single-space your documents. Indent paragraphs instead of leaving a blank space between them. Leave one letter space between sentences instead of two; it looks better on desktop-published documents, anyway.

No cover Reset your laser and fax to omit cover sheets. To replace the fax cover sheet, redesign your letterhead to include the fax number, date, time, and number of pages in the document (some word processors will stamp these automatically).

Use the backs Use the blank back side of used sheets for drafts. This is okay for inkjets and sheet-fed dot-matrix printers, but used paper will jam in many laser printers. To flatten jam-causing wrinkles, press the paper under a heavy weight. Buy laser printers and fax machines that can do duplex (double-sided) printing. Adobe's newest PostScript printer driver supports duplex printing.

Use print utilities Printing utility programs can help you squeeze more service out of your printer by allowing you to print several reduced sheets on one page or to print on two sides of the paper. That could potentially cut your printer paper use in half. Several of these programs are listed in the Green-PC resources section.

Small is beautiful Got a small message? Use a small piece of paper. Most sheet-fed printers can handle paper as small as 5½ by 8 inches, half the size of a letter-sized sheet.

Draft dodging Don't print drafts at all. Learn to edit right on the PC. Distribute draft documents on disk or via network for editing and approval. Dispense with multiple page proofs when doing desktop publishing.

Make one do for all Post, share, and circulate memos instead of printing one for each employee. Better yet, use electronic mail; see the e-mail section later in the chapter.

How to be a paperlite office

While offices are getting comfortable with paper conservation, they can work toward an even higher plane of paperlite existence. Here are some suggestions for moving in the right direction, starting with simple ideas and moving to the more ambitious.

Study your paper flow How much paper do you really use? Where does it come from? Where does it go? How much does it cost you? Where is the best place to start replacing paper? Analyze what functions are performed by paper in your organization, and identify at least one area where going paperlite makes financial sense. Then develop a plan of action and assign someone to see it through.

Educate the office Educate everyone in the office about the value of paperlite communications. Make sure all employees are up to speed in each paperlite application program you use. Set a practical, intermediate goal for reducing paper use—say, 75% of current levels in three months—and keep track of your progress.

Install paperlite tools Even if the paper is gone, the need to communicate remains. If PCs are to be the basis of paperlite office communications, then employees need PC tools that replace paper. Many companies offer integrated paperlite office systems that provide most of the tools you'll need in one package. See the section on integrated systems for more. You can also assemble your own paperlite system a piece at a time. Depending on how extensive a program you plan to install, you'll need some or all of the tools in the following list. The cost depends on what systems you choose and how many PCs will be connected; it can run into the hundreds of thousands of dollars for larger organizations. Here's what you'll need:

- An office PC network.
- Electronic mail for interpersonal communications.
- Fax modems to send out mail.
- Telecommunications software for remote file transfer and database access.
- Optical character recognition (OCR) scanners and software to scan archived and incoming paper documents.
- Basic group software: notepad, contact manager, and calendar.
- Form-processing software and a form database manager.
- Universal digital document software for unrestricted document interchange (see the section on universal documents later in this chapter).
- Tape or optical-disk mass storage for archives.

Switch to fax modems The standard fax machine is one of the biggest paper wasters in an office. Every day, millions of PC users print letters and run them through fax machines only to have the recipients take the faxed documents and type them back into a PC. And thermal fax paper isn't recyclable. More efficient than a stand-alone fax is a fax modem, a board or external device that functions both as a fax machine and a data modem for telecommunications. With a fax modem, any document you prepare on your PC can be sent directly to another fax modem for storage and display on the receiver's PC. No paper is involved. See the section below on fax modems.

Reduce mail Forget sending letters via the Postal Service (snailmail) or expensive express services. Use a fax modem or e-mail to send all documents over long (or short) distances—it's faster and cheaper. Reserve postal or express services for packages that contain something other than documents.

Eliminate paper memos Use electronic mail to send messages among coworkers on your office network. The habit of copying a two-line memo on two hundred sheets of paper and sending an administrative assistant to hand it out all over the building deserves a quick death. There's more on e-mail later in this chapter.

Get rid of your filing cabinet Many offices print a copy of PC documents and keep them in an old filing cabinet "just in case." Presumably, that means in case PCs disappear and we go back to the obsolete office practices of three decades ago. That's more likely to happen if we don't conserve our resources with paperlite computing. Don't print and file unnecessary paper. If you're worried about keeping an extra copy in case your PC is stolen or your files are corrupted, make backup copies on floppies, tape, or other storage media and lock the copies away in a fireproof safe.

Archive on disk The alternative to the traditional file cabinet is disk archiving. Because disk media are so much more efficient at storing text, you'll save valuable space in the office. The trick is to scan all your paper documents into the computer—which can be a daunting task, especially if you have millions of pieces of paper on file. But you might as well get started now. You can get to work with a relatively simple and inexpensive system that includes your PC, basic optical character-recognition or document-imaging software, a scanner, and enough mass storage to hold all your files. The hardware and labor cost will be anywhere from $1,000 for a small archiving job to millions of dollars for major corporate archiving.

Scan it Most offices receive as much paper—letters, applications, bills, invoices, etc.—as they send out. Filing these documents takes time and space, and more often than not you can't put your hands on them later when you need them. Consider using an optical character-recognition system (OCR for short) to scan these documents into your archiving system. If the documents are properly identified in the retrieval system, and if you keep secure backups, you'll be able to find these documents instantly and transmit them over your office network. And you can always print out a copy if you must. Remember to recycle the original paper document.

Process forms on your PC A study by the research firm Datek Information Services shows that one-third of all business documents are forms, and that U.S. businesses spend $6 billion a year to buy preprinted paper forms and up to $120 billion a year to process them.

Forms don't have to be on paper, however. There are many form-processing software packages now on the market that, in conjunction with a database-management system, can eliminate much paper and reduce the cost of processing forms significantly. You start saving immediately. Half of the large corporations in the United States have turned to computer-based form systems. Smaller organizations can benefit, too.

Here's one real-world example. I used to order 4,000 three-part NCR preprinted questionnaire forms every year to compile information for a directory. The top sheet of the form was mailed to directory listers; the second sheet was mailed only if there was no response to the first; the third sheet was for filing and was hardly ever referred to. Those unused parts, comprising more than half the total print job, became instant landfill waste.

Switching to electronic forms eliminated the need for the second and third sheets because additional forms could now be printed in-house, on demand, using a laser printer and plain paper. The investment was $1,500 for a simple forms layout program and database running on an existing Macintosh and 50 hours of in-house development time. The yearly savings was 7,000 sheets of paper and 150 hours of paper handling, or about $3,300. With additional programming, the form database was turned directly into a formatted desktop publishing document, saving about 2,000 sheets of galley and mechanical pages, about 75 hours of manual paste-up work, and a quart of solvent-based rubber cement. We have recently begun publishing the directory on disk, eliminating paper almost entirely.

Investigate integrated paperless systems Many vendors now offer complete paperless document systems that integrate paperless communications, OCR, form processing, and archiving with networked PCs, scanners, and mass storage. Such systems are usually expensive, and their full complexities are beyond the scope of this book. They do, however, represent the logical goal of paperlite computing. Carefully investigate several such systems before you commit to one to be sure that it meets the needs of your organization. One company, Pinnacle Micro, makes a donation to the World Wildlife Fund with every installation of its paperless system. A list of paperless office system vendors is included in the Green-PC resources section.

Paperlite networking

Telecommunication is always more environmentally benign than paper communication. Sending a message in electronic form uses few resources and meets the computer-age requirement of near-instantaneous transmission and global reach. Telecommunication to nearby PCs is best accomplished through a local area network, or LAN; distant telecommunications can be done using a data or fax modem over phone lines.

Installing a network to provide direct data communications between local PCs is the key to reducing most in-house paper waste. When files, letters, memos, and reports can be zipped directly to the interested parties or archived electronically on the server for retrieval by any networked PC, the pressure to print is greatly lessened. Most organizations notice a sharp reduction in in-house printing within days of getting up to speed with a network.

E-mail

An electronic mail system makes it possible to send memos, letters, documents, files, faxes, "while you were out" messages, and voice mail anywhere your network can reach, without using paper. Here's how it works: You compose a letter to a coworker on your PC and then send it to her at her e-mail address; she reads it online, composes a reply, and sends it back to you at your address. If sender and receiver are both online and monitoring their mailboxes, then messages can be read and exchanged in real-time. The instantaneous nature of e-mail means that you can read a document on your PC and immediately respond. Or you can store messages for later perusal.

Electronic mail has advantages over ordinary paper mail, but it beats telephone contact, too. The main advantages of e-mail over phone calls are that there's a text record of everything communicated, and that entire documents such as reports and press releases can be exchanged and collaboratively edited. E-mail is also inexpensive; messages cost at most only a few pennies apiece.

E-mail software usually comes in two parts: a messaging application for composing messages on each PC, and a server-based central post office that receives, stores, and forwards messages around the network. Networks with gateways to other networks can forward messages around the world. Most organizations don't have to be sold on e-mail; the benefits are obvious, both in environmental savings and in increased speed of communications. By 1995, according to an estimate by International Data Corporation, there will be 35.6 million LAN-based e-mail addresses, an estimate that frankly sounds rather low given that the same report suggests that more than 60% of corporate PCs are already linked to a network. Many e-mail systems will incorporate voice mail and speech synthesis, even video teleconferencing. E-mail will ultimately supplant telephones and answering machines in most organizations. That means less hardware to eventually clog our landfills.

E-mail without a network You can send e-mail even if you aren't on a network and don't have e-mail software. Most of the larger information services can forward messages to any e-mail address on a network linked to the Internet, the network of networks. Such calls often cost less than a direct connection because the call to the service is local. You'll need a telecommunications program and log-on privileges with the service. E-mail software developers offer gateway utilities so their products can easily connect to online services. Some services that offer e-mail are listed in the Green-PC resources section.

Modems

A modem translates digital data from your PC into pulses that the telephone system can transmit, and vice versa. It differs from a fax in that faxes transmit compressed images of documents, while a modem can transmit the document file itself. Modems can cost as little as $50 today; many people purchase a fax modem, a device that performs the functions of a fax machine as well as a modem, for $80 to $150.

Most green computerists find a modem invaluable, not only to avoid sending paper documents or disks by mail, but also for tapping into the wide range of environmental information sources online. (See chapter 12 for more on online environmental databases and other resources.) A modem is also necessary to link a local network with distant networks.

The green-PC fax

Faxing is a fact of modern life. Few businesses can afford to be without one, and many live or die by the information that curls out of the office fax machine. Faxing is also one area of office communications where paper can truly be eliminated.

Sending a single-page fax anywhere in the world typically costs less than a letter sent to the same address and requires no envelope, stamp, or transportation. Faxing saves gas and lowers air pollution, and the energy required to send a fax is far less than the energy required to manufacture and distribute the paper in a letter and deliver the letter to its destination. And the fax arrives instantly, at the time of day you choose. Faxing is even more environmentally beneficial if you send the same communication to multiple destinations, a capability included with most higher-quality fax machines and fax modems. You can instantly save the paper in multiple pieces of mail and receive confirmation that all your communications have reached their destinations.

Fax modems

A fax modem is a combination fax machine and data modem, sized to fit in your PC or on your desk. With it, you can fax most documents in your computer simply by activating the fax modem software, in a process that is usually as easy as printing to a printer. It's faster than a stand-alone fax, uses less power, and transmits clearer copy. Best of all, it doesn't require paper and a printer. Send your fax modem document to another fax modem, and no paper is involved in the communication at all. When you need to sign on to an online service or send a file to a friend, your fax modem (plus telecommunications software) can do that too.

Receiving a fax through a fax modem is also easy. The fax modem receives an incoming fax and stores it as a snapshot that you can view in your fax software. Keep in mind that your PC has to be powered up to receive a fax transmission with a fax modem, even when you're not there. Consider using a timer to turn your PC on and off when a fax comes in. See chapter 3 for more on timers.

As long as you fax only documents created on your PC, a fax modem should meet all your needs. If you want to fax other documents—book pages, signed contracts, photographs, and the like—you'll need a scanner to scan the document into your PC. A good hand-held scanner costs as little as $300 today.

Keep in mind that all faxes, including fax modems, transmit only pictures of text, not text that can be edited and used in other computer documents. You can't grab an ordinary fax document and paste it into your word processor. But suppose that's just what you want to do? There's a solution to this problem. You can buy fax software that not only sends and receives faxes, but also converts them to editable text using optical character recognition techniques. Most of these programs will also compress your faxes so they don't take up too much room on your hard disk.

A stand-alone fax machine isn't as green as a fax modem, but there's still something to be said for it. It can be on and ready to receive while your computer is off, and a fax in idle mode uses less power than a PC equipped with a fax modem. In fact, it isn't always easy to choose between reducing fax paper use by switching to a fax modem or reducing fax power use by leaving on a stand-alone fax.

If you already own a stand-alone fax, it probably makes sense to leave it on all the time to receive (assuming you get faxes during nonoffice hours), and use an inexpensive fax modem to send faxes (so you don't have to leave on your power-hungry PC all the time). It's important to keep your paper-saving strategies flexible. Don't be dogmatic about saving every last bit of paper when it will mean wasting electricity or buying a new piece of hardware you'll use only once in a while. Additional fax modem considerations include the following:

Internal or external Internal fax modem boards use fewer materials and draw less electricity, so they're the greener choice. Buy an external model only if you plan to use it with another PC now or in the future.

Send or receive Make sure the fax modem you choose will both send and receive fax transmissions (not all do). Another invaluable feature is fax management, which allows you to screen unwanted faxes, broadcast faxes to many destinations, and schedule fax transmissions for hours when rates are lowest.

Telecom switchbox Telecommunications switchboxes automatically route incoming calls to your modem, fax, or voice phone. These inexpensive units (under $100) eliminate the need for separate lines and thus save you money. Home businesses benefit the most from telecom switchboxes. The more telecommunications equipment you have, the more you'll need one. Some fax modems come with this feature already built in.

Scanners As already mentioned, in order to send fax modem documents that include paper-based information like photographs and pages of books, you'll have to scan the pages or photos into your PC with a scanner. Scanners work a lot like photocopiers, except they create a computer graphics file that can be incorporated into other computer documents. Hand-held scanners are probably best for most people because they're small, easy to handle, and cost around $300 or less.

No-fax faxing

Fax modems are the best choice for green paperlite communications. But not everyone can afford a fax modem or a fax machine. You can still enjoy many of the green benefits of faxing by exploring the following alternatives:

The corner fax If you don't have a fax of your own, most copy shops and stationers will send or receive a fax for you. There are even fax kiosks. But most of them require hard copy to send a fax, which means you have to print out a paper document to bring with you. Faxes sent to you will also be printed on paper. If you send and receive many faxes this way, check around for a neighborhood fax service that has a fax modem so you can bring a reusable disk instead of paper. Keep in mind that your disk and files will need to be compatible with the service's PC.

Online fax services Many online services will send a fax for you, and you don't need a fax machine or fax modem of your own—only a standard modem and telecommunications software. Sign on to the service, upload the file you want to send, and give the recipient's fax number. The service will take it from there. The charge per fax might be one or two dollars (America OnLine, for example, charges two dollars for each transmission). Most services will send text files only, not graphics or other file types. If you don't have access to a fax machine or fax modem yourself, you can't receive a fax this way; you can only send one. But if you already spend a lot of time online and don't have fax access, this might be the quickest, easiest, and most cost-effective way to send a fax letter. The Green-PC resources section lists online services with faxing capabilities.

Printer fax Another approach is the printer fax. This is a low-power, low-cost unit, about the size of a small modem, that attaches to an HP LaserJet or other printer and gives it plain-paper fax capability. This is how printer faxes work:

1. Install the hardware and printer fax software.
2. Create a document to send.
3. Print the document, but choose the printer fax as the printer.
4. The printer fax intercepts the document and sends it over the phone lines instead.

To receive a fax, your PC and printer don't have to be on; the printer fax will store incoming messages in memory until you're ready to retrieve them. As with fax modems, however, you won't be able to send book pages or other non-PC documents unless you scan them into your PC first.

Paperlite publishing

Of the many promising developments for publishing without paper, several are now on the market or will be by the mid-1990s. All of these depend on PCs and online or disk-based document distribution. Two important technologies are universal digital documents and electronic books and periodicals.

Universal digital documents

Most complex documents—that is, documents with elaborate text formatting, color illustrations, mathematical formulas, and the like—are still published on paper. It's easy to understand why; the intended audience can easily read them and pass them around. With computer documents, it's a different story. If you've worked much with PCs, you already know that every application program creates its own kind of file, which usually can't be read by most other programs running on the same PC, much less by programs on other computer platforms. It's difficult to incorporate different kinds of files, such as text files, scanned photos, and database reports, into one document. You can't even look at most files if you don't have the application that created them.

So how do modems and fax modems send and receive different types of documents between different types of computers? The answer is that files sent between machines are mainly of two universal kinds. Fax modems send snapshots of documents that can be interpreted and displayed by all other faxes and fax modems. These snapshots can be read on the screen, but can't be edited or used in another application, like a word processing or database program. Fax modem snapshots are also of poor visual quality, don't include color, and can be viewed only with the fax modem software. You can convert the fax into editable text using an OCR program, but that's a troublesome step, and the results often need correcting by hand.

Most modem traffic, on the other hand, consists of straight unformatted ASCII (text only) documents. ASCII (American Standard Code for Information Interchange) is a standard way of encoding letters, numbers, punctuation marks, and some other special symbols understood by all PCs. Most word processors and other programs that deal with text will allow you to edit ASCII documents. The main problem with ASCII is that it doesn't preserve any of the formatting or graphic elements in the document, like margins, indentations, tab settings, typefaces and sizes, bold and italic letters, embedded illustrations, and so on. Without these elements, a great deal of the total information content of a document can be lost.

Neither fax modem transmissions nor ASCII files are really satisfactory ways to exchange documents from PC to PC. What's needed is a universal electronic document format that can be read on any PC, can include all the formatting from the original document, and can be edited or incorporated into other documents.

Acrobat Several developers are working on universal digital document formats, also called cross-platform documents. Adobe Systems, developer of PostScript, the *lingua franca* of page-layout and high-end printing, is probably closest to finding an answer. In 1993 Adobe released a suite of utility programs called Acrobat that provides a standard way to exchange electronic documents among programs and across Macintosh and PC platforms. The Acrobat Exchange or Distiller programs convert any document created with any program to a single universal file format, with most formatting intact. As long as you have the Acrobat Viewer program running on your Mac or Windows PC (UNIX and other versions will be available by the time you read this), you'll be able to view any Acrobat file without having to own the application that created the original document.

Naturally, Adobe hopes that everyone who has a PC will also want to purchase Acrobat. The company is distributing the Viewer free or nearly free in various formats. Unfortunately, the Exchange and Distiller programs are fairly expensive for single users. If you manage in-house publishing for a medium- to large-size corporation, however, Acrobat's expense will not be a major issue, and you can definitely save plenty of paper.

For single users, a better digital-document solution might be Common Ground, a lower-cost program from No Hands Software (for Windows and Macintosh). Common Ground works best for smaller and text-only documents. You can distribute a free "miniviewer" along with each document so that recipients don't have to own Common Ground themselves to look at what you send. Not only will Acrobat, Common Ground, and programs like them make electronic document interchange simple, but they will also simplify document archiving. Archives of digital documents will be accessible to any PC or other computer.

The digital document downside Until all computer monitors display text and graphics at the resolution of the printed page—at least 300 dots per inch—electronic digital documents won't have the information density and readability of paper. You'll have to strain your eyes more to read digital documents than you currently do to read paper documents. Eventually, high-resolution displays will become common, as demand drives down their price. The other problem is that the various digital document programs aren't compatible with one another. We can only hope that a standard document type emerges that everyone will agree on.

EDI The Electronic Data Interchange standard (EDI, also called ANSI protocol X.12), allows organizations to exchange purchase orders, invoices, shipping notices, and more than 100 other forms of standard business information in a universal digital format. EDI software codes and tags the information in your electronic forms so that other EDI-equipped PCs can read it. Unlike Acrobat documents, EDI documents are fully editable. Even at an average of $2,000 for EDI software and up to $125,000 for a complete EDI network, the technology is so useful and economical that more than 18,000 organizations now use it, according to an industry consulting firm. EDI users agree that the savings in paper, postage, rekeying labor, and time justify the expense.

Use of EDI is growing fast, mainly because large companies and government agencies are requiring their suppliers to adopt it. If it's large enough, your business might need to add EDI capability in the near future. See the Green-PC resources section for sources of information on EDI.

Electronic books, documentation, & magazines

The age of the book on disk is here. Individual novels are being published on disk for reading on portable computers, and CD-ROMs already offer vast collections of modern literature. Not that printed books are likely to vanish anytime soon. They might use a lot of paper, but books are attractive to look at, long-lasting, inexpensive, light, and portable. They need no batteries and are readily biodegradable.

There are, however, immediate practical benefits to publishing some types of material on disk. Documentation for complex machines and systems is now published routinely on CD-ROM. The 50,000 pages of text and images in the maintenance manuals for a Boeing 727 can be encoded on one CD-ROM disk and read on a PC equipped with a CD-ROM player, all of which takes up less room and costs less to produce, both in dollars and in environmental impact, than the multivolume paper version. Florida Power & Light put all the documentation required to license nuclear power plants on CD-ROM; the $75,000 conversion cost was estimated to be one-third that of publishing on paper. Even software documentation is getting out of hand. The paper documentation for both Microsoft Windows 3.1 and IBM's OS/2 2.0 weighs several pounds; that's why IBM is increasingly publishing all its documentation on CD-ROM. Apple publishes its monthly developer mailings on CD-ROM, saving tens of thousands of dollars in postage. Soon, all large documents and databases will be published primarily on CD-ROM.

Major business software is also appearing on CD-ROM. Microsoft publishes its best-selling applications on a CD-ROM called The Microsoft Office. One disk holds four programs and all the documentation. Lotus Development publishes a similar CD-ROM suite of its business applications. Many professional graphics programs, including Adobe Photoshop and CorelDraw, are also available on CD-ROM.

Sales of CD-ROM drives have skyrocketed, making CD publication a viable economic venture. *Disk/Trend* magazine estimates that worldwide shipments of CD-ROM drives will top 3 million in 1994. Apple Computer alone claims to have shipped about 1 million drives in 1993. According to industry projections, some 5,000 CD-ROM titles will have been published in 1994.

Do-it-yourself CD-ROMs Want to publish your own documents on environmentally benign CD-ROMs? Professional duplication services will master a CD-ROM from your data, which you provide in tape backup format or on a portable hard disk, for between $800 and

$3,000, depending on how quickly you want it. Each copy thereafter costs $2 to $3, with a minimum order of at least 200 units. It's an expensive process if you need to publish only a small number of disks and you need to publish them often—the typical situation for publishers of technical documentation.

If you plan to do a lot of CD-ROM publishing in small runs, and you need to publish material fast, then it makes more financial sense to purchase your own CD-ROM mastering system. Desktop CD-ROM mastering systems cost between $4,000 and $12,000 and are available for IBM-compatible, Macintosh, and Unix platforms. Even at the higher prices, these systems pay for themselves after only a few runs, making it far easier to justify getting into CD-ROM publishing in the first place. And the price of desktop mastering will go down as CD-ROMs become more common.

What laser printers did for paper publishing, desktop CD-ROM mastering systems will do for CD-ROM—put high-quality publishing tools into the hands of nearly everyone who wants them. The difference is that desktop publishing has led to an exponential increase in paper use, while CD-ROMs save paper and trees. (True, the disks use polycarbonate, but they potentially can be recycled and made from recycled stock.)

Desktop mastering system manufacturers are listed in the Green-PC resources section of this chapter. There's more on the issue of CD-ROM recyclability in chapter 6. Environmental databases on CD-ROM are listed in chapter 12.

Electronic magazines Many computer magazines cull articles, reviews, news, and program listings from their printed publications and republish them on the major commercial online information services. (See the following section for a list of major online computer magazines, and chapter 12 for more on online services.) Downloading material from electronic magazines (called e-mags or e-journals) generally costs less, both in money and in environmental resources, than buying a paper copy, even with the surcharge some e-mags add to the usual downloading costs.

Not only computer magazines, but also environmental publications are available online. For example, one Internet-mag is The GreenDisk Paperless Environmental Journal. See the Green-PC resources section for contact information, and chapter 12 for more on the Internet.

This trend is now being followed by general-interest magazines. *The Atlantic Monthly*, *Time*, and *Omni* are three of a number of national magazines that publish selections of current issues on the commercial service America OnLine. CICNet, a university cooperative network accessible through the Internet, publishes some 350 e-journals. Many, on obscure topics of specialized interest, would be unable to find their market as paper publications, but the low cost of electronic network publishing makes it possible for anyone with a computer and modem to publish e-mags.

The main current drawback of e-mags is that they contain only unformatted ASCII text, without the design, color graphics, and advertising that make the printed versions so attractive. Soon, however, e-mags will begin taking advantage of universal digital document systems to publish reasonable simulations of slick paper magazines—even with ads.

Computer magazines online Tired of saving all those dusty back issues of computer magazines? Here's how to acquire some of the larger computer publications online:

- The full text of *Byte Magazine* appears on BIX, the Byte Information Exchange. For current access fees and information, call 800-695-4775 for more information.
- *PC Magazine* runs an online service on CompuServe called PC MagNet, where you can read some of the material published in the magazine, download utilities, and gain access to other services as well. Call 800-848-8199 for CompuServe customer service and information on how to enroll. If you're already logged on to CompuServe, type GO PCMAG at the prompt.
- PC/Computing's online service on CompuServe is called PC/Contact. Call 800-848-8199 for CompuServe customer

assistance. If you're already logged on to CompuServe, type GO PCCONTACT at the prompt.

- MacWorld maintains a folder on America OnLine. Call America OnLine at 800-227-6364 ext. 5254 to request a free enrollment kit. If you're already logged on to America OnLine, go to the MacWorld folder by typing MACWORLD at the keyword prompt.
- *Compute* magazine publishes articles and reviews from the magazine as well as Compute Book extracts in the COMPUTE MAGAZINE or OMNI folders on America OnLine. Call America OnLine at 800-827-6364 ext. 5883 for an enrollment kit. If you're already logged on to the service, type the keywords COMPUTE or OMNI.
- *Computer Shopper's* online forum on CompuServe is part of the ZiffNet service. Call 800-848-8199 for CompuServe customer service and information on how to enroll. If you're logged on to CompuServe, type GO COMPSHOPPER at the prompt. The ZiffNet service, the electronic publishing arm of Ziff-Davis, publishes material from *PC Magazine*, *PC/Computing*, *PC Week*, *MacWeek*, *Computer Shopper*, and *PC Source*. Call 800-666-0330 for a free sign-on kit. ZiffNet is also on the Prodigy online service. Contact Prodigy at 800-776-3449, or jump ZIFFNET if you're already logged on. For AppleLink subscribers, selections from Macintosh-related Ziff publications are available in the ZiffNet Selections folder. These will also be available from Apple's new online service, eWorld (which should be in operation by the time you read this.) Ziff-Davis also publishes Computer Select, the full text of 50 computer magazines on CD-ROM.

Choices that make a difference

- ❒ Educate coworkers about the paperlite office.
- ❒ Conserve paper by reformatting documents.
- ❒ Use print utilities to print more efficiently, with less paper.

- Install an office network with paperlite features.
- Archive on disk.
- Employ e-mail instead of printed memos.
- Send files by modem; don't send paper.
- Use a fax modem instead of overnight or courier services.
- Use universal digital documents.
- Read and publish electronic books, documentation, and magazines.

Green-PC resources

Paper-saving print utilities include:

4Print
Provides flexible page printing for HP LaserJets, DeskJets, and other popular printers. It allows double-sided printing, reduced-size pages, multiple pages per sheet, and pages in book order. It's available from most shareware libraries, user groups, and online services.

PRNCOL
from Steve Fox
11515 113th Place, NE
Kirkland, WA 98033

TreeSaver
DiscoverSoft, Inc.
1516 Oak St., Suite 307
Alameda, CA 94501
510-769-2902

This catalog offers many other paper-saving print utility programs (mostly shareware):
The Software Labs
3767 Overland Ave., 112-115
Los Angeles, CA 90034
800-359-9998

E-mail software is available from:
CE Software
P.O. Box 65580
West Des Moines, IA 50265
800-523-7638

Lotus Development
cc:Mail Division
2141 Landings Dr.
Mountain View, CA 94043
415-961-8800

Microsoft Corp.
One Microsoft Way
Redmond, WA 98052
206-882-8080

Sitka Corp.
950 Marina Village Pkwy.
Alameda, CA 94501
510-769-9669

WordPerfect Corp.
1555 N. Technology Way
Orem, UT 84057
801-225-5000

A few of the many integrated paperless office system manufacturers include:
Blueridge Technologies, Inc.
703-675-3015

FileNet Corp.
714-966-3400, fax 714-966-3490

Flagstaff Engineering
602-634-5100, fax 602-634-0100

IBM Corp.
914-765-1900

Odesta Corp.
708-498-5615, fax 708-498-9917

Pinnacle Micro
800-553-7070, fax 714-727-1913

Xerox Corp.
203-968-3000

The annual National Fax Directory is one of the most useful fax phonebooks.
National Fax Directory
Compiled by General Information, Inc.
Gale Research
Book Tower
Detroit, MI 48226

Information about online e-mail and/or faxing services is available from:
America OnLine
800-227-6364 ext. 5254

CompuServe
800-848-8199

GEnie
800-638-8369

MCIMail
800-999-2096, operator 22 for information
800-444-6245

Prodigy Information Services
800-776-3449

Acrobat is available from:
Adobe Systems
1585 Charleston Rd
PO Box 7900
Mountain View, CA 94039
800-833-6687, fax 415-962-0850

Common Ground is an digital document-sharing program that offers features similar to Acrobat:
Common Ground
No Hands Software
415-321-7340

Information on EDI is available from:
Data Interchange Standards Association, Inc.
1800 Diagonal Rd., Suite 355
Alexandria, VA 22314
703-548-7005

EDI, Spread the Word!
P.O. Box 811366
Dallas, TX 75381
214-243-3456
This organization publishes an international yellow pages of EDI users.

6

Recycling & your PC

CHAPTER 6

EVERY WHITE-COLLAR WORKER in the United States produces about three pounds of office waste, mostly paper, every day. Thirteen 50-employee offices generate a ton of office waste daily. The cost to dump each ton of waste in a landfill ranges from $70 to $200 per ton.

The high cost of waste disposal is beggaring many municipalities, especially in the northeastern United States. Worse yet, according to the Environmental Protection Agency, half of the 5,500 operating landfills in the United States will be full in less than 5 years, and few new ones are being opened.

Waste conservation, or precycling as it's sometimes called, is an excellent approach to the waste problem. Not using that extra sheet of paper or printer ribbon is better for the environment, and less expensive, than trying to dispose of it responsibly later. (For more on reducing paper use, see chapter 5.) But waste conservation programs are often slow to take root for a variety of reasons, including the pressure from manufacturers to consume first and ask questions later. Recycling, the practice of harvesting waste to make new consumer goods, is recognized as the quickest way to alleviate the solid-waste problem and save money at the same time.

In the United States, there is intense interest in recycling on the state and local level. The majority of states have enacted recycling statutes during the last few years. In my area of the United States (the northeast), waste disposal is so expensive that many towns and cities find it cheaper to recycle waste paper than to dump it in a landfill. In the last two years, most communities in western Massachusetts joined a regional recycling program for glass, metal, cardboard, paper, and some forms of plastic. The participation rate from businesses and homes is 70% to 80%.

Many businesses are now required by law to meet strict recycling goals or have undertaken recycling programs voluntarily. To take one example from the computer industry itself: Microsoft Corporation, the world's largest software developer, has instituted a recycling program in its main manufacturing plant that has already made a real difference to the local environment. According to Ray Emery, Microsoft's general manager of manufacturing and distribution, the company's Canyon Park manufacturing center recycled 426 tons of paper between January and August 1992, almost double the amount recycled the entire previous year. By Microsoft's reckoning, that saved 13,082 trees, 1,308,213 gallons of water, 1,924 barrels of oil, and 2,309 cubic yards of landfill.

And the market for recycled products is expanding quickly, despite some growing pains. According to the Buy Recycled Business Alliance, its membership of nearly 500 large and small companies spent $10.5 billion on recycled products and materials during 1993.

PCs are great consumers of disposable goods. Think of all the computer paper, ribbons, toner cartridges, disks, and packaging you use and throw away in a year. Much of that waste—perhaps all of it—is recyclable and reusable.

Recycling PC paper

According to the American Paper Institute, the use of recovered/recycled paper fiber by U.S. paper mills is growing at twice the rate of that of virgin paper fiber. The paper industry as a whole hopes to reach the goal of 40% recycling by 1995. To do that, it needs a constant supply of waste paper from consumers. That means more business and consumer recycling programs.

If you're thinking of initiating a recycling plan for your green-PC office, paper recycling is the logical place to begin. Paper is easy to handle, easy to sort, and everywhere. Recycle a ton of waste paper, and you'll save three cubic meters of landfill space. You'll also reduce your waste-removal bill and maybe even get enough together to sell at a tidy profit.

Recycling paper in your office

For the home office, getting a recycling program underway shouldn't pose a great challenge. But recycling programs for the corporate office can be hard to start. Few office recycling programs are born with a major initiative from top management. Recycling usually begins in one department or even in a small group of workstations. One person has to serve as the evangelist who gets things started—the person who educates and encourages other workers.

Let's say the evangelist is you. Start by keeping a box labeled recycling next to your workstation to catch waste white paper: ruined print jobs, drafts, memos, and the like. Get your associates to do the same. At the end of the day, dump the boxes into one large box.

Once you're collecting an appreciable amount of paper, approach your supervisor and ask for permission to draw up a recycling plan for your department or for the entire office. Pitching recycling as a money-saving measure rather than as a moral obligation is more likely to get results. Explain that while your office might not get a high price for its waste paper—you might even have to bring the paper yourself to a recycling center if there's not enough volume (more than 500 pounds) to interest a waste paper buyer—the company will still save money on trash service.

These are the steps you'll need to take in order to get an officewide recycling program off the ground:

1. Nominate a recycling evangelist. (They're usually self-selected.)
2. Enlist management backing.
3. Define the extent of your recycling ambitions—just paper, or more?
4. Determine the type and quantity of recyclable waste your office produces.
5. Find a paper buyer. Call around for the best price per load.
6. Research the best pickup options.
7. Set up a consistent, convenient collection method.
8. Involve and educate everyone in the office.
9. Keep coworkers informed. Start a recycling message center on e-mail.

⑩ Coordinate recycling programs with other businesses in your building.

Preparing waste paper for recycling Your buyer might ask you to remove paper clips, plastic tape, and other contaminants from waste paper. Because envelopes often contain clear plastic windows, folding metal clasps, tape, gummed labels, and other elements that can't be recycled, your buyer might ask you not to recycle envelopes at all.

Wastepaper buyers prefer well-sorted paper, and you'll get a better price for it. Sort your paper for recycling into the following categories, listed below in approximate order of value:

1. Plain white office paper (letterhead, memos, copier and laser printer paper, and tractor-feed computer paper).
2. Data-processing paper with blue or green stripes.
3. Corrugated cardboard.
4. Magazines.
5. Newspapers.
6. Mixed papers (folders, card stock, and brown paper products).
7. Unrecyclables (envelopes, thermal printer and fax paper, post-it notes, express-service packs, dark-colored paper, and mixed shredded paper).

A note about magazines Most PC users and computerized offices collect PC magazines, and most stash them away after a month, never to be looked at again. What can you do with those computer magazine back issues you've been collecting? Most recycling programs will accept the clay-coated paper in magazines, but first try donating your back issues to a local library, user group, or school. Many public libraries don't subscribe to more than one or two computer publications, but they would be happy to add them to their periodicals collection for free. If you need to consult reviews from back issues, keep the magazines for a year and then recycle them. Developments in computing move so quickly that reviews from computer magazines that are more than a year old are usually worthless.

Using recycled paper

Sending out your own paper to be recycled is a good start, but if you aren't buying recycled papers you're not recycling. By buying recycled paper, you combat deforestation, reduce wastewater pollution in mill communities, save about half the energy it takes to make paper from virgin pulp, and make sure waste paper gets at least one more use before it enters the waste stream.

Today, paper manufacturers offer recycled paper in every style and quality. Not all recycled papers are created equal, however. You need to know something about the finer points of recycling to evaluate the industry's claims.

What is recycled paper? Until the late 1980s, there was no widely accepted definition. Paper mills could claim "recycled content" when the only things that had been added to the virgin pulp were scraps, trimmings, and overruns, which had been reused by mills all along. In 1988, the EPA offered its own definition and recommended that mills label their products with the percentage of recycled content.

Mills can still claim that paper containing manufacturing scraps—or preconsumer waste as it's now called—is recycled paper. But the thing you should look for on the label is the percentage of postconsumer waste—that is, paper used previously in a finished product that was obtained by the mill through recycling programs. The higher this postconsumer waste percentage, the better, from the green point of view.

Deinking Another term to watch for is the paper's percentage of deinked paper. This is pretty much equivalent to the paper's postconsumer waste content because nearly all recycled papers must undergo an ink-removal process to make them suitable for incorporation into new paper.

Rag content All papers with rag content actually contain some recycled material—not paper, but cotton rags. These rags can be pre- or postconsumer.

Bleaching Another factor to consider is whether the paper has been bleached, and how. As a rule, choose unbleached paper over bleached paper. The chlorine process used by most manufacturers to make paper white is the biggest source of water-polluting chemicals in the paper-making process. These toxic by-products include dioxin, a well-known carcinogen. Safer bleaching processes, such as oxygen bleaching, are used by some companies and result in excellent-quality stock. Time Inc., for example, recently announced its intention to use nonchlorine-bleached stock in all its mass-market magazines.

Many paper products don't need to be bleached at all. The slightly uneven buff or gray tones of unbleached paper are fine for general printing. Use bleached paper only for documents that will be reproduced by photocopying or offset printing (and the fewer of those, the better).

Durability Paper can be recycled more than once. Current technology allows about seven or eight cycles before the paper fibers wear out. You needn't worry about your recycled papers falling apart, though. A good-quality recycled paper can actually be better than virgin stock for laser printing because it's more flexible and less likely to warp when exposed to heat and stress.

Recycling printer consumables

Paper isn't the only printer consumable you can reuse and recycle. Machines that re-ink printer ribbons and companies that recharge laser toner cartridges can also save you quite a bit of money, as well as saving space in landfills. Of course, you'll save immediately on printer ribbons and toner cartridges if you're doing less printing. See chapter 5 for ideas on creating a "paperlite" office.

Ribbon facts Dot-matrix and daisywheel printers still crank out much of the world's PC-printed matter, though lasers and inkjets are catching up fast. And they must be fed with ribbons—more than 100 million of them per year worldwide. Ninety-five percent of ribbons are used once and thrown away. The waste produced by ribbons includes not just the approximately 10% of the ribbon unit that actually provides ink to the printhead, but also the plastic, cardboard, and shrink-wrap packaging that goes with it.

Ribbon conservation You can stretch out the life of your fabric ribbons with a few tricks. Always print in draft mode except for important documents. Use the light density setting on your printer. Re-ink the ribbon and use it again.

Ribbon re-inkers Did you know that in Japan, workers are required to re-ink printer ribbons and to return worn-out ribbons to the manufacturer? Given the high price and short life of disposable printer ribbons, the practice of re-inking fabric ribbons is increasingly popular even in the United States. A top-quality tabletop ribbon re-inking machine costing about $400 can pay for itself in a year if you need to re-ink ribbons at least six times a month. An individual ribbon can be re-inked up to 100 times. (Mylar ribbons aren't re-inkable.) In fact, a well-inked ribbon helps your printer last longer because the ink lubricates the printer head. Sources for ribbon re-inkers are listed in the Green-PC resources section that ends this chapter.

Inkjet refills Many of the same firms that sell re-inkers also sell refills for the printer cartridges in the popular Hewlett-Packard, Canon, Brother, and Apple lines of inkjet printers. Instead of throwing away empty cartridges, as the inkjet cartridge manufacturers would like you to do, refill them through the tiny pinhole at the top of the cartridge. If you really want to save money, you can try refilling the inkjet cartridge yourself. Use a hypodermic syringe (available from your local surgical supply house) to inject the empty cartridge with fresh ink from a bottle of standard Shaeffer or Scripto, which can be purchased in any stationery store. Or use a vegetable-based ink of similar viscosity (see the following section). This trick saves packaging, waste, and money, but is only recommended for the daring. Hint: wear an apron.

Vegetable inks Unlike ordinary printers' inks, which use petroleum as a vehicle, environmentally friendly inks based on soy or corn oil contain no petroleum. These new inks are formulated from a renewable resource; require fewer hazardous, smog-producing solvents; and in many cases produce brighter, cleaner colors. (The ink pigments still contain heavy metals, but the ink industry is years from developing "green" pigments.) If you plan to print many copies of a desktop-published document at a commercial press, ask the press to use vegetable inks; many do it already.

To date, no printer ribbons loaded with vegetable inks are available commercially, but you might be able to use vegetable inks in your re-inking machine or inkjet refills. Contact the American Soybean Association for more information (see the Green-PC resources section).

Toner cartridges The toner cartridges that keep laser printers rolling out page after page of nice black type are eminently recyclable. And there are many reputable companies who will take your spent cartridge, refurbish it, refill it, and return it to you at a price well below that of buying a new one. Yet, according to a 1991 study by BIS Strategic Decisions of Norwell, Massachusetts, only one out of five U.S. corporations recycles its toner cartridges or sells them to remanufacturing outfits. Overall, fewer than 5 million of the 15 million toner cartridges used in the United States every year are recycled or remanufactured. The remaining 10 million unrecycled toner cartridges add 40 million pounds of carbon, plastic resins, selenium, and other metals to U.S. landfills annually—all material that's manufactured in Japan (primarily by Canon) and disposed of in the United States. It has been estimated that the materials in cartridges could last 1,500 years without deteriorating, so these items will be in landfills for a very, very long time. By 1995, BIS estimates, Americans will be using 28 million toner cartridges a year, doubling the problem.

Most toner cartridges are rated for about 3,500 pages before the toner runs out. Even if you're near the end of the cartridge's rated number of pages and your pages are light or streaky, you might be able to squeeze out as many as 500 additional pages. Remove the cartridge and hold it horizontally. Then seesaw it gently a few times and replace it. This redistributes toner that might have been bunched up at the ends. Replace it, and your pages should look better.

Extending cartridge life One bad idea for increasing the life of nearly empty toner cartridges is to turn up the toner density. That might produce blacker dots, but it uses up toner even more quickly. The cartridge will die sooner rather than later. Your printed pages will look fuzzier, too.

A better idea is to extend the life of toner cartridges with Toner Tuner, a software utility for Macs that allows you to print in a draft mode that uses less toner. Experiments with Toner Tuner show that printouts at only 60 to 70% of normal toner density are still quite readable. Densities of 40 to 50% are fine for drafts with most fonts (small or thin fonts might not be too legible). Toner Tuner, which lists for $25, can pay for itself by extending the useful life of just one or two cartridges. See the Green-PC resources section for more information on Toner Tuner.

Recycling cartridges Once the toner cartridge is really spent, there's no reason not to recycle it, except pure laziness. It's easy to pack the cartridge in the same box it came in and send it to one of the remanufacturers (also called refurbishers) listed in the Green-PC resources section, or to a local refurbisher. You can usually find them through local stationers or computer stores.

Look for remanufacturers who belong to the International Cartridge Recyclers Association (ICRA), which sets professional standards for recyclers. Reputable remanufacturers don't just drill a hole in the cartridge and pour in new toner, a process called "drill and fill"; they completely disassemble the cartridge, replace worn-out parts, fill it with toner, and then reassemble and test it.

Most laser printer manufacturers, including Apple, Lexmark, Qume, Hewlett Packard, and Canon, will take back used toner cartridges. Some companies even make a small charitable donation to environmental organizations and causes for each returned cartridge. Qume will pay you $5 for each returned cartridge, plus shipping.

These manufacturers reuse cartridge parts but don't refurbish the entire cartridge the way remanufacturers do. This has prompted some critics to complain that manufacturers accept used cartridges mainly to boost sales of new cartridges by keeping the parts out of the hands of remanufacturers. Whether you choose to return the spent toner cartridge to the manufacturer or recycle it through a remanufacturer is up to you; either choice is far better than simply throwing the toner cartridge away.

Cartridges can be refurbished and refilled up to six times before they wear out. Keep track of the number of times a particular toner cartridge has been recycled by putting a small scratch or grease pencil mark on it each time; this will also tell you whether you're receiving back the same cartridge you sent. You'll save plenty of money, too. New toner cartridges go for $70 to $100 on the street, but they can be recycled for 30% to 50% less.

Drum recycling You can also recycle the drum in your laser printer by recoating it with new photosensitive material when the original coating wears out. This can be done once or maybe twice. Better yet, have the old drum replaced with a new drum with a super-hard coating that lasts up to ten times longer. Ask your toner cartridge remanufacturer if it supplies this service.

A green laser printer Laser printers are notorious not only as power hogs and paper wasters, but also as dollar eaters. Add up the cost for power, toner, paper, and wear-and-tear on the print drum, and it costs two to three cents to print a page on most laser printers. That's about three times the cost per page of dot-matrix printers.

Kyocera, one of the first printer manufacturers to incorporate green principles into its laser printer designs, claims to have reduced the page cost of its Ecosys aSi laser printer to less than one penny, cheaper than any other current laser printer. The key to the Ecosys's economic design is its long-lasting drum, which is coated with a superhard layer of amorphous silicon, and the fact that the printer doesn't use toner cartridges. Toner refills are packaged in a biodegradable container made from kelp; you pour the toner in yourself. For more information, contact Kyocera at the address given in the Green-PC resources section.

Floppies forever

Floppy disks, of course, can be used again and again, and that's what most people do. But you might be surprised at how many disks you have around, stashed away in boxes of old software, piles of outdated backup disks, and so on. Every one of them can be made to hold as much as 10 megabytes of data (the equivalent of 5,000 pages of typed text). Perhaps you have hundreds of megabytes of storage space you didn't even know about. Here are a few tips for getting the most from your disks:

Resectoring As floppies get older, they develop bad sectors (usually due to dust or some other contaminant on the disk itself) and can't be formatted. If you fail after two or three tries to format the disk, try using a disk repair utility program to isolate the bad sectors so it can be formatted.

Floppy repair Three-and-a-half-inch floppies with damaged or missing write-protect tabs can still be rescued. With a thin screwdriver or other instrument, pry out the remainder of the tab, if any, and fit a small piece of thin cardboard into the hole. Or pop in a write-protect tab you've pried out of a bad disk.

File compression Use a file-compression utility to get more bytes on your floppies. Files can often be compressed to 25% of their uncompressed size. You might be able to fit as much as 10 megabytes of compressed files on a 1.44-megabyte disk. Some compression programs will do this for you automatically, without requiring you to enter the compression program itself—a real time saver. Chapter 1 has a detailed discussion of file-compression software.

Hole punchers You've probably heard about the inexpensive devices that will cut a hole in double-density (720K or 800K) 3.5-inch floppies and make them compatible with the high-density (1.4 megabyte) 3.5-inch standard, thereby "doubling" the disk's storage capacity. The theory behind these devices is that there's no difference in media between double-density and high-density, no matter what disk manufacturers claim; the only difference is in the high-density disk casing, which has an extra hole in it. So once a hole is punched in the disk, you should be able to use it as a high-density disk with no problem. In theory, this should mean you need fewer floppies, a good green goal.

This sounds too good to be true, and it is. Double-density disks don't make it through the more stringent quality-control tests that all high-density disks must pass. So they're more likely to develop disk errors if they're formatted as high-density. Hole-punch manufacturers always warn that converted disks shouldn't be used for archival purposes. But what else would you use floppies for? A more reliable way to increase floppy disk storage capacity is to use file compression software, discussed in the previous section.

Used floppies Some companies offer used, reconditioned floppies at a considerable discount. Make sure they've been degaussed (demagnetized) and relabeled. You can take your own old disks, reformat them, and donate them to schools and charitable organizations. Companies that deal in used disks are listed in the Green-PC resources section.

Recycling commercial software

Reusing and recycling commercial software poses some legal problems. You can always reuse or recycle the physical materials, of course, copying over the floppy disks and putting the manuals in the paper recycling bin (remove the ring binding first, if there is one). But the end-user license agreement that you accepted when you first used the software (it's usually printed on the envelope containing the original floppy disks) severely restricts your legal right to donate, sell, or copy the program and its documentation. If you're thinking of donating a well-used program to your child's elementary school, for example, you'll be legally safe if you:

- Write a letter assigning to the recipient all rights to the software. Such a letter can come in handy at tax time, as well. You might be able to deduct the cost of the software as a charitable donation.
- Hand over all original floppy disks and other materials, including a copy of the end-user license agreement.
- Erase all other copies of the program.

WordPerfect Corp., publisher of the popular word-processing program, has a formal program for donating old copies of WordPerfect to schools. Just fill out a form supplied by the company and send it in. WordPerfect will send you a new copy of the license that you can give to the school along with the software.

Organizations that have purchased multiple copies of software under a site license agreement are under further restrictions. The site license probably forbids the donation of older versions of a program. Legally, at least, it's safer, when disposing of multiple copies of commercial programs, to reformat the old floppy disks and recycle the old manuals.

Recycling PC plastics

Durable goods, including computers, make up 22% of landfilled municipal waste by volume, according to the EPA. In the case of computers, most of that waste is plastic. Ten years ago, steel was the material used in most PC casings. Today, PCs are made mainly of various plastic resins, as are most peripherals and consumables other than paper.

Many plastics used in making PCs can be recycled. The problem is recognizing which plastics have been used because there are dozens of resins used in the industry, and many of them look alike to the untrained eye.

The plastics industry's Partnership for Plastics Progress has developed a coding system for the plastic resins used in cars that will make it easier to group disassembled parts by resin type; these codes will eventually be stamped by the manufacturers on all plastic durable goods, including computer parts. IBM is already doing this on a limited basis. At the same time, manufacturers will likely redesign PC components for easy disassembly, using screwless, snap-together construction, and a single resin for each part rather than hard-to-recycle plastic laminates.

Don't bother to strip down one or two PCs for the plastic in them. It makes more sense to recycle individual PCs as intact units. Should you happen to have large quantities of PC casings and other plastics on the premises, The Council for Solid Waste Solutions can provide detailed profiles of plastic recycling firms in your area that can take them off your hands. (See the Green-PC resources section at the end of this chapter.) Many PCs still have some life in them even after they're no longer useful to you. See the section in this chapter on reselling and donating your PC.

CD-ROMs

CD-ROMs, the polycarbonate disks that are becoming increasingly popular as a storage medium for computer publishing, are produced in the millions every year. By the mid-1990s, according to most experts, the silvery disks will replace floppy disks as the preferred way to distribute software. (See chapter 5 for creating your own CD-ROMs, and see chapter 12 for sources of environmental information published on CD-ROM.)

Because many CD-ROMs contain time-dependent information such as directories and mailing lists, the CDs become useless as soon as the information on them is outdated. Unlike floppy disks, however, CD-ROMs can't be written over, and most people just toss them away. As yet there's no company that recycles used CD-ROMs, audio CDs, or the jewel box and plastic tray that CD-ROMs and audio CDs are packaged in.

Some CD-ROM distributors are turning away from jewel boxes entirely. For example, Apple Computer, which sends out thousands of CD-ROMs to developers every month, now protects its CD-ROMs with a recycled cardboard and plastic sleeve instead of a jewel box, as does Educorp, a publisher and distributor of Macintosh CD-ROMs.

Interestingly, a small crafts industry has grown up in California around discarded CD-ROMs. Local craftspeople use discarded disks to make clock faces, mirrored wall decorations, and jewelry. That's not the only unusual use of recycled plastics from computers. McDonald's, the fast-food giant, is using plastics recycled from old computer casings to shingle the roofs of its restaurants. Several avant-garde designers incorporate discarded chips and other computer parts into jewelry and even clothes. One company markets a line of clipboards made from old printer circuit boards.

Dealing with foam

Polystyrene and polyurethane packaging foams are ubiquitous in the computer industry. At one time, foam manufacturers used halogenated chlorofluorocarbons (CFCs) as gaseous foaming agents to create packaging foams, but concerns about the effect of CFCs on the earth's ozone layer have prompted most manufacturers to switch to HCFC-22, a somewhat less ozone-destructive gas, or to non-CFC gases like pentane and butane. Nonetheless, packaging foams are not exactly earth-friendly. Once the foam is made, it doesn't biodegrade. So you should avoid using plastic foam whenever possible.

Ironically, if you've accumulated a lot of computer equipment, then you've also collected plenty of foam packing material. New computers and other electronics are invariably packaged in molded foam inserts. Electronics manufacturers and mail-order vendors, following United Parcel Service guidelines, pack smaller items in larger boxes full of polystyrene foam loose-fill (popularly known as foam peanuts). The loose-fill is ideal in some ways; it's cushiony, extremely light, inhospitable to vermin, inert (unless burned), and requires relatively little energy to make. But, as everyone knows, the peanuts last forever, cling to your clothes, and are difficult to handle. What can you do with all that foam?

Save the inserts Don't throw away foam inserts; store them away so that you can repack components in them when you move or when you return your PC for servicing.

Recut to fit Foam inserts can sometimes be recut to fit components other than the ones for which they were made. A sharp knife or small handsaw is all that's needed. Cut the foam to make a very tight fit; it will compress. Repair crumbling edges with masking tape.

Break & reuse If you have no more use for a foam insert, break it up into pieces and use it as loose packing material.

Collect & reuse loose fill Foam peanuts can be reused many times before they crumble. Keep a large garbage can for peanuts and dump them right in as each box is opened.

Recycle it Yes, there are recycling centers for foam packaging. The Association of Foam Packaging Recyclers operates more than 45 foam recycling plant locations nationwide. They handle both molded foam inserts and loose-fill foam peanuts. Mailboxes, Etc., a national chain of mailing and shipping service centers, will also accept your unwanted foam peanuts and reuse them. See the Green-PC resources section.

Don't burn it Don't burn polystyrene to get rid of it; it will give off toxic gases.

Foam alternatives

There are some alternatives to foam peanuts. Several companies offer biodegradable packing material, some based on cornstarch; see the Green-PC resources section in this chapter.

A good, cheap, do-it-yourself packing material is crumpled or shredded wastepaper. Wastepaper packing material costs nothing, works about as well as foam, and reduces the amount of paper around the office. Just think: you can finally put all those out-of-date issues of computer magazines and newspapers to work. The disadvantage is that paper requires manual labor to prepare, can't be dispensed from a hopper like peanuts, and is somewhat heavier.

One major PC mail-order vendor, PC Connection/MacConnection (Marlow, New Hampshire), has come up with a neatly circular packaging solution. According to staff environmental research specialist Phil Blaisdell, the company at first tried crumpled newspaper, then recycled foam peanuts, and even air-popped popcorn. None of these methods was entirely satisfactory. Now the company sends out its wastepaper to two local mills that recycle it into packing tissue that's lighter than foam and completely biodegradable.

Recycling PC batteries

The rapid growth in the notebook PC market has been accompanied by a parallel rapid increase in the use of batteries incorporating toxic heavy metals. Nickel-cadmium batteries, the rechargeable "ni-cads" most commonly used in notebook computers, contain toxic cadmium, one of two metals recently singled out by the EPA as a particular landfill hazard. (The other metal is lead, present in household batteries but not in most computer batteries.) Ni-cad batteries are good for up to 1,000 charges or about two years (whichever comes first), depending on such variables as the number of times they've been fully charged and discharged.

But once ni-cads are dead, they're dead forever, and they become a serious waste disposal problem. If discarded batteries are burned in incinerators, vaporized metals are released into the air. If the batteries are dumped in landfills, the metals can leach into the soil to pollute groundwater and wells. Most people, unaware of the hazardous nature of ni-cad batteries, toss them away in the regular trash. The result is that discarded ni-cads from portable electronics are the largest source of cadmium in the waste stream.

Alternatives to ni-cads are now on the market. Nickel-metal-hydride (NiMH) batteries contain no cadmium and pose less of a health and waste problem. They are starting to appear in midrange and high-end notebook PCs. NiMH batteries are the greenest notebook batteries developed to date, and their availability should be a factor in your purchasing decisions. Toshiba America is one PC manufacturer that has switched entirely to NiMH batteries in its high-end notebooks, and Apple now uses them in its PowerBook Duo notebooks.

All desktop PCs and many notebooks also use small, nonrechargeable batteries to back up the system setup memory. These small batteries are usually long-lasting lithium types that will probably outlive your PC. Sooner or later they also become part of the waste stream, too. And there are far more of them than ni-cads. Some PC manufacturers, including Hewlett Packard and Amkly, are turning to flash memory, a type of memory chip that doesn't require constant power to retain information, as an alternative to system-backup batteries.

Battery care The first thing to do is to make your PC batteries last as long as they can. There's not much you can do to prolong the life of nonrechargeable desktop PC batteries. With rechargeable ni-cads, the trick is to use them until they are fully discharged before recharging them, and then to recharge them fully. Otherwise ni-cads develop an annoying phenomenon called "memory effect," in which it becomes impossible to fully charge them. Ni-cad batteries with memory effect tend to go dead sooner than ni-cads that are properly cared for. This might be a problem for notebook users because the battery management software shipped with many models tends to shut down before the battery is fully discharged (so that no data is lost). Most users then recharge the battery without completely draining it first. The result is batteries that hold less power and go dead sooner than they should. If possible, circumvent the power management software and let your notebook run right out of power each time battery levels get low, or switch to newer versions of software that allow deeper drainage cycles.

You can restore some of the lost capacity of ni-cads with memory effect by running them through a series of ten or more deep-discharge/full-recharge cycles. Some third-party power-management utility programs, such as Battery Watch Pro, have a "deep-discharge" function that drains the battery to the dregs before recharging. So do some third-party battery chargers. Or you can send out your batteries to a company that will do the job for you. See the Green-PC resources section for more information.

NiMH batteries do not suffer from "memory effect," but they have shortcomings of their own. Unlike ni-cads, which hold their charge for a long while, NiMHs lose most of their charge if you leave them sitting on the shelf. You'll get the best performance from your NiMH battery if you use and charge your notebook every day.

Battery recycling There are currently no federal laws regarding battery disposal, but as of January 1994, 19 states had laws or were considering legislation controlling disposal or collection and recycling of batteries. The Portable Rechargeable Battery Association (PRBA), a trade association, is preparing a "National Rechargeable Battery Collection Plan" that will be promoted by PRBA members (most battery and small electrics manufacturers). Federal programs await the adoption of the EPA's proposed "universal waste rule," which might be implemented in 1994.

What can you do with the dead batteries you have now? Some PC manufacturers have started battery-recycling programs for their products. Apple Computer will accept spent lead-acid batteries from the Macintosh Portable and ni-cads from Mac Powerbooks. Return them to any authorized Apple Service Provider, or contact Apple at the address and phone in the Green-PC resources section for more information. Apple then recycles or disposes of the batteries according to EPA hazardous waste guidelines. Other manufacturers, including IBM, Toshiba, and Compaq might be offering notebook battery recycling programs by the time you read this.

Local communities are also getting into the act. Call your municipal department of public works to see if your community has a battery collection program. Municipal programs might take button and lithium batteries as well as household lead-acid batteries and ni-cads.

Recycling your PC

There's no reason why PCs can't live a long, long life. Manufacturers want you to trash your old PC every two or three years and get a new one. But there is much useful computing work that can be done with an older machine even after you've moved on to bigger and better things. Alex Randall, the prophet of PC recycling who founded the Boston Computer Exchange and the East-West Educational Development Foundation, claims, "It's a sin for any computer to be idle. It is imperative that we recycle this stuff until it dies."

Germany and Japan are leading the way in PC recycling. A strict German law set to take effect in 1994 mandates that electronics manufacturers are completely responsible for disposal of all packaging and products, including PCs. NEC, the Japanese electronics giant, has a factory in Kawasaki City, Japan, that annually recycles thousands of tons of machinery, separating the gold and other precious elements from used electronics. IBM does the same in its plants in the United Kingdom. Even Russia has a plant in the Ural mountains dedicated to stripping discarded circuit boards of every usable chip.

Computer recycling efforts Efforts to recycle PCs in the United States are mainly ad hoc and informal. However, there are a few working computer recycling sites in the United States. One of the first is an experimental operation run by the University of Massachusetts in Amherst. In 1990, R. Marc Fournier, newly hired as recycling coordinator, began stockpiling the university's old computers, typewriters, and other electronic equipment, waiting for the market for recycled electronics to mature. In 1993, a pilot "electronics deconstruction system" at the university's Solid Waste Department began taking old computers and breaking them down into dozens of basic components, using the labor of students and disabled workers. The program now sells gold from chips, lead from CRTs, and plastics from enclosures to local recycling companies. The program might eventually be expanded to handle computers from other colleges and from local municipalities.

Companies are also planning or operating commercial electronics recycling plants. Every month, Advanced Recovery, Inc., a Belleville, New Jersey, firm, strips down some 400,000 pounds of computers and other electronics bought from corporations. Chips are pulled from printed circuit boards and sold to parts wholesalers; gold and other metals are separated and sold to metals recovery firms; recyclable glass and some plastics are sold to recyclers. French International, Inc. has developed a completely modular, easily transportable electronics recycling and reuse factory called the Wemex plant. Already in operation in Germany, this plant uses a dry mechanical method to dismantle, sort, crush, and recover all but a few percent of the valuable materials in PCs, televisions, and other electronics. (See the Green-PC resources section for contact information on these two companies.)

Corporations that upgrade to new machines too often leave outdated models rusting in warehouses because they simply don't know what to do with them. Organizations like Randall's East-West Foundation have the contacts and the expertise to find new homes for large numbers of PCs that still have plenty of computing life left in them. East-West picks up warehoused components, refurbishes them, and discards the small percentage that's truly useless. It then sends half of the PCs to U.S. charities selected by the donor and ships the remainder to charities overseas, mainly in Eastern Europe. East-West takes individual donations, too. "Every single donation is precious to us," says Randall. "We're glad to know that one person out there cares about our work."

Randall believes that his organization provides an indispensable service for the computer industry. "If old machines are kept by users because they can't get rid of them, fewer new machines are bought. With us, the industry stays healthy; without us, it drowns in its own garbage."

What to do with your PC

You've grown disgusted with your old clunker of a PC while others are zipping past you in their PowerMacs and Pentiums. You've postponed buying a new PC for as long as possible while squeezing every ounce of performance out of your old one, using the tips collected in chapter 1 of this book. Finally, you make the move. A brand-new, lightning-fast PC arrives in the mail. What to do with your old computing partner, about whom you suddenly feel nostalgic?

Keep it Why not keep your old PC? You can use it to format disks, perform telecommunications, or print long reports while you use your new machine for other things. Think of it as free parallel processing.

If you're a hardware hacker, older IBM compatibles are worth having around for parts. (Macs and Amigas are harder to pillage, but not impossible.) Disk drives, video cards, RAM chips, cables, connectors, and so on can all be stripped out of an old machine and installed into a new one.

Sell it You can always try to sell it, but be realistic about what price to ask. Don't expect to make anything close to your money back unless you're selling a PC of recent vintage that's close in computing power to the typical mainstream PC being sold in computer stores. There's little point trying to sell an XT-class PC, Apple II, Amiga 1000, or Mac 128K or 512K, much less a truly obsolete Radio Shack, Texas Instruments, or Kaypro computer. These outdated machines might still have some computing life left, but there's no resale market for them. Give them away, if anyone wants them (see the following section).

If you decide to sell, try advertising in local papers and in the newsletters of local users groups. Check with the Boston Computer Exchange or the National Computer Exchange for the latest used-equipment prices (see the Green-PC resources section). These brokerage firms and others will help you connect with buyers; in return they'll charge you a 10% to 15% commission. Brokerages put the buyer's money in an escrow account for a few days until the buyer has had time to check out the computer. Then you receive payment directly from the brokerage. Perhaps the biggest advantage for you as the seller is that you stay anonymous. You won't personally have to provide support to the buyer in the future.

Consider buying a used PC for your new machine, too. A "slightly used" brand-name PC can cost 40% less than new merchandise purchased at street value. Many local computer dealers have reconditioned PCs to sell. Likewise, a local users' group is a good place to find a used PC.

The latest wrinkle in computer recycling is the used-PC superstore, where new, used, overstocked, surplus, closeout, demonstration, and liquidated units can be had for 50% to 90% off list prices. These stores will sometimes take your old machine as a trade-in, just like car dealers do.

Donate it The "trickle-down theory" might be outdated economics, but it still makes good sense for computing. Give away that clunker to someone who would be happy with less computing power than you need now. Most companies do that, passing once-top-of-the-line PCs from engineering to accounting to the typing pool. That system even pertains in government. Former vice president Dan Quayle got his first PC, a 286 PC-compatible, as a hand-me-down from the Agriculture Department. Still, sooner or later you might have to hand on an old computer to someone outside your organization.

When you're ready to upgrade, clean up your old PC, make sure it's in working order, round up all necessary cables and expansion cards, and donate it to a local school. Most schools are desperate for computers, especially any computer that's not an Apple II. Give them all your outdated software, too (but see earlier in the chapter for a discussion of the legal issues involved in donating commercial programs).

Older PCs, with their rugged steel casings, often last longer in the brutal environment of elementary schools. Your local church, temple, or community center could probably use a PC, too. Older PCs are fine for such places because they rarely do more than write letters, keep member databases, and do mailmerges.

The National Christina Foundation is another organization dedicated to finding new homes for older PCs. The group takes donations of PCs and matches them to people with disabilities and to schools in disadvantaged areas. In less than 10 years, says founder Yvette Marrin, the group has placed 100,000 computers with carefully screened recipients. Foundation members work with user groups, whose members repair donated machines and see that PCs are loaded with appropriate software.

Corporate donations are also welcome. Packard Bell recently donated a truckload of computer equipment worth $104,000. Insurance giant Metropolitan Life donated 250 laptops to the foundation. All donations are fully tax-deductible. A list of organizations that will accept PCs and route them to charities can be found in the Green-PC resources section.

Charitable donations are generally tax-deductible at the computer's depreciated value, which you can calculate using the formulas on the IRS form for amortization and depreciation. The IRS considers computers to be fully depreciated after five years, at which time they're worth nothing, at least for tax purposes. (Most corporations try to depreciate computers in three or four years, which is still too long, given that today's obsolescence cycle for PCs is more like two years.) For your tax records, get a receipt from the charity that spells out the nature of the transaction.

Choices that make a difference

❐ Conserve printer paper.

❐ Recycle waste paper.

❐ Use recycled paper with a high postconsumer waste content.

❐ Re-ink ribbons and recycle or recharge toner cartridges.

❐ Increase floppy disk storage.

❐ Reuse PC foam and cardboard packaging, and then recycle it.

❐ Recycle your software and your PC.

Green-PC resources

The following industry and federal organizations can provide more information on recycling:
American Forest and Paper Association
1111 19th St., NW, 8th Floor
Washington, DC 20036
800-878-8878
Information on paper manufacturing and recycling.

American Plastics Council
1275 K St., NW, Suite 500
Washington, DC 20005
800-243-5790, 202-371-5319
Plastic and paper recycling information; its Durables Program is aimed at manufacturers seeking sound plastics recycling practices for computers and other durable goods.

Institute of Scrap Recycling Industries
1325 G St., NW, Suite 1000
Washington, DC 20005
202-466-4050
Where to get rid of industrial leftovers.

International Cartridge Recycling Association (ICRA)
1101 Connecticut Ave., NW
Washington, DC 20036
202-857-1154
Member companies are required to adhere to a code of ethics that's intended to promote professionalism in the cartridge-recycling industry.

National Recycling Coalition
1101 30th St., NW, Suite 305
Washington, DC 20007
202-625-6406
Has general recycling information.

National Office Paper Recycling Project
1620 I St., NW, Suite 305
Washington, DC 20007
202-293-7330
Information on recycling office paper.

Solid Waste Assistance Program (SWAP)
P.O. Box 7219
Silver Spring, MD 20907
800-677-9424, fax 301-585-0297
A joint project of the U.S. EPA and the Solid Waste Association of North America (SWANA); it provides technical information and assistance on solid-waste issues to any interested party.

Sellers of recycled printer paper products include:
Atlantic Recycled Paper
800-323-2811, fax 410-747-8778

PaperDirect
P.O. Box 618
205 Chubb Ave.
Lyndhurst, NJ 07071
800-A-PAPERS, 201-507-5488, fax 201-507-0817

Manufacturers and distributors of recycled paper composed of 50% or more postconsumer waste include:
Alte Schule USA
704 E. Palace Ave.
Santa Fe, NM 87501
505-983-2593

Crestwood Recycled Paper Co.
315 Hudson St.
New York, NY 10013
212-989-2700

Earth Care Paper
Ukiah, CA 95482
800-347-0070
Also carries unbleached papers.

Forest Saver, Inc.
1860 Pond Rd.
Ronkonkoma, NY 11779
800-777-9886, fax 718-631-0104

Simpson Paper Co.
One Post St.
San Francisco, CA 94104
415-391-8140

This company makes chlorine-free brown paper:
Eco Paper Source
312-720-1943

Recycled fax paper is available from:
JP Atlanta
Dept GM
2157 Tucker Industrial Rd.
Tucker, GA 30084
800-874-1905

Paper Systems
185 Pioneer Blvd.
P.O. Box 150
Springboro, OH 45066
800-950-8590

The Recycled Paper Co.
617-737-9911

For information on soy- and corn-based inks, contact:
American Soybean Association
540 Maryville Centre Dr., Suite 400
P.O. Box 27300
St. Louis, MO 63141-1700
314-576-1770, fax 314-576-2786

National Corn Growers Association
1000 Executive Pkwy., Suite 105
St. Louis, MO 63141-6397
314-275-9915

Inkjet refill units and ribbon re-inking machines are available from:
Computer Friends
14250 N.W. Science Park Dr.
Portland, OR 07229
800-547-3303, 503-626-2291, fax 503-643-5379

DGR
1219 W 6th St, Suite 205
Austin, TX 78703
800-235-9748

Market Share Associates
285 Messner Drive
Wheeling, IL 60090
800-GO-REFILL
Also remanufactures laser cartridges and stocks labels made of recycled paper.

The Ribbon Factory
2300 E. Patrick Lane, #23
Las Vegas, NV 89119
800-275-7422, fax 702-736-1054

Toner Tuner, a utility program that extends the life of toner cartridges, is available from:
Working Software
408-423-5696

The following laser printer manufacturers will accept spent toner cartridges for recycling. Some pay shipping and donate money to a charity for every toner cartridge returned. Call for more information:
Apple Computer
800-776-2333

Canon
516-488-6700, 800-962-2708

Hewlett Packard
800-752-0900, ext. 1872

Lexmark
800-848-9894

Qume
800-421-4326

Xerox
800-822-2200, 714-836-8042

For information on the EcoSys laser printer, contact:
Kyocera Electronics, Inc.
100 Randolph Rd.
Somerset, NJ 08875
800-323-0470

The following are three of the many companies that will refurbish, recharge, and return your spent toner cartridges. Call for prices:
American Ribbon Company
800-327-1013, 305-733-4552, fax 305-733-0319

EcoCartridge
202-483-1200

Market Share Associates
800-GO-REFILL

These companies buy and sell used floppy disks at a discount:
EcoDisk
800-ECO-6175

Covenant Recycling Services
619-792-6975, fax 619-792-1599

For more information on recycling commercial software, call the Software Publishers Association hotline:
Software Publishers Association
800-388-7478

For more information on notebook battery recycling, contact:
Norm England, President
Portable Rechargeable Battery Association (PRBA)
1000 Parkwood Circle, Suite 430
Atlanta, GA 30339
404-612-8826, fax 404-612-8841

Information on recycling Macintosh Portable and Powerbook batteries is available from:
Apple Computer, Inc.
20525 Mariani Ave.
Cupertino, CA 95014
800-776-2333

The Complete Portable will recondition your ni-cad batteries or dispose of them for you.
The Complete Portable
505 Shawn Lane
Prospect Heights, IL 60070
800-328-4827 ext. 3317, 708-577-6342, fax 708-577-6551

A utility program that helps you conserve battery power and make your batteries last longer is:
Battery Watch Pro
Traveling Software
18702 N. Creek Pkwy.
Bothell, WA 98011
800-472-4735

This book offers a balanced picture of plastics recycling in the United States:
A Plastic Waste Primer: Handbook for Citizens
by The League of Women Voters
Lyons & Burford Publishers
31 West 21st St.
New York, NY 10010

For the foam-packing industry's view of foam-packing materials, contact:
Plastic Loose-Fill Producers' Council
P.O. Box 601
Grand Rapids, MI 49516

Polystyrene Packaging Council, Inc.
800-242-7434

Contact the following companies for more information on alternative packing materials:
American Excelsior Co.
1111 duPaige Ave.
Lombard, IL 60148
708-627-3200

Deltapaper
2925 State Rd.
Croydon, PA 19021
800-444-6700, 215-788-1800

Free-Flow Packaging Corp.
1093 Charter St.
Redwood City, CA 94063
415-364-1145

For locations of foam-recycling sites and other information, contact:
The Association of Foam Packaging Recyclers
1025 Connecticut Ave., NW, Suite 515
Washington, DC 20036
800-944-8448

Local franchises of Mailboxes, Etc., will accept foam peanuts for reuse. Contact their corporate offices for more information:
Mailboxes, Etc. International Headquarters
6060 Cornerstone Court W.
San Diego, CA 92121
619-455-8800

Contact the University of Massachusetts computer recycling program at:
University of Massachusetts
Physical Plant
Amherst, MA 01003
Attn: R. Marc Fournier
413-545-4386

For more information on Advanced Recovery, Inc., and the Wemex electronics recycling/reuse system, contact:
Advanced Recovery, Inc.
201-450-9797

French International, Inc.
Attn: Peter M. Smeets
305-563-4070, fax 305-563-2750

Donate your old PC to one of the following organizations:
East-West Educational Development Foundation
49 Temple Place
Boston, MA 02111
617-542-1234, fax info line 617-542-2345

Educational Assistance Limited (EAL)
708-690-0010
Donates PCs to colleges in exchange for tuition credits that are awarded to underprivileged students.

National Christina Foundation
42 Hillcrest Dr.
Pelham Manor, NY 10803
800-274-7846
Among other uses, donates PCs to help physically challenged people telecommute or set up small businesses.

The following companies buy and sell used PCs:
American Computer Exchange
800-786-0717

Boston Computer Exchange Corp.
800-262-6399, 617-542-4414

Computer Exchange Northwest
206-820-1181

National Computer Exchange (NaComEx)
800-359-2468

PreOwned Electronics
800-274-5343
This company specializes in used Apple equipment.

Western Computer Exchange
505-265-1330

The following company buys older computers and remanufactures them for resale to corporations:
Heritage Computer Company
9555 James Avenue South
Minneapolis, MN 55431
800-426-3695

7

Telecommuting

CHAPTER 7

CARS ARE ONE of the defining inventions of the 20th century, but their effect on the environment has been a disaster. According to the U.S. Department of Transportation, America's 140 million cars burn more than 200 million gallons of gasoline every day. That's about 55 barrels of gas every second. When each gallon of gasoline is burned, 20 pounds of carbon dioxide are released into the atmosphere, adding to the greenhouse effect and possibly increasing the overall temperature of the earth's atmosphere.

But that's only the beginning of the problem. Every year, cars emit millions of pounds of gaseous hydrocarbons, which cause ozone smog, and more than 7 million tons of nitrogen oxide, a leading cause of acid rain. Gas and oil leaked from gas stations and petroleum storage areas foul our sources of fresh water. Tankers carrying the crude oil from which gasoline is made spill millions of barrels of fossil fuel into the world's oceans. Town greens and open fields have already been replaced by mall parking lots. The mountains of discarded cars and tires are growing daily. And every year, between 30,000 and 40,000 U.S. citizens are killed in motor vehicle accidents.

Auto manufacturers are working to make cars safer, more efficient, and less polluting, but progress is slow. There is a limit to how safe you can make a 2-ton object moving at 55 miles per hour that is controlled only by the skills of a human driver. Slower methods of transportation, like walking and biking, provide a partial answer to the problem of cars. Bicycles are widely used as commuting vehicles in Denmark and China, for instance, but many Americans can't get to work safely by bike. Most cities have bus systems, but buses are inconvenient and unreliable for commuting, and they pollute, too. High-tech mass transit is expensive and provides point-to-point transport within or between urban areas only. So cars remain the principal mode of transportation in the U.S. and much of the industrialized world.

Most people who use cars during business hours are commuting to or from work or traveling on business. During a 40-year career, a commuter who spends two hours each day driving to and from work—a typical commute for U.S. workers—will spend 2.3 years of his or her life on the road. And consider that daily commutes of two or three hours each way are no longer rare.

The U.S. Department of Transportation has compiled yet more disturbing statistics about commuting:

- The average commuter drives 4,000 miles per year and consumes 190 gallons of gas.
- 23 billion gallons of gas are burned annually by U.S. commuters.
- 11 million tires are worn out on commutes.
- Each year, commuting cars emit 219 million tons of CO_2, 1 million tons of nitrogen oxides, and 1.4 million tons of nonmethane hydrocarbons such as benzene.

Commuting not only damages the environment and subtracts years of irreplaceable time from our lives, it also contributes to social problems. Those extra hours spent on the road are hours not spent with our families. While we're stuck in traffic, our children are being raised in day care, or watching television in an empty house, or wandering the neighborhood.

The real key to reducing the environmental, social, and personal costs of cars is to use them less, and especially to commute less. That's where the computer, another defining invention of our time, can come to the rescue.

The personal computer allows new kinds of work to be done at remote locations and sent instantly to a central place of business. Nearly all work done on a PC, and that includes an increasing amount of all the work done in the world today, can be done anywhere. Using networks, e-mail, fax modems, and online services, computer commuters can work at home in comfort, leaving their cars in the garage and their suits in the closet.

This is called *telecommuting* (or telework), and it's a prime example of how computers can supplant more harmful technologies, like the car—and give more freedom to workers at the same time.

People in the Los Angeles area discovered the advantages of telecommuting in the aftermath of the earthquake of January 1994. With several major arteries closed for repair, workers turned to telecommuting as a way to avoid lengthy and possibly dangerous commutes to downtown LA Pacific Bell and GTE California announced "telecommuting relief" packages, offering to waive installation fees for services such as business phone lines, ISDN, and voice mail, and many businesses formerly closed to the idea rushed to take advantage of the offer.

How telecommuting works

The New York research firm Link Resources estimates that there were more than 6.6 million telecommuters in the United States in 1992, an increase of about 20% over 1991. According to surveys by the Gallup Organization and other research groups, the typical telecommuter is 35 to 45 years old, married, with young children, well-educated, and employed in a white-collar job in a service industry.

Informal telecommuting Most telecommuters are employees of large corporations or government agencies. They generally work at home on an informal part-time or temporary basis, coming into the office several times a week and taking work home to finish on their PCs. They often use modems or faxes to return finished projects. Other telecommuters are independent contractors who specialize in certain tasks, such as database services or computer consulting, that the employer can't provide in-house. They often work out of home or local offices and meet with employers on an irregular basis, staying in touch by phone and modem. Some telecommuters, dubbed "lone eagles" by environmental writer Jeremy Rifkin, deliberately move to isolated rural communities, dealing with employers and clients solely by electronic means.

Formal telecommuting programs In *The Telecommuter's Handbook* (Pharos Books, 1990), author Brad Schepp lists 100 companies that already employ telecommuters on a formal basis, offering well-thought-out telecommuting programs with all the work aspects carefully calculated. These pioneering firms include such computer industry giants as Apple Computer, AT&T, Control Data Corporation, DEC, Hewlett-Packard, IBM, and UMI/Data Courier. Organizations that are heavily dependent on computers are more likely to institute such programs because they're already used to the idea that work can take place anywhere there's a phone jack and an ac outlet.

Hewlett-Packard, for example, set up a telecommuting program for its western-region sales force in December 1991 and expects to recruit half its regional salespeople into the program within a few years. Even government agencies can be good candidates for telecommuting programs. Los Angeles County employed more than 1,200 telecommuters in 1991, saving the county $30,000 per month in reduced expenses and increased productivity, and helping to meet California's strict environmental laws by keeping cars off the highways. Apple Computer is one of the many California-based computer companies that has an active telecommuter program.

Satellite computing centers Another approach is for an employer or group of employers to set up satellite computing centers near the residential areas in which their employees live. In Los Angeles, a group of companies including Pacific Bell, Southern California Edison, Xerox, IBM, and Disney leases office space in the Riverside Telecommuting Center, an unassuming office building located in the residential suburb of Riverside, 60 miles southeast of the city. The rewired and remodeled center offers computing workspaces equipped with PCs, computerized phone systems, faxes, modems, and network connections.

Instead of adding to Southern California's smog problem by commuting three or four hours a day to central LA, employees can drive or bike to the Riverside Center in a matter of minutes and get their work done without the endless distractions of the typical corporate office. The companies who participate also save on rent because space in Riverside goes for far less than similar space in central LA. Managers who are uncomfortable with work-at-home arrangements might prefer this approach.

Telecommuting communities Some communities actively seek telecommuters. Two examples are Telluride and Sky Field, Colorado. Telluride, with its breathtaking natural scenery and clean air, attracts Californians who have had enough of smog and crowding. Sky Field has gone further. This developing community is putting a high-tech telecommunications system in place, so lone eagles will be able to tap into the latest high-speed network services.

Telecommuting jobs Not every type of job is well suited for telecommuting. Until remote-manipulation stations ("waldos," in the jargon of robotics) are cheap enough to install in a spare room at home, factory workers and machine operators won't be telecommuting. Jobs that do adapt well to telecommuting share these traits:

- They can be performed outside the office and on a flexible schedule.
- They don't depend on a central, nonportable physical resource.
- They don't require constant supervision.
- They can be performed with the aid of a computer and telecommunications equipment.

Many jobs that involve routine clerical tasks, data entry, forms processing, telemarketing, and other white-collar duties are good candidates for conversion to telecommuting. Architects, computer programmers, consultants of all kinds, editors, graphic designers, lawyers, legal and medical transcription typists, mathematicians, theoretical scientists, stockbrokers, writers, and other professionals who regularly use computers are also likely candidates. So are employees of housing, community-development, and social-services agencies who must maintain close contact with local neighborhoods, yet report to distant central offices.

Who telecommutes? In the same way that not every type of job is right for telecommuting, not every type of worker can handle the demands and responsibilities. Successful telecommuters tend to fit the following profile:

- They're self-motivated.
- They're hard workers who enjoy their work.
- They're flexible-minded, creative problem solvers.
- They work best without close supervision.
- They're comfortable with computers, networks, and other technologies.
- They have a personal stake in the success of the telecommuting programs in their organizations.

Benefits to the earth

Telecommuting's environmental benefits are significant and are becoming more important as telecommuting becomes more common. Most of the benefits center on reducing the use of automobiles.

Less gas consumed Telecommuting's most important single benefit is saving gasoline and reducing all the pollution and waste problems that stem from its use. According to EPA estimates, some 10 million American workers drive an average of 75 miles round-trip to work in cars that get an average of 25 miles per gallon. If these workers all telecommuted, they would save 30 million gallons of gas every workday and keep 600 million pounds of carbon dioxide out of the atmosphere.

Reduced traffic Telecommuters don't add to the ever-increasing urban traffic problem, and they reduce the need to spend millions on the construction and upkeep of roads and parking lots, traffic control, and car-related waste disposal.

Fewer resources required Telecommuters do consume energy whenever they use their PCs, but the increase in electrical consumption is more than offset by reduced gasoline consumption. In fact, home-based telecommuters tend to be more conscious of energy and paper use, especially if they pay for office expenses themselves, so they're more likely to use fewer resources overall than office workers doing the same tasks with the same equipment. It's also easier to implement the suggestions for green computing in this book if you can do it in your own home office.

Benefits to workers

Few telecommuters go back to the 9-to-5 grind once they've tried the telecommuting life. While telecommuting has many tangible benefits for workers, like saving money on gas and clothes, it's often the intangible gains that workers cite as most important.

Typical are the reasons given by telecommuter Ian Gilman, a computer programmer who currently lives in Washington state but works mainly for California employers. At first, Gilman telecommuted for economic reasons. "To start with, I couldn't afford to move. I had a programming job that I was able to telecommute to, and to do otherwise would've meant moving from Washington to California," he says. But soon telecommuting became less a matter of economics and more a way of life. "Recently, I did go to down to California, and stayed there for several months while finishing up a program. I've since moved back to Washington, and I'd say it's now much more a matter of choice that I telecommute."

Gilman enjoys the feeling of not having to live two separate lives, a work life and a personal life. "There isn't this separation between work and the rest of my life," he says. "I live where I work, and I work where I live. I'm fortunate in that I enjoy my work, so I have no need to force a division between work and nonwork. The division happens naturally enough without living and working in separate places." Among the other benefits to workers are the following:

Higher morale Telecommuters are happier. They've succeeded in adapting work to their lives, rather than fitting their lives to the arbitrary structures of work. Telecommuting parents are able to form stronger bonds with their families because they're at home more often.

Increased employability Physically and mentally challenged workers and workers who live in areas remote from a central office are excellent candidates for telecommuting. In most cases, telecommuters can live anywhere they want, as long as there's a phone line to connect them to their employers. All that matters is the quality of the work produced.

Reduced work expenses Telecommuters waste fewer hours on the road and spend less money on gas, tolls, parking, business lunches, and pollution-causing dry cleaning. Day-care expenses are generally less as well. (Health-care and insurance costs might be higher, however; see later in this chapter.)

Benefits to employers

Employers also reap important benefits when they support telecommuting. These include:

Lower cost per employee Employers soon find that telecommuters cost less than in-house employees. Telecommuters take up little or no room in the office, which means lower overhead. They require less supervision, reducing the need for middle managers. They can supply their own PCs, and many telecommuters are contract employees who pay for their own benefits and insurance.

Higher productivity Many studies have shown that home-based telecommuters are generally more productive than workers who perform similar tasks in a typical office environment. This is in part because most telecommuters are self-motivated, high-energy pioneers with a real stake in making telecommuting work. But there are other factors as well. Telecommuters aren't interrupted by meetings and trivial office communications, they're less engaged in office politics, and their work is almost entirely computerized.

Retention of valuable personnel Telecommuting reduces absenteeism, enhances an organization's ability to retain experienced personnel (reducing the need for expensive job-training programs), and attracts talented new personnel. In fact, these were some of the goals of Hewlett-Packard's telecommuting program.

Compliance with environmental laws Amendments to the Clean Air Act that took effect in November 1992 require that employers in some high-pollution urban areas sponsor alternatives to commuting by car. California, where pollution from cars is rising to life-threatening levels, has passed state clean air laws that set a strict timetable for reducing car commuting, and the responsibility for change is placed mainly on employers. Other states might soon follow with similar laws. Telecommuting is a low-cost and environmentally benign way to achieve this goal.

Becoming a telecommuter

If your organization has had no experience with a telecommuting program, it might be difficult to convince managers to start one. Telecommuting programs rarely originate from managers. As with recycling programs, an employee is needed to get things started, someone who is comfortable with PCs, who can handle the responsibilities and isolation of telecommuting, who has a good reason to work off-site, and who's willing to try new things on a trial basis.

Telecommuting experts and consultants agree that the best way is to start small and work up. If you aren't telecommuting now and would like to begin, here are the steps you'll need to take:

1. Ask the hard questions

Few employers are ready for telecommuting. It isn't covered in the standard management texts, and it runs counter to the main rule that managers learn about supervision: if employee is at desk, all is well. Research the feasibility of telecommuting before you speak to anyone. Is it really right for you? Can you work long hours in isolation? Is your job suited to telecommuting? Do you have or can you get the organization to provide the necessary hardware and software? Do you have a good working relationship with your boss? Can you afford to pay more of your benefits yourself in return for greater freedom?

Employers rarely have problems with or reservations about telecommuting once things are underway. But telecommuters do sometimes encounter work-related difficulties that should be mentioned right at the start. The success of your telecommuting effort and its environmental impact depends on overcoming the following problems:

Loss of contact Telecommuters lose the face-to-face contact that builds close relationships between coworkers. Working independently, they might also not be immediately aware of changes in the office. So telecommuters must make a special effort to maintain contact, usually by coming in for meetings and special events and keeping in daily touch by phone.

Lack of advancement Telecommuters often fear that out of sight is out of mind, and that they'll be passed over for promotions in favor of someone who's on the scene. Telecommuters who are concerned about promotion need to make sure that managers know about their work and their commitment to the job. Many telecommuters find that the benefits of telecommuting are worth the risks.

Isolation Telecommuters must be able to work alone for long periods, without the stimulation of a large office. For some, this is the hardest telecommuting problem to overcome.

Exploitation Some employers attempt to take advantage of telecommuters by assigning them more work than can reasonably be completed in an eight-hour day or 40-hour week. According to experts, employers are more likely to try this if the telecommuters are women working at low-paying jobs like form processing. The best defense against exploitation is to be well-informed about the workload of in-house employees, and not to allow yourself to work 10- and 12-hour days.

Self-imposed overwork More common than employer exploitation is telecommuter workaholism. Because the home office never closes, overachieving telecommuters are tempted to squeeze out "just one more bit of work."

Loss of benefits As long as telecommuters put in a full week's work for their employers, they can't be denied the benefits owed to in-house employees. However, employers might not be legally required to cover telecommuters moving from full-time work to part-time work. So you could lose valuable insurance benefits. Workers' compensation still covers home workers in most states, however.

2. Make a plan

Once you've decided that telecommuting is for you, draft a written explanation of why you want to telecommute and how it will benefit the organization. Work out a schedule of off-site and in-house work that covers all your job responsibilities. You might have to do things that were previously done by your employer, such as purchase insurance and provide maintenance contracts on your equipment. And you might have to become an expert in areas such as telecommunication and online research that formerly weren't part of your job. Also detail what computers and computing resources you'll need, where they'll come from, and what they'll cost.

Arguments based on telecommuting's earth-friendliness might not be as impressive to your boss as arguments based on financial savings and productivity gains. Employers are generally more concerned about such matters as:

- The red tape required to get a program off the ground, or even to let one employee try it for a week.
- Who will supply and be responsible for the PC and other hardware involved, and who will pay for supplies, maintenance, and computer insurance.
- Whether and how to reimburse for expenses such as phone calls and express courier service.
- Issues of worker's compensation, insurance, and other benefits. Will your employer extend the same benefits to you even if you work part-time at home?
- Determining who can handle telecommuting (because others in your office will ask for it as soon as they see you doing it).
- Keeping tabs on telecommuting employees (such as how to make sure they aren't goofing off when surprise managerial inspections aren't possible). Your boss might fear losing control. This will likely be a major point of contention and negotiation, at least at first.

Present your plan coolly and objectively, and answer all questions honestly. Be willing to try it for a couple of days without a firm commitment, but make sure that you can get an evaluation in writing from your supervisor of how the experiment worked. If things don't work out, find out why and offer an alternative plan that will work.

3. Set up a green home office

Once you're a telecommuter, you have more responsibility for green computing than you did as an in-house worker because you have more control over your methods of work, the kinds of hardware and software you use, and the ergonomics of your home office. You won't be constrained by poorly thought-out office practices that are bad for you and for the environment. For example, you don't have to allow smoking if you don't like it, or suffer from the noise pollution of other people's printers, or use paper with no recycled content.

All the green computing rules of thumb described in this book apply to home offices as well as company offices. Get more from your hardware, save energy, compute without paper, recycle PC consumables, be a green consumer, and take advantage of low-cost, low-impact online sources of information. Keep in mind that simply by choosing to telecommute you're helping to do your share to keep the environment healthy.

4. Work toward full-time telecommuting

The less commuting you do, the better it is for the environment. It's unlikely, however, that your organization will approve full-time telecommuting right off the bat. Start by telecommuting one day a week, or even one day a month. Once you've proven that it can work, increase it to two or three days a week. Within a year, management might be comfortable with allowing you to appear in the office just one day a week for meetings and mail, assuming your type of work allows for that. Few telecommuters are willing to sever the cord entirely, but most prefer going to the office as seldom as possible. And most managers, once they've had a taste of successful telecommuting, are willing to oblige.

5. Set up a formal telecommuting program

Build on your success by extending telecommuting's benefits to others. Work to create a formal telecommuting program in your organization. Again, draft a report giving hard numbers on dollar savings and productivity gains based on your own experience, and enlist your boss's support. Research what other firms are doing. Quite a number of Fortune 500 firms have been enjoying the advantages of telecommuting for years.

Green telecommuting on the road

Computing, even telecommuting, is generally a sedentary, solitary activity. Isolated from the world in a makeshift office, parked behind a desktop PC, cradled by an ergonomic chair—that's the standard image of the telecommuter at work. But for a growing number of telecommuters, computing can be the central activity in a life literally off the beaten track.

Steven K. Roberts, author of the popular book *Computing Across America* (Learned Information, Inc., 1988), is the chief spokesman for and wizard of a loose network of computerized wanderers who ramble around the world in vans, trailers, and computerized bicycles. Roberts himself threw over his "standard technoid life" as an engineer and freelance writer in the early 1980s to become a "high-tech nomad."

He hit the road on a succession of custom bicycles that could take him anywhere and perform any computing task. His solar-powered recumbent bike (the Behemoth) packs enough computing power to equip a small office and every imaginable telecommunications tool, from ham radio, fax modem, and cellular phone to a microwave satellite link. With this rig, Roberts can compute anywhere on earth he can bike to, whether high in the Rockies or in the middle of Death Valley. "The key to nomadic technology," he says, "is to reduce the significance of where 'here' is." Best of all, from the green point of view, the Behemoth is essentially pollution-free and energy-self-sufficient; the only energy input is from the sun and from the food that powers Roberts's biking muscles.

Roberts is a gifted tinkerer who has made nomadic computing his life's work. While you might not have the technical expertise to build a computerized bike or the rock-hard quadriceps to pedal it thousands of miles cross-country the way he does, you don't have to be stuck at home or hovering near a phone jack and ac outlet to do your computing. Equipped with a notebook PC, cellular modem, and cellular phone service (or wireless radio modem and packet radio service), you can send in your work from many metropolitan areas in the United States and Canada. (See the Green-PC resources section for contacts.)

By the time you read this, several companies, including Hewlett-Packard, Tandy, Sharp, Casio, and Apple, will have announced notebooks or palmtops that have two-way radio networking built-in. Because you'll have to subscribe to a cellular or radio packet service, as well as purchase an expensive wireless modem, don't expect such capabilities to come cheap. But for nomads, no price is too great for total computing freedom.

The ultimate goal of telecommuting is to decentralize and democratize the workplace. In a world where the worker's home is not only his or her castle, but a corporate branch office as well, it will be harder to continue practices that aren't in the best interests of workers or of the earth. As Timothy Leary once quipped, "mobility is nobility."

Choices that make a difference

- ❐ Telecommute to save gas, time, and money.
- ❐ Work from part-time toward full-time telecommuting.
- ❐ Design a green home office.
- ❐ Start a formal telecommuting program at your place of business.

Green-PC resources

Four helpful books on telecommuting are:
The One-Minute Commuter
by Lisa Fleming
Acacia Books
1309 Redwood Lane
Davis, CA 95616
916-753-1519

Telecommuting: How to Make It Work For You and Your Company
by Gil Gordon and Marcia Kelly
10 Donner Court
Monmouth Junction, NJ 08852
908-329-2266

The Telecommuter's Handbook
by Brad Schepp
Pharos Books, World Almanac Education
1278 West 9th St.
Cleveland, OH 44113
800-521-6600

Computing Across America
by Steven K. Roberts
Learned Information, Inc.
available from:
Nomadic Research Labs
Box 2390
Santa Cruz, CA 95063
408-459-9780

These organizations can provide valuable assistance to telecommuters:
Association of Part-Time Professionals
7700 Leesburg Pike, Suite 216
Falls Church, VA 22043
703-734-7975

AT&T Home Office Network
800-446-6311 ext. 3010, fax 800-446-6399

Online services geared to telecommuters include:
Home Office Roundtable
GEnie
800-638-8369

Nomadic Computing Forum
America OnLine
800-227-6364 ext. 5254 for a free enrollment kit

Office.at.home
BIX
800-695-4775 for registration information

Working From Home Forum
(includes AT&T Home Office Network forum)
CompuServe
800-848-8199

Telecommuters with disabilities can get help from:
Office of Special Education
Apple Computer, Inc.
20525 Mariani Ave.
Cupertino, CA 95014
800-776-2333, 408-996-1010

IBM National Support Center for Persons with Disabilities
800-426-3333

A power converter that runs a Macintosh PowerBook off the 12-volt battery of an electric wheelchair is made by:
Don Johnston. Inc.
800-999-4660, 708-526-2683

Mobile communications services useful for off-road telecommuting include the following (call for current area availability, connect requirements, and rates):
ARDIS
800-992-7347
Motorola/IBM's national wireless packet radio network.

EMBARC
800-EMBARC4, x330
Motorola's paging and messaging service.

SkyTel
800-759-6206, extension 507
A radio-paging and messaging system.

Notify! is an application for DOS, Windows, and Macintosh that allows any compatible application to send a message via modem to any paging service and then to a pager or data receiver. It's available from:
Notify!
Ex Machina, Inc.
718-965-0309, fax 718-832-5465

8

Healthful computing

CHAPTER 8

WHAT PART of the earth's environment is most affected by PCs? The answer isn't landfills or the ozone layer. PCs make their greatest impact on their immediate environment: the computerized workplace and the human beings who work there. A green-PC workplace isn't truly green if the people who run it devote lots of attention to conserving energy and recycling paper while ignoring the health of PC workers. And, with tens of millions of people using PCs every day, computer-related health problems affect a larger percentage of the world population than do high-profile environmental hazards such as toxic waste spills from chemical plants or radiation released from nuclear reactors.

Using computers on a daily basis can lead to a variety of strain injuries and stress-related diseases that currently afflict millions of computer users. These injuries are often difficult to diagnose and treat, more so because employers and insurance companies are sometimes reluctant to acknowledge their seriousness. This chapter will examine the health aspects of personal computing and suggest ways to design a comfortable, productive, and health-supportive green-PC workstation.

Ergonomic computing

Ergonomics is the study of people in relation to their working environment. An ergonomic computing workplace is one in which PCs, keyboards, monitors, peripherals, chairs, desks, and other office furniture have all been designed for comfortable, efficient, and safe work. A good deal of ergonomic data has been compiled about the complex physical interaction between human bodies and computer equipment, covering everything from the right height for a keyboard to the proper level of illumination on the screen. Well-designed computer equipment takes into account human comfort and safety.

It's rare, however, to find a computerized office that doesn't in some way inflict strain and stress on PC users. This is especially true of home offices. Home-office workers are likely to compute on tables and chairs left over from dining-room sets. They wedge their offices in a dark corner of the dining room or in other small spaces not intended for computer work. Some corporate offices aren't much better. In fact, it's a good bet that your workspace is an ergonomic disaster.

In the face of poor worker health and rising insurance costs, some companies are now developing comprehensive ergonomics programs. The Occupational Safety and Health Administration (OSHA) is expected to institute a workstation-ergonomics standard in late 1994, which will encourage more companies to recognize and deal with the problem.

Ergonomics questionnaire

How ergonomically helpful is your computer workplace? To find out, sit down at your PC in the position you normally take. Spend a few minutes doing the kind of work you normally do. Now stop and listen to what your body is telling you. Where are your arms and legs? At what angle are they bent? How do they feel? Are your hands relaxed and comfortable? Now you can answer the following questions about your posture and computing environment:

- Are all components and materials within easy reach?
- Is your upper arm resting vertically near your chest?
- Are your hands slightly lower than your elbows?
- Are your wrists flexed when typing or using a mouse?
- Is your mouse arm supported?
- Does your mouse fit comfortably in your hand?
- Is your mouse at the same height as the keyboard?
- Are the heights of your monitor and keyboard adjustable?
- Can you move the keyboard away for manual work?
- Is the edge of your worktable rounded?
- Are you using a comfortable keyboard?
- Can you adjust the height and angle of your seat?

- ➢ Does your chair offer adjustable back support?
- ➢ Does the front of your seat round downwards?
- ➢ Do your feet rest flat on the floor?
- ➢ Is your workstation fitted to suit any disabilities you might have?

A "no" answer to any of these questions indicates that there's something uncomfortable, and therefore ergonomically wrong, with your computing environment. The result, sooner or later, is likely to be some form of injury or physical disorder that endangers your health and reduces your productivity.

Computerized businesses feel the pinch not in the neck but in the pocketbook. The total cost of treating work-related neck and back pain in the United States exceeded $80 billion in 1992. Much of this was paid by business as part of worker's compensation claims. (This figure includes injuries to physical laborers like stevedores and steelworkers, but there are many more claims from office workers than laborers these days.)

While it might take years for a work-related health problem to develop, these are problems that it's better not to ignore, as many long-time computer users have discovered. (See the section on stress and strain injuries later in this chapter.) Most ergonomic problems can be prevented or relieved by simple measures: changing your computing habits, rearranging components, or replacing one or two pieces of furniture. You'll see immediate improvements in comfort and productivity. Keep in mind that your PC feels no pain, but you can. Don't try to make yourself fit the PC. Make the PC fit you.

How to improve workstation ergonomics

When you work at your computer, your body should be relaxed and comfortable. Your back should be straight, but not rigid. Your neck should be inclined slightly forward to look at the screen. Your neck and shoulders should be relaxed, and your upper arms should fall straight down from your shoulders. Your forearms should incline slightly downward as your hands rest on the keyboard or mouse. Your thighs should be parallel to the floor, and your feet should rest fully on the floor or a footrest.

If your body is positioned correctly, you will feel comfortable, avoid strain, and be better able to concentrate on your work. If any part of your body isn't in the optimal position, however, it will throw off all the rest, leading to poor posture and unnecessary strains. Most of these strains by themselves are rather minor, and you might not even notice them at first. But over time, with hundreds or thousands of repetitions, the strains accumulate, and real health problems can result. Here are some suggestions for improving the ergonomics of your workstation:

Keep things within easy reach One of the primary causes of back and arm strain is having to reach for peripherals, supplies, and books. You're likely to strain yourself if you reach frequently for things that are just a little too far away, so that you're tempted to get them without leaving your chair. To minimize strain, everything that you need should be close at hand and easily reached, neither too high nor too low. Materials that you don't need to use often should be placed far enough away that you have to get out of your chair to get them. Your desk might be way too crowded to hold one more thing, so consider installing shelves nearby to hold books, software, and other materials.

Maintain the proper upper-body posture Achieving a strain-free upper-body posture is crucial to healthful computing. But that's not as easy as it might seem. There are many factors involved, including the height of your chair and table, the relative positions and heights of your keyboard, monitor, and mouse, and the proportions of your own body.

The keyboard, mouse, and work surface should be a little below the level of your elbows with your arms straight down, so your forearms are angled slightly down as you type. If the keyboard is too high, you will unconsciously pull up your shoulders and strain your shoulder and neck muscles. Unfortunately, many worktables have surfaces too high for proper typing. Most desks are about 30 inches high, a good height for eating dinner but two to four inches too high for typing.

Having to reach up or down to the keyboard flexes your wrists, which can lead to carpal tunnel syndrome. (For a fuller discussion of carpal tunnel syndrome, see a following section.) Your wrists should be in a straight line with your forearms, parallel to the floor. Possible solutions to flexed wrists include raising the level of your seat and getting a foot rest, getting a new desk with a keyboard shelf, or installing a pull-out keyboard shelf under your desk.

Keyboard and mouse should be within easy reach, so that your upper arms hang down alongside your chest, rather than extending forward or angling back. Reaching out, even a small distance, encourages you to bend forward and puts a strain on your spine. The result is fatigue and reduced productivity. If your arms are angled back—that is, if you're sitting too close to the keyboard or input device because there's not enough room behind your chair—you'll tend to lean back, again stressing your spine and producing arm and shoulder fatigue.

One way to achieve correct arm position is to adjust the distance between keyboard and chest by moving your chair until your arms are at a comfortable angle. This will be easier if you're sitting on a chair with casters. If necessary, use a carpenter's square to check that the angle of your arms isn't less than 90 degrees.

Support your mouse arm Using a mouse certainly makes many PC operations easier, but it can be hard on your mouse hand. It's a considerable strain to hold your arm out to the side for long periods, resting only on your wrist or the heel of your hand while making small, precise movements. The condition called "mouse arm" is a real occupational hazard among Macintosh and Windows users, and especially among graphic artists. The best solution to this problem is a height-adjustable padded armrest that can support the forearm of your mouse hand. The manufacturer of your chair can probably supply you with one.

Mouse at the right height Your mouse or other pointing device should be at the same height as the keyboard. Don't put it on a pile of books or down on a side table; your arms will be at unequal angles and you'll soon begin leaning to one side, which is bad for your back. Make sure there's enough room for your mouse next to the keyboard. You don't need the square foot of mouse space that experts often cite; set your mouse on a quicker speed, and you can mouse around in a few square inches. (Less mouse movement means less stress on your mouse wrist and elbow, too.) If you just can't make the room, try a stationary pointing device such as a trackball.

Use the right mouse You don't have to keep using the mouse that came with your computer if it's uncomfortable. It might be too big or too small, too heavy or too light, too wide or too narrow, or the buttons might not be easily accessible to or clickable by your mouse finger. Using an unsuitable mouse will soon lead to strain injuries of your mouse hand.

The number of brands and types of computer mice seem to multiply nearly as fast as their biological namesakes, and each mouse is shaped differently. Try several at a computer store until you find one that seems to fit, but be sure you can return it because it might take some time to tell if it's right for you. The newest models are generally more comfortable to use and require less arm motion than do older models.

Some people hate mice and prefer trackballs, pointer pads, tablets with cordless pens, and other exotic input devices. Consider these alternatives if you just can't get along with a mouse. Trackballs are especially good for children, who might not have the large motor skills or the arm reach to move a mouse with accuracy. Some suppliers are listed in the Green-PC resources section.

Adjust keyboard & monitor The two main ergonomic components of a PC are the monitor and the keyboard. The keyboard should have legs that can be flipped up and down to lower or raise its height and change its angle. It's also important to obtain the right relation between the height of your keyboard and the line of sight of your monitor. Because that relationship depends on the distance between your eyes and the ideal position of your typing hands, it's different for everybody. (See a following section on monitors.)

It's essential, therefore, that the heights of the monitor and keyboard be independently adjustable; otherwise one or the other will probably be at the wrong height. Unfortunately, not all computer equipment is designed this way, notably older one-piece data-entry terminals. Upgrade them to modular units if possible, even though that's a landfill problem; here's an instance where human health is more important than solid waste reduction.

It's a good idea to be able to swing away the keyboard when you need your desk space for reading or writing on paper. Otherwise you'll have to twist to the side to do these tasks, straining your spine. And it's important to realize that a table set at the correct height for keyboarding is too low for comfortable manual writing and reading. Ideally, the keyboard area on your desk should be easily height-adjustable, so you can raise and lower it to suit the kind of work you're doing.

Your desk should feature a rounded front edge. A sharp edge will cut into your wrists as you type. Even better, place a foam pad in front of your keyboard to cushion and support your wrists. These cost around $15 and are widely available from PC product catalogs.

Use the right keyboard Keyboards, like mice, come in different shapes and sizes; the one that came with your PC might not be the right one for you. Very small differences in the size and spacing of keys and the amount of force needed to push down a key can affect the comfort of your hands. Try different keyboards at a PC store and see if any of them reduce hand strain. Again, be sure you can return any keyboard that doesn't work out.

Use a copy stand Many computer users refer to information on paper documents as they type. Usually, the paper is perched precariously on top of a pile of books, and you must look back and forth from paper to screen, typing only as much as you can remember from your last glance. The result is strained eyes and a sore neck. One good idea is to use a copy holder positioned next to the screen, so you don't have to look down at your desk to read copy as you type. If you position the copyholder the same distance from your eyes as the screen, your eyes won't have to refocus when looking from the screen to the paper and back again, which helps to prevent eye strain.

Sit correctly Your chair probably has more effect on your posture and comfort than any other piece of equipment you own. Chair adjustments can go a long way toward making up for the ergonomic deficiencies of your desk and other equipment.

In a good computer chair, the height of the seat and the angle of the back should be easily and independently adjustable. It should be possible to tilt the back of the chair up to 15 degrees. The back of the chair should supply support to the middle of your back, so that you sit upright and relaxed in a natural position, and this back support should be adjustable, too. The chair should have height-adjustable, padded arm rests to support your elbows and take stress off your wrists. The seat of the chair should extend far enough forward to give your thighs full support and curve down in the front to avoid cutting off the circulation in your thighs when you lean forward. And the chair should swivel and roll smoothly on casters.

Chairs with all these features aren't inexpensive—they might cost anywhere from $300 to $1,000—but consider the money an investment in your health. It will cost you hundreds more in a few years when you need to have your spine attended to by a chiropractor.

Find your footing Finding the correct position for your lower legs and feet can make a big difference to your sitting comfort and productivity. Your thighs should be parallel to the floor and your feet should be planted comfortably on the ground. Dangling your legs from your chair puts all the weight of your lower legs on the underside of your thighs, preventing proper blood circulation to your legs. People with diabetes and other illnesses involving reduced circulation in the legs need to be particularly cautious about leg position. If your chair height doesn't allow a flat-footed position, use an adjustable footrest.

Is your PC handicapped-accessible? The Americans with Disabilities Act (ADA) of 1990 requires larger U.S. companies to make "reasonable accommodations" in designing handicapped-accessible workplaces. Workers with disabilities, particularly workers in wheelchairs, have special ergonomic requirements. Disabilities can involve sight, hearing, speech, access, and mobility. To make computer workstations comply with the ADA, your organization needs to consider such measures as:

- Widening doors and lanes of access to PC cubicles.
- Mounting PCs on height-adjustable worktables that are either of a roll-away or swing-away design.

- Installing trackballs or other stationary pointing devices.
- Installing alternative interface hardware such as text-to-speech and voice recognition devices.
- Installing special software that enlarges the screen image or aids in typing.

The most comfortable and effective ergonomic solutions are those worked out individually between the employer and the disabled employee. Often, ergonomic improvements made to aid disabled employees result in improved working conditions for all employees. (Sources of information on computers and the disabled are listed in the Green-PC resources section.)

Eye strain & vision issues

You might not be able to achieve a comfortable working position at the computer until you understand how your vision affects your posture. Ergonomics experts have found that we unconsciously move our bodies to see better. If the computer display isn't in your natural line of sight, you'll move your body into an unnatural position to correct the situation. So proper positioning of the computer display is essential.

That's not the only vision issue associated with PC work. Looking at computer screens for long periods has created a whole new kind of stress on our visual system that it was never designed to handle. Our eyes are best suited to spotting complex patterns and motions at middle and long distances—a skill that was used all the time by our arboreal ancestors as they leaped from branch to branch. But the PC users of today spend all their work hours concentrating on a fixed surface only a few inches from their eyes. We stare much longer and more closely at the screen than we do at most other objects in our world. To make matters worse, the screen is likely to be too close, at the wrong angle, and poorly illuminated as well.

There's considerable evidence that long hours at the PC can lead to eyestrain, blurred vision, nearsightedness, changes in color perception, and visually induced headaches, including excruciatingly painful migraines. In fact, a 1982 study by the Canadian Labor Board found that users of video display terminals (VDTs, a term that includes PCs and dumb terminals connected to mainframe computers) changed their glasses prescriptions twice as often as other workers as they tried to compensate for the stress on their visual systems. Ophthalmologists have coined a term, computer vision syndrome (CVS) to describe the range of vision-related disorders that can be caused by computing. As many as 10 million people suffer from CVS, according to one recent study. If you spend much time in front of a PC, there's a high probability that you're one of the 10 million.

Vision questionnaire

To check the vision ergonomics of your PC, sit down at your computer in the position you normally take. Work for a while—a minimum of half an hour. Now stop and make some observations. Note the relative positions of your head and the monitor screen. Using your arm or a meter stick, measure the distance from your eyes to the screen, between your eyes from the table, and between the table and the top of the screen. At what angle is the screen tilted? Note which areas are well lit and which are in shadow. Finally, take note of any tension in your eyes, face, neck, shoulders, and upper back. Now answer the following questions:

1. Is your monitor screen at arm's length from your eyes?
2. Is your line of sight perpendicular to the screen?
3. Is the top of the screen lower than your eyes?
4. Does the monitor tilt and swivel?
5. Does the screen look clear, bright, and sharply focused?
6. Is your screen free of glare and reflections?
7. Is your work area evenly illuminated?
8. Do your eyes feel comfortable looking at the screen?
9. Is it easy to focus on other work when you look away?
10. Are the muscles in your face and upper body relaxed?

If you answer "no" to any of these questions, you might already be experiencing vision problems with your PC.

What to do about vision problems

Researchers in ergonomics have come up with a number of recommendations that could help reduce CVS and possibly help you avoid more serious vision problems.

Position your monitor properly Vision experts agree that the main error most people make is to position the screen too close to their eyes. Keep the screen at least an arm's length away (20 inches or so) and farther away if possible. If the screen is too close, you'll force your eyes to maintain a steady focus on a nearby object—a recipe for nearsightedness, some ophthalmologists claim. The best arrangement is to position your monitor so there's a long open space behind it. Then you can easily glance up and focus your eyes on a distant object.

If you can't make out screen text at arm's length, don't move the screen closer. Try enlarging the characters on the screen. This is an easy task if you're using an operating system such as Microsoft Windows or the Mac's System 7. These give you a lot of control over the display of characters. Or you can switch to a multiresolution monitor (also called an autosynchronous monitor) that can enlarge things on the screen by making the pixels larger.

If you have trouble reading the screen at a resolution of 72 pixels per inch, you can switch to a resolution of 40 pixels per inch and get screen characters almost four times bigger. The trade-off is that less of your document will fit on the screen. Some software will do this for you as well. For example, Apple supplies a program called CloseView with every Macintosh. CloseView lets you magnify any area of the screen and even invert the screen image from the Mac's usual black on white to white on black, which some people find easier to read.

A monitor that's farther away has other benefits as well: it won't cause dust buildup on your corneas from the static charge on the screen, and you won't be exposed to as much low-frequency radiation (see chapter 9 for more on monitor emissions).

The monitor should also be at the right height and angle to your line of sight. If your desk and chair are at the right height (see the previous section), and if you're sitting in a comfortable position, the natural line of sight of your eyes should be perpendicular to the screen. Position the top of the screen so that it's at your eye level. As you sit, your head will naturally bend slightly forward, and your eyes will be looking directly at the center of the screen at about a 15-degree angle. You shouldn't have to roll your eyes up or down or duck your head to do your work. If you do, you can expect constant neck pain.

These adjustments will be easier if your monitor can tilt and swivel freely, and if it can be adjusted for height. There are a wide variety of tilt-and-swivel monitor stands available for under $50 from most PC accessories catalogers. Avoid computer desks that hold the monitor underneath the desk tilted up toward you. You'll be forced to tilt your head too far forward to see it, and the glass plate that protects the monitor will create glare and reduce the contrast of your screen. Moreover, you won't be able to reach the monitor controls without lifting the glass cover from the desktop.

Choose the right monitor Computer displays vary widely in such characteristics as focus, contrast, sharpness, clarity, flatness of the screen, resolution, pixel size, refresh rate (flicker), color purity, and overall color cast. The characteristics that have the most immediate effect on your vision are focus, screen flatness, and refresh rate.

First of all, the screen should be in clear focus in the corners as well as the center. If it isn't, your eyes will strain to bring it into focus. Have a technician adjust the screen for maximum focus and linearity (a measure of linear distortion) in your presence so that you can give the technician feedback.

Screen flatness is also important. Most monitors have curved screens, some more curved than others. The more curve to the screen, the more distorted it appears, especially at the edges. A flat screen has less distortion at the edges. Flatness is a characteristic of certain monitor tubes, such as Sony's Trinitron and Zenith's FST monitors; switch to one of these types, or any other that doesn't have an exaggerated curving distortion at the corners of the screen.

Finally, make sure your screen doesn't flicker. The picture on a monitor has to be refreshed (drawn by the electron gun that beams the image onto the inner side of the screen) many times a second. The more times per second the screen is refreshed, the less your eye will notice any flicker between refreshes. A refresh rate of under 60 times a second (60 hertz) will result in a noticeable flicker on the screen; your eye is just quick enough to see a trace of the screen being redrawn. Most people find flicker fatiguing to the eye. Use a monitor with a refresh rate of 70 hertz or more to reduce flicker-induced eye fatigue. You'll also want to consider choosing a monitor that reduces low-frequency radiation emissions. See the section on monitor emissions in chapter 9.

Properly light your workspace Good illumination of your work area is crucial, but it's difficult to achieve. You need to have enough light in the right places, but you also want to avoid glare. Finding the right balance might take some time.

First, make sure that you have the right kinds of lights. There should be overhead lights to provide an even overall illumination, and desk lights by your PC to direct bright light where you need it. The ratio of light from various sources in your work area is important, too. Looking from areas of shadow to areas of bright illumination strains your eyes. No area of your workstation should be in deep shadow or in very bright light. Overhead and desk lights should certainly be no more than three times brighter than the screen—that would be far too bright for comfort—nor should the screen be more than three times brighter than the ambient light level. If you like, you can use a simple light meter to check the illumination levels in various areas of the office.

Once you've achieved balanced illumination, you have to adjust the various components of your workstation to reduce glare. Glare, or light reflecting off your screen, makes it hard to see your work clearly. Your eyes will strain to resolve what's on the screen and deliver you a nice headache at the end of the day.

Reducing glare could be as simple as swiveling your monitor a few degrees one way or another and moving a light or two. It's more likely, however, that you'll end up moving everything around—your lights, your PC, and even your desk. You'll have to keep experimenting until you've minimized the glare. There are a few principles to keep in mind:

- Never position your monitor so a window is behind your back as you work. Glare from the window will reflect off the screen and into your eyes. If the window is in front of you (that is, behind the monitor), you'll get light from the window directly in your eyes, making it hard for you to see the screen. Position your screen so it's perpendicular to the windows. If necessary, pull down the blinds in your office or install shades that let in a soft, glare-free illumination. Or place a room divider so that it blocks glare from windows.
- Reposition desk lights so they don't reflect into the screen. Consider reducing the overall level of desk and overhead lighting, but don't let it get too dark.
- Wear a baseball cap to keep glare from overhead lighting out of your eyes. This is especially helpful for people who catch glare on their eyeglasses.
- If all else fails, try an antiglare filter for your monitor. These devices are glass screens that fit over the front of your monitor and are available from several manufacturers for around $100. They reduce glare, all right, but they also reduce contrast on the screen. Many newer monitors come with antiglare coatings.

If you've attained a glare-free state of bliss, there's one more thing to do: adjust the screen image for optimum contrast. The ratio between the light and dark areas of your screen should be no more than ten to one: that is, the white areas of the screen should be no more than ten times brighter than the black areas. This is especially important when using Windows or Macintosh applications where most of the screen is white. Turn down the contrast on your monitor if the picture seems too bright, but not so far that characters become difficult to resolve.

Be aware of eyestrain If, after a session at the PC, your eyes are tired, red, or sore, or you have a headache or neckache, it's likely that you're already suffering from CVS. (You might also be reacting to low-frequency radiation from your monitor or ozone emissions from printers; see chapter 9.) Don't shrug off the problem as temporary or unrelated to PC use. Have your eyes checked regularly and explain your concerns to your ophthalmologist or optometrist. Work with your employer to reduce eyestrain by installing good lighting and improving the ergonomics of your workstation. Above all, be kind to your eyes. Take frequent short breaks from looking at the screen and rest your eyes by closing them or looking into the distance.

Seek help for CVS If you're already experiencing vision problems, you should seek expert help without delay. A behavioral optometrist might be the right specialist to see. Behavioral optometrists are experienced in diagnosing vision problems related to work, especially computer work, and can perform tests to determine the nature and extent of your problem. If you're still experiencing problems after you've addressed the ergonomic and lighting problems of your computer workstation, you might need special eyeglasses just for computer work.

Stress & strain injuries

Each year, tens of thousands of computer users around the world suffer from strain disorders. Medical researchers haven't yet settled on an overall name for computer-related stress disorders, so you'll see them referred to as repetitive strain injuries (RSI), cumulative trauma disorders (CTD), cumulative strain disorders (CSD), repetitive motion injuries (RMI), overuse syndrome, and work-related musculoskeletal disorders.

Whatever the name, they're caused by the strain of performing small, repetitive motions thousands of times per day. The injuries are mainly to the hands and forearms, and involve painful, even paralyzing damage to nerves, ligaments, and muscles. The neck and back can also be affected if the workstation ergonomics are poor (see the earlier section on ergonomics).

Carpal tunnel syndrome Perhaps the best-known example of repetitive strain injury is a form of nerve damage known as carpal tunnel syndrome (CTS). CTS is a disorder of the nerves and tendons of the hand and wrist caused by the unnatural strain of a repetitive motion, such as playing a musical instrument, cutting meat, or typing at a keyboard. In CTS, the transverse carpal ligament, which spans the front of the wrist, becomes inflamed. The inflammation compresses the median nerve of the arm, which runs into the hand through a bundle of nerves and tendons called the carpal tunnel. If untreated, CTS can cause numbness, loss of motor control, and eventually severe pain. In serious cases, surgery might be required to relieve the pain and swelling.

According to the Occupational Safety and Health Administration, CTS now accounts for about half of all workplace illnesses in the United States. Employers, who are reluctant to address the problem of CTS, or even to admit it exists, end up paying a heavy price in worker's compensation or lawyers' fees and settlements. The pinch is being felt even by the computer companies. As of mid-1993, employees with CTS were suing Apple, AT&T, Digital Equipment Corporation, and IBM.

Stress Stress is another health factor in the computerized workplace. Stress is defined as the human body's reaction to physical, emotional, and environmental demands. Stress can be physical and/or psychological, and it can have positive or negative effects on health, depending on the nature, intensity, and duration of the stress. Healthy exercise is an example of positive stress. A major emotional or physical trauma causes negative stress.

Stress doesn't have to be major to put your health at risk, however. Even small levels of negative stress, if you must cope with them every day, can lead to health problems such as heart disease, high blood pressure, ulcers, and a host of psychological and emotional problems. For example, several studies have shown that working in a highly competitive office is stressful for employees and contributes to a higher rate of ulcers and other gastrointestinal problems among workers. The same studies show, however, that stress doesn't affect everyone equally; some employees thrive under high pressure and do their best work in competitive office environments.

In the case of computer work, stress can be caused by several factors in any combination: poor workstation ergonomics, the lack of body movement for long periods, the need for extreme care in doing monotonous, abstract tasks, unpaid and unacknowledged overwork, and excessive managerial monitoring and control. Also involved are factors that aren't well understood, such as radiation from computer monitors (see chapter 9).

In fact, the sedentary working conditions of computerized offices can be more stressful than the physically demanding conditions of working on a manufacturing assembly line. The human body needs and thrives on a higher level of physical activity than is afforded by computer work; reduced activity lowers your general fitness and is especially bad for your heart.

Data entry & stress The kinds of work that computer users perform, and the social conditions under which the work is done, can be extremely stressful. Data-entry workers, such as phone order takers and claims processors, are typically required to sit for long hours in one position while making repetitive typing movements. They're often isolated in tiny cubicles. The work itself is dull, but it still requires extreme precision. It is also expected to be perfect, even though many data-entry workers are at the mercy of poorly designed software that actually encourages mistakes.

PC networks and multiuser software enable supervisors and managers to enforce an Orwellian level of control over data-entry employees. In modern "electronic sweatshops," supervisors can observe every keystroke made by any worker on the network and issue instant productivity evaluations based solely on keying accuracy and speed. This level of control destroys trust in the workplace and can be extremely stressful for workers, who feel that someone is always looking over their shoulders.

Many data-entry workers are poorly paid and few are unionized; they have little say about the conditions in which they work or the amount of work they're given. As PCs grow ever faster and more capable, keyboard workers are expected to increase their own speed and productivity as well. The result is that human beings are held to the work standards of machines, which is why stressful, health-destroying overtime is pandemic in the world of computer work.

An NIOSH (National Institute for Occupational Safety and Health) study reported in mid-1992 that 22% of 593 US West VDT operators were afflicted with various strain injuries, even though the company had made a serious effort to provide an ergonomic workplace. Even more important, apparently, were psychological stress factors such as constant demands for high productivity, real-time electronic monitoring, and worker fears about job security.

And such stress isn't limited to data-entry workers. A famous T-shirt worn by the Macintosh development team read, "Working 90 hours a week and loving it," but in fact members of the team suffered from a variety of strain and stress disorders, including CTS, chronic exhaustion, and depression. The same pattern was repeated during the crash development of Apple's Newton personal digital assistant. Several engineers burned out, and one committed suicide.

Computer-related overwork, and the stress it causes, won't easily be banished from the workplace. The very managers who push for ever-greater productivity are themselves under stressful pressure from boards of directors who must produce quarterly profits for corporate shareholders.

Efforts to reduce strain injuries and lower the general stress level in the computerized workplace must start with each individual worker. Before you try to change the way work is done in your office, first analyze your own strains and stresses using the following questionnaire.

PC strain & stress questionnaire

Keep track of the number of hours you work in a week and the amount of work you produce. As you work, pay attention to the sensations in your hands and forearms. Note your emotions during the day and how you feel after the workday ends. Honestly assess your relationships with your supervisors and your future expectations in this job. Then ask yourself the following questions about the stresses and strains of your computing work.

- Are your hands and arms in pain when you compute?
- Does this pain persist even when you aren't working?

- Do you frequently work at the PC for hours without a break?
- Is your software difficult to use?
- Are there frequent down times due to software problems?
- Do you work in an isolated cubicle or office?
- Do you work at the PC more hours now than you did before?
- Do you do the same task the whole day?
- Do your supervisors monitor your work on their PCs?
- Do supervisors ignore complaints of work stress and strains?

If you answered "yes" to any of these questions, you might already be under stress that could hurt your health.

What to do about PC strains & stress

It's probably impossible to eliminate strains and stresses in the computer workplace, but there are some measures you can take to reduce them.

Address ergonomic problems The best way to deal with repetitive strain injuries is to prevent them. Improve the ergonomics of your workstation, following the recommendations in the previous sections. Many physical sources of strain and stress will disappear, and you'll feel better.

Take regular breaks Continuous work and overwork lead directly to strain and stress. You can avoid repetitive strain injuries by taking regular breaks to do other tasks or simply relax. As you type, briefly vary your position, stretch your hands, move your keyboard to your lap—anything to reduce continuous strain. Some experts recommend a break of ten minutes every hour; others recommend fifteen minutes every two hours. The important point is to interrupt the harmful routine of computing strain and stress, and the more often you can do this, the better.

Get up from your chair, stretch, and walk around. Exercise your hands by gently stretching them in the direction opposite to the way they are held for typing, then shaking them to relax the muscles. Stretch your neck, arms, and shoulders, too. Remember to rest your eyes as well.

Use software to relieve stresses & strains Software can come to the aid of habitual overworkers and people with incipient strain injuries. Several programs on the market will pop a message on the screen to remind you when it's time for a break. The better ones monitor key and mouse movements, so they know when you're working and when you're away from the PC. Some programs also include online ergonomic recommendations and diagrams of helpful exercises. See the Green-PC resources section for more information.

Try alternative keyboards A number of radically designed keyboards are available, most of which require you to learn new hand and key positions. For example, the Bat keyboard, made by a company called Infogrip, contains just seven keys and is operated with one hand. You type by pressing combinations of keys, which Infogrip calls chords.

Ergonomically, Bat is superior to a standard keyboard because it firmly supports the entire hand, preventing the wrist-flexing that can lead to carpal tunnel syndrome. And it's a good keyboard solution for disabled workers whose hand mobility is limited or who have the use of only one hand. However, a trained typist can type faster on a standard keyboard than on a Bat or some of the other alternative keyboards. If you're interested in checking them out, see the Green-PC resources section.

Seek medical help for severe strains If you're already in real pain, don't just grit your teeth and type on. Try wrist braces and wrist pads to relieve the strain on your hands. Braces and other strain relievers are available from SelfCare and other catalogs. (Keep in mind, though, that no device is as important in alleviating the pain of repetitive strain injuries as frequent breaks from typing.) Continued strain will only make things worse and can lead to painful, expensive surgery. If you're self-employed or are a freelance or part-time worker, surgery for a condition like CTS could be a financial disaster. So get medical attention, including physical therapy, if necessary.

Assess software for ease of use The software you use every day can actually add to strain and stress. Some poorly designed programs, for example, require users to type more with one hand than another. Programs that are difficult to use, unforgiving of errors, or prone to crashes are stressful to use. Even something as simple as online help is often left out of business software.

These problems can often be expensive to fix, especially for networked databases or other custom software used by many workers. If new software is needed, the people who will actually have to use it should be involved in the selection process.

Arrange work to decrease isolation One of the most stressful aspects of working with a PC is isolation. Many offices increase the natural solitariness of computer work by sequestering workers in small cubicles and setting up a workplace that prevents social interaction. The result for most people is high worker stress and lowered productivity.

Studies in the 1970s and 80s by management researchers Kurt Lewin, Wendell L. French, William G. Dyer, and others have shown that teamwork is more efficient, more productive, and less stressful than the efforts of isolated workers. Set realistic team goals, arrange the office for cooperative work, and watch productivity improve.

Combine data entry with other tasks To minimize strains and stress, data-entry work should be limited to four hours per day and combined with other tasks that don't involve PCs at all. If that isn't possible, then rethink the job to include related work like proofreading and phone calling that will at least alter the rhythms of PC work. Ideally, these other tasks would increase workers' autonomy and responsibility as well.

Enlist your boss's help PC-related strain and stress are real health problems, with real economic consequences. Retrograde workplace practices like using ergonomically poor furniture, monitoring data entry in secret, requiring unpaid overtime, and designing office layouts to increase worker isolation ultimately cost employers heavily in health care costs, workers' compensation claims, lost productivity, poor morale, and high worker turnaround. In many cases, however, employers don't even understand that there's a problem, assuming instead that complaints of pain and stress are signs of laziness. It's up to you to inform them.

Make the case to management, drawing on information from resources listed at the end of this chapter, and present a plan for reducing PC-related strain and stress in your office. Focus on the fact that management can reduce workers' compensation costs by setting reasonable PC working standards and rewarding responsible health practices among employees. In many places, such standards won't long be voluntary. The city of San Francisco already has an ordinance establishing ergonomic standards for computer workstations and requiring regular rest periods for computer workers.

PCs are at the center of a heated controversy over the health effects of electromagnetic pollution. Computers and their peripherals can also pollute the workplace environment by releasing ozone and emitting harmful levels of sound. See the next chapter for more.

Choices that make a difference

- ❒ Maintain the correct computing posture to reduce discomfort.
- ❒ Invest in ergonomic hardware and furniture.
- ❒ Make your PC handicapped-accessible.
- ❒ Reduce vision problems with the right monitor and lighting.
- ❒ Take regular breaks from repetitive tasks.
- ❒ Find ways to reduce the stress of computing and monotonous data-entry work.
- ❒ Seek medical help for severe vision problems, stresses, and strains.

Green-PC resources

The following publications contain more information on material in this chapter:

Computers and Visual Stress
by Edward Godnig and John Hacunda
Seacoast Information Services
401-364-6419

Stretching
by Bob and Jean Anderson
Stretching, Inc.
P.O. Box 767
Palmer Lake, CO 80133
800-333-1307, 719-481-3928
Includes a series of stretches that reduce the stress and strain of computing.

Visual Display Units: Job Content and Stress in Office Work
by Fe Josefina F. Dy
International Labor Organization
A thorough discussion of data-entry work and how to make it more bearable.

These organizations can provide more information on workplace health hazards, including PC hazards:

American Conference of Governmental Industrial Hygienists
1330 Kemper Meadow Drive
Cincinnati, OH 45240
513-742-2020

National Institute for Occupational Health and Safety (NIOSH)
Technical Information Branch
Mail Stop C-19
4676 Columbia Pkwy.
Cincinnati, OH 45226
800-35-NIOSH

Alternative pointing devices are available from:
Communication Intelligence Corporation
800-888-9242, x5026, fax 415-802-7777

Curtis Manufacturing
30 Fitzgerald Dr.
Jaffrey, NH 03452
603-532-4123

Kensington Microware Ltd.
800-535-4242

Logitech
6505 Kaiser Dr.
Fremont, CA 94555
510-795-8500

MicroTouch Systems
55 Jonspin Rd.
Bloomington, MA 01887
508-694-9900

Wacom Inc.
501 S.E. Columbia Shores Blvd., Suite 300
Vancouver, WA 98661
206-750-8882

Alternative keyboards are made by:
Infogrip
1145 Eugenia Place, Suite 201
Carpinteria, CA 93013

Industrial Innovations
10789 N. 90th St.
Scottsdale, AZ 85260
602-860-8584

Ergonomic computer furniture is available from:
Anthro
3221 N.W. Yeon St.
Portland, OR 97210
800-325-3841, fax 800-325-0045
Height-adjustable rolling carts for PCs and Macs.

Ergosource, Inc.
2828 Hedberg Dr.
Minnetonka, MN 55305
800-969-4374
Ergonomic furniture and accessories.

ScanCo
800-722-6263, 206-481-5434
Offers an excellent line of office furniture tailored to the Macintosh.

Contact the following organizations for information on the Americans with Disabilities Act and how to comply with it:
Alliance for Technology Access
800-992-8111, 415-455-4575

National Organization on Disability
202-293-5960

Worldwide Disability Solutions Group
Apple Computer
408-974-7910

These inexpensive programs alert you when it's time to take a break from the PC:
EyeCise
RAN Enterprises
One Woodland Park Dr.
Haverhill, MA 01830
800-451-4487
For Windows and OS/2

LifeGuard
Visionary Software
1820 SW Vermont, Suite A
Portland, OR 97129
800-877-1832
For Macintosh

User Friendly Exercises
FingerTip Info/Technically Innovative Computer Accessories
Distributed by
PM Ware
800-274-8422, 619-738-6633
For DOS and Windows

Take Five is a stress-relieving CD-ROM that teaches stretching exercises and relaxation techniques. It also offers digitized photos of landscapes and plays soothing music and natural sounds.
Take Five
Voyager
578 Broadway
Suite 406
New York, NY 10012
212-431-5199
For Macintosh

The SelfCare catalog has braces and other aids to relieve the strain of computing:
SelfCare Catalog
5850 Shellmound St.
P.O. Box 8813
Emeryville, CA 94662
800-345-3371, fax 800-345-4021

9

PC pollution in the workplace

CHAPTER 9

IF YOU DON'T LIVE NEAR a manufacturing plant, a toxic waste dump, or a polluted river, you might feel that pollution isn't really your problem. But did you know that pollution is emitted from your own PC? Not in the form of sludge and smog, but as invisible electromagnetic radiation, sound, and noxious gases.

Some researchers suspect that electromagnetic emissions from PCs, especially PC monitors, cause a variety of illnesses, including cancer, miscarriages, vision problems, and stress-related disorders. Others believe that such fears are groundless. We'll look at the evidence for and against in this chapter.

PCs can also emit radio waves that interfere with the operation of other electronic devices. Ozone gas is emitted from certain kinds of printers, and some printers generate unhealthy levels of sound. We'll also examine these other forms of computer-generated pollution and what you can do about them.

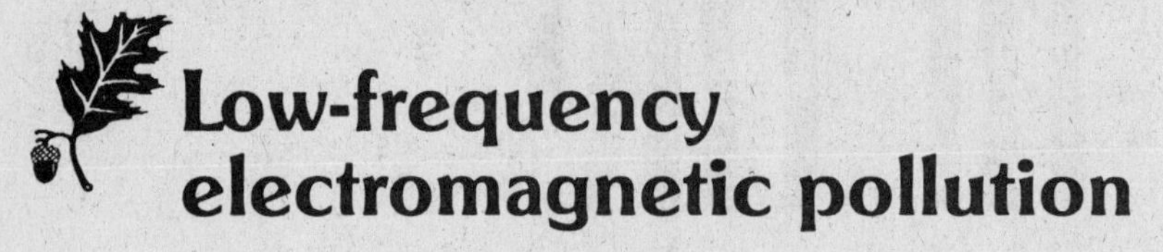

Low-frequency electromagnetic pollution

Computers, along with many other electronic devices, emit radiation along the entire range of the electromagnetic (EM) spectrum, from X-rays at the energetic upper end of the band to extremely low-frequency (ELF) radiation at the low-energy end. Light and heat, in the form of infrared rays, are two harmless types of electromagnetic radiation with which we're all familiar. What concerns some researchers today are the electromagnetic fields that pervade the space surrounding every PC, which usually encompasses one or more human bodies.

The health effects of EM emissions from computer terminals have been a matter of debate in the scientific world since the 1960s, though there was little publicity about the topic until the late 1980s. Scientists have long known that X-rays and very strong electromagnetic fields can damage living tissue by breaking apart the very atoms that make up cells.

The fields emitted from PCs and other electrical and electronic devices are so weak that most researchers assumed that there would be no biological effects at all. But there's some disturbing evidence to the contrary. Several studies since the 1970s have found possible correlations between computer use and leukemia, breast cancer, miscarriages, cataracts, and debilitating stress. Most researchers now admit that the biological effects of lower-frequency EM fields like those emitted by PCs are complex and poorly understood.

ELF

Inside every conventional computer monitor (and every television, too) is a cathode-ray tube, or CRT for short. The CRT is the part of the monitor that actually generates the image you see on the screen. At one end of the CRT is a scanning electron gun; at the other is the glass screen. The electron gun shoots a beam of electrons toward the screen. Encircling the path of the beam is a set of powerful magnets, the deflection coil. The magnetic fields generated by the deflection coil deflect the beam in a back-and-forth, up-and-down pattern so the point of the beam scans the screen corner to corner every $\frac{1}{60}$ of a second. Dots of phosphor on the back of the screen light up when they're hit by the beam, making the screen image that you see in front of the monitor.

The electronics of CRTs generate several types of radiation, including electrical fields from the scanning electron beam and magnetic fields from the deflection coil magnets and the flyback transformer that controls the coils. At one time, X-rays were thought to be the major health risk from cathode-ray tubes. However, today's CRT designs emit very little X-ray radiation—so little that X-rays are virtually undetectable outside the monitor enclosure, and they pose no measurable health risk to humans.

Recent research has focused on the potentially harmful effects of emissions from the other end of the EM spectrum, specifically on extremely low frequency (ELF) electromagnetic fields. These low-level, low-power EM emissions are produced by all electrical transmission equipment, including high-tension power lines and ordinary household wiring. During the last few years, ELF fields have become the focus of a raging debate among epidemiologists, cancer researchers, and physicists.

A 1979 study by Denver, Colorado, epidemiologists Nancy Wertheimer and Ed Leeper produced the first evidence that low-frequency fields from power lines caused a higher-than-average rate of leukemia among children living nearby. The incidence of leukemia among children living closest to the power lines was double the national average, they discovered. These findings have since been supported by studies by the University of Colorado in 1986, the New York State Department of Health in 1987, and the University of Southern California in 1990. Most recently, two Swedish reports published in the fall of 1992 found the same correlation between EMF, power-line proximity, and leukemia in children and adult men.

Also in 1979, a Johns Hopkins University study cited higher-than-average levels of several different cancers among male telephone cable splicers, who often work near power lines. This finding was confirmed by several other studies, including a 1982 study by the Washington State Department of Health in which electricians, power station operators, and others who were routinely exposed to ELF fields from power transmission equipment were found to have a higher-than-expected rate of leukemia. (In all studies, however, the actual number of cases linked to ELF of all kinds has been very small, no more than one or two a year.)

Two 1992 studies appear to contradict the results cited above. A report by Sir Richard Doll, the British scientist who established the link between cancer and cigarette smoking, came to the conclusion that the evidence linking cancer and EMF was too tenuous to prove a cause-and-effect relationship. Another study, by the Oak Ridge Associated Universities, concluded that "epidemiologic findings of an association between electric or magnetic fields and childhood leukemia or other childhood or adult cancers are inconsistent and inconclusive."

ELF fields aren't just a matter of concern for telephone technicians and power-line workers. ELF magnetic fields are emitted by the power and flyback transformers and the magnetic coils that control the scanning guns of CRTs. While the computing part of PCs also emit ELF magnetic fields, they aren't as powerful as those from computer monitors, which are now seen as the source of greatest potential emissions risk.

ELF and other EM fields from computers have attracted great interest because PCs are used everywhere and workers in many different fields spend so much time near them. Over the past few years, several studies, including one by Kaiser Permanente in 1988 and the National Institute for Occupational Safety and Health (NIOSH) in 1991, have investigated the effects of these fields on computer workers, with mixed results. The KP study found a correlation between computer work and miscarriages, while the NIOSH study didn't. Researchers now agree that the methodology of both studies was flawed.

Several things complicate the task of determining the health hazards of low-frequency emissions. One is the difficulty of eliminating from any study other factors that could contribute to PC-worker health problems. For example, the researchers in the NIOSH study claimed that the miscarriage rate in the KP study was caused by job stress rather than ELF emissions. (All the more reason to follow the stress-relieving recommendations in chapter 8.)

The biological effects of ELF emissions themselves appear to be complex. The intensity and frequency of the EM field, the length of exposure, and the distance from the field might all be involved. There are less obvious factors as well, such as whether the field is pulsed, the frequency of the pulse, and whether the field is electrical or magnetic. (Magnetic fields are considered to be potentially more harmful.) Researchers investigating the effects of ELF on living cells were surprised to discover that in some cases, certain cells were affected by low-frequency fields only at certain power levels or for a certain length of exposure. And less exposure didn't necessarily result in fewer biological effects.

The bottom line For all the research that has been done, no irrefutable correlation has been proven to exist between power-line or PC-generated low-frequency EM fields and health effects on human beings. Some writers have claimed to find a conspiracy by governments and the electric industry to suppress evidence of harm.

Yet the sometimes hysterical nature of such claims does not mean that those reputable studies that show a positive correlation should be dismissed out of hand. We simply don't know enough about the biological effects of low-frequency emissions to say with absolute certainty whether they're safe or not. It is possible that we never will know.

What you can do about electromagnetic pollution

In the absence of definitive data one way or another, prudence suggests that you take reasonable steps to reduce your exposure to electromagnetic pollution from PCs and monitors. Here are a number of suggestions for lowering your ELF exposure; most of them concentrate on reducing emissions from monitors:

Keep your distance Emissions intensity decreases with the inverse square of the distance from the source. That means that you're better off the further away you are from the monitor, so keep your distance from the monitor and PC. Emissions at 24 inches from the screen are one-quarter as strong as at 12 inches. It so happens that 24 inches is a good distance for your eyes, too. Emissions levels are stronger at the sides and back of the monitor than at the front. Arrange the office furniture so that no one in the office is sitting to the side or back of a monitor. Four feet away is the minimum distance. Laser printers and copiers also generate EM fields, so position them well away from desks.

Turn off equipment No electromagnetic fields are generated by devices that aren't drawing power. To minimize your exposure, turn off your PC when you aren't using it; you'll save power, too. See chapters 3 and 4 for more power-saving tips.

Use a smaller monitor Larger monitors generally emit more radiation of all kinds than smaller models. Measured in terms of diagonal screen size, use the smallest size monitor that you can to get your work done comfortably. Instead of using a large 21-inch monitor, you might be able to choose a 16-inch model.

Go monochrome Monochrome monitors emit half the low-frequency radiation of color monitors. If your work doesn't require color—and much computer work doesn't—then opt for a low-emission monochrome monitor. It will also cost less. Unfortunately, good mono monitors are becoming hard to find for PC-compatibles; you can still find them for Macintosh.

Make sure your monitor conforms to MPR 2 or TCO Invest in monitors that meet or exceed the electromagnetic emissions standard set by the Swedish National Board for Measurement and Testing (MPR). Make sure the monitor meets the board's MPR 2 standard (also called the NUTEK standard, after another Swedish organization, the National Board for Industrial and Technical Development), which limits ELF and other emissions. Don't purchase a monitor that conforms to the older MPR 1 standard, which is less restrictive. Most new monitors made by Apple, IBM, NEC, Sigma, Sony, Supermac, and other manufacturers already meet this standard, but monitors manufactured before 1992 most likely don't. It's easy to tell which monitors conform to MPR 2 because manufacturers are certain to advertise MPR 2 compliance.

MPR 2 is the strictest emissions standard currently available in monitors you can easily buy. However, it is not the ultimate standard because it is not based on medical studies, only on a low-emissions level that is easily achieved with current manufacturing techniques. MPR 2 might not afford sufficient protection from the possible harmful effects of low-frequency fields.

Recently the specifications for a third, tougher emissions standard were published by TCO, the Swedish office-worker's union. TCO measures emissions of ELF and VLF at 12 inches from the monitor screen, where fields are stronger, as opposed to MPR 2, which measures fields at about 20 inches. At the time of writing, only a few monitors, notably the T-series models made by Nanao, comply with TCO. The United States currently has no standard for monitor emissions, though one is being developed by the Institute of Electrical and Electronics Engineers (IEEE).

Use an LCD screen The liquid-crystal display (LCD) screens of notebook computers use a display technology completely different than the older CRT technology. LCDs emit no detectable low-frequency fields. You can now buy no-emission LCD screens for desktop PCs. However, you'll have to balance this advantage against the relatively poor visual quality of LCD screens, which can cause eyestrain. Active-matrix and thin-film transistor LCD screens, like the one for IBM's PS/2 E (see chapter 4), are much brighter and clearer than older LCDs, but they are still pricey—up to $2,000.

Radiation shields Some manufacturers sell emissions shielding that they claim can reduce radiation health hazards. Shielding can be installed inside the monitor, or a clear shield can be fitted over the screen. No shielding has been shown to provide complete emission protection, and over-the-screen shields do little to block the magnetic fields that are of greatest concern. For the curious, several shielding manufacturers are listed in the Green-PC resources section.

Don't bother with lead aprons Lead aprons were a popular remedy a few years back. They do nothing to shield you from the low-frequency fields that are the focus of current research.

Test magnetic emission strength If you are truly concerned, you can measure the strength of the magnetic fields emitted from your PC equipment with a handheld magnetic-field meter, called a gaussmeter. (A *gauss* is the standard unit of measure for magnetic fields.) These devices measure field strength in milligauss (thousandths of gauss) and can sense magnetic fields surrounding the electronic device in your office or home. Meters can be purchased for as little as $100, but a good meter (one that is going to give you accurate and reliable information) will cost at least $1,000; high-end meters go for $6,000. Check into the possibility of borrowing, renting, or leasing a unit from one of the companies listed in the green-PC resources section.

Even a top-rated gaussmeter won't tell you how much of the magnetic field is ELF, though, only whether a magnetic field of some kind exists and how strong it is. The recommended maximum magnetic field exposure from any electronic or electrical device is 1 milligauss.

On average, if you hold a gaussmeter 2 feet away from your PC when it is running you'll get a reading between 1 and 2 milligauss in front and about double that at the sides and back. That's more than the maximum recommended, but way less than the 7 to 10 milligauss you're exposed to when you blow-dry your hair or drive your car. On the other hand, you presumably don't sit in front of your blow dryer all day. (But you might consider getting rid of your electric blanket and driving less. See chapter 7 for tips on telecommuting.)

Radio-frequency interference

ELF isn't the only worrisome electromagnetic emission from computers. Computer equipment also emits *radio-frequency waves* (abbreviated rf)—electromagnetic radiation that occupies the same part of the EM band as radio and television. The rf in PCs and printers is generated by the rapid switching of electronic circuits and the strong, pulsing magnetic fields in monitors. There are many different frequencies of rf in any computer setup, and if the rf isn't contained within the equipment by adequate shielding (usually some type of metallic lining on the inside of the casing) it will escape to become radio-frequency interference (rfi), which I'll discuss later.

What are the health effects of radio-frequency radiation? Long-term, high-levels of exposure to rf and microwaves (powerful radio waves from the more energetic end of the radio band) have been shown to quadruple spontaneous abortion rates in mice and to produce cataracts in humans. Other human health effects, including changes in blood chemistry, reduction in the effectiveness of the blood-brain barrier, and psychological symptoms such as chronic depression and weariness, have all been cited as the result of rf exposure.

There's no study to date that provides incontrovertible data that the lower-power rf from PCs has any adverse health effect on computer users. But it has one very important indirect effect on human health. Rfi from PC equipment that isn't properly shielded can interfere with emergency radio communications, aircraft-control signals, and medical life-support systems. In one recent case, rfi crippled operation of the Search and Air Rescue Satellite, which helps pinpoint emergency beacons from ships and mountain climbers. The source of the rfi turned out to be a single poorly shielded computer monitor in an Internal Revenue Service office in Maryland.

Lest you imagine that this is an isolated circumstance, note that the Federal Communications Commission (FCC) fined more than 100 companies at the Fall 1991 COMDEX computer show for displaying and selling computer equipment that failed to comply with the FCC's rf regulations. Sixty-six companies were fined at the 1992 Spring COMDEX. That unshielded modem you bought on sale could be blocking an ambulance radio right now, perhaps at the cost of someone's life.

What you can do about radio-frequency interference

Unlike low-frequency magnetic fields, rfi is already recognized as a problem by PC designers and is regulated by the federal government. Rfi can easily be detected and prevented by people who use PCs.

Buy only FCC-certified equipment The best way to make sure that your PC and peripherals don't emit rfi is to make sure that they fully comply with the federal regulation called FCC Part 15, which specifies the maximum rfi that can be emitted by any consumer electronic device sold in the United States. The FCC has two classifications of rfi-free electronic devices: Type A equipment, which is suitable for business use, and Type B equipment, which can be used in homes as well. Type B is the more stringent specification, and the one that appears on almost all computers. Once the FCC approves a machine, the manufacturer is required to attach an FCC certification number to each unit manufactured.

Most reputable manufacturers comply with the FCC regulations (though apparently not at computer shows, where many prototypes are shown). However, certification costs money and takes time, and some computer manufacturers bypass the whole process. Unscrupulous vendors even attach old FCC certification numbers to uncertified equipment. So it's up to you to ask for proof when there's a question of compliance—that is, when there appears to be damage to the FCC number on the machine, or when there's no number at all. All your PC equipment should have an unmodified FCC certification number permanently attached to the device; you can check the number with the FCC if you're really in doubt. (FCC contact information is in the Green-PC resources section.) Let vendors know you'll return equipment that isn't FCC certified. If you're buying recycled equipment, test it for rfi first, as described in the following section.

Test for rfi If your PC interferes with other electronic equipment, such as your neighbor's TV, or crashes whenever you turn on the Cuisinart, you know you have an rfi problem. No special equipment is needed to check for rfi. You can do it with any portable radio. First, turn off all other electrical or electronic equipment in the room. Tune the radio to a quiet place between stations on the AM band. Set it next to the operating PC. Listen for rfi noise—loud static that occurs only near the PC. Now gradually move the radio away until the noise stops. If you can still hear static when you leave the office, your PC is putting out a potentially hazardous amount of rfi. Try moving the PC and plugging it into another outlet, and if that doesn't work, get the shielding fixed at a local PC repair shop. If the PC is certified and under warranty, the repair should be free. Many reputable PC manufacturers will fix shielding problems for free even if the PC is no longer under warranty.

Other sources of workstation pollution

Electromagnetic pollution from PCs has attracted the most interest from researchers, but health problems can also be traced to chemical and sound pollution from computer equipment. Printers, copiers, and fax machines emit ozone, and impact printers generate high-decibel sound. We'll look at these sources of workstation pollution in this section.

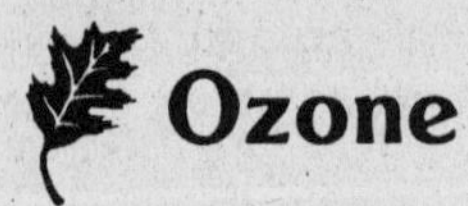

Ozone

Ozone gas is a variant of plain old oxygen. You can smell it in the air after a thunderstorm. (The word ozone comes from the Greek ozein, "to smell.") The ozone gas that collects up in the stratosphere acts as a protective layer against the sun's rays, and ozone is refreshing to breathe occasionally after a heavy rain, but down in the office it's considered an air pollutant. Concentrated ozone is bad for your lungs, eyes, and general well-being. Ozone-sensitive people, especially asthmatics, can suffer reactions that include migraine headaches, nausea, depression, and severe asthmalike symptoms.

The main source of ozone pollution in the modern office is the drum-charging process used in laser printers, some plain-paper fax machines, and copiers. The culprit is the corona wire inside the toner cartridge. Whenever a printout or copy is made, a high-voltage current is sent through the corona wire, which in turn generates a powerful electrical field to charge the imaging drum. The electrical field breaks down oxygen from the air around the corona wire, creating ozone. Unless it's filtered or carried away, that ozone leaks out into the office air, where it gets into your eyes, nose, mouth, and lungs. In some cases, ozone concentrations near laser printers can rise well above the EPA's recommended maximum of 0.1 parts per million for continuous exposure and 0.3 ppm for peak exposure. Here are some suggestions about reducing ozone pollution:

Change the filter Many older laser printers (including the popular Hewlett-Packard LaserJet, LaserJet II, and LaserJet III series, Lexmark's IBM LaserPrinter 10, and NEC's SilentWriter Model 95) use an ozone filter to catch ozone emissions from the corona wire. For most of these printers, the ozone filter should be replaced after 50,000 copies or every two years. (Check the manufacturer's recommendations for the exact replacement schedule.) Newer lasers, such as the LaserJet 4 series and Kyocera's EcoSys laser, don't need filters because they use low-voltage charging systems that produce little or no ozone.

Ventilate the office Make sure the area around the machine is well ventilated. If your office has a window, put the laser printer, copier, and fax machine near it and use a small exhaust fan to vent ozone fumes. If you don't want to open the window, or you don't have one, then at least move the devices as far from your desk as possible. Consider moving all devices that use photocopying or laser-printing processes to a separate room away from desks, and ventilate that room. The air in all parts of the office should be circulated regularly, otherwise, ozone as well as many other kinds of air pollutants can build up inside the office and affect your health.

Note: Beware of aerosol products for cleaning laser printers, copiers, and the like that claim to provide an "ozone guard." Some of these products contain HCFC-22, a chlorofluorocarbon that does nothing to guard against ozone from your laser but is classified as a Class II, stratospheric-ozone-depleting chemical under the Clean Air Act. Use a plain old damp cloth to clean the plastic enclosures of your equipment. A little vinegar or citrus cleaner will help to remove greasy fingerprints.

Sound pollution

PCs themselves aren't especially noisy, but dot-matrix and other impact printers are. An office full of whining dot-matrix and clattering daisywheel printers can reach ambient sound levels about the same as those on a factory floor. High levels of sound create stress, make it hard for people to concentrate on their work, and interfere with conversation. A study conducted by Columbia University in the late 1970s found that excessive noise in the office was the factor with the highest correlation to job dissatisfaction and high levels of stress. Many people find the whine of a high-speed dot-matrix printer, with its ultrasonic, insectlike overtones, especially irritating.

Segregate noisy printers There are several ways to reduce printer sound. One of the easiest is to segregate printers in one corner of the office away from desks, shielded with a couple of acoustically padded movable screens (available from office-supply stores). Or you can relegate all printers to a separate room. If the printers aren't networked, you'll need extra-long cables to connect distant printers to your PC, but keep in mind that parallel connections don't work on cables longer than 12 feet or so. Another solution is to cut down the number of printers in the office. Many workers can share a few distant printers by using a parallel or serial-port switchbox, as discussed in chapter 1.

Install acoustic shielding If segregating printers isn't possible in your office, then consider putting an acoustic hood over each noisy printer. Acoustic hoods can reduce the level of noise from printers, often to half the former level. Inexpensive shielded plastic hoods that fit over most dot-matrix printers can be purchased from office supply catalogs. Even a sturdy corrugated cardboard box used as a hood can cut down on printer noise by 20% to 30%. To absorb sound, you can also install acoustic tiles and carpeting in especially noisy areas.

Choose quiet printers You can always switch from dot-matrix or daisywheel printers to quieter printer technologies such as inkjets or lasers. Inkjet printers cost about the same as dot-matrix printers, and laser printers cost three to ten times as much, depending on speed and maximum printout size. There are also some relatively quiet dot-matrix printers on the market, though they aren't as quiet as inkjets or laser printers. Citizen offers one, the GSX-240, that has patented acoustic shielding. Panasonic also markets dot-matrix printers with so-called "quiet technology." See the Green-PC resources section for contact information.

Choices that make a difference

- ❐ Be aware of potential PC pollution problems in your workplace.
- ❐ Keep your distance from computer monitors.
- ❐ Use low-emission MPR 2 monitors.
- ❐ Buy only FCC-certified computing equipment.
- ❐ Change filters on laser printers to reduce ozone emissions.
- ❐ Install adequate ventilation in offices.
- ❐ Shield, segregate, or retire noisy printers.

Green-PC resources

The following publications contain more information on topics covered in this chapter:

Cross Currents: The Promise of Electromedicine, the Perils of Electropollution
by Robert O. Becker
Jeremy P. Tarcher, Inc.
5858 Wilshire Blvd., Suite 200
Los Angeles, CA 90036
213-935-9980, fax 213-935-9986

Currents of Death: Power Lines, Computer Terminals, and the Attempt to Cover Up Their Threat to Your Health
by Paul Brodeur
Simon & Schuster
1230 Ave. of the Americas
New York, NY 10020
212-698-7000
Brodeur believes there is a threat and a conspiracy to hide the medical effects of EMF; he amplifies this theory in a more recent book, *The Great Power Line Coverup* (Little, Brown, 1993). For an opposing view, read the next resource.

"ELF and Cancer FAQ Sheet"
by John Moulder
Radiation Biology Group
Medical College of Wisconsin, Milwaukee
available by calling:
414-266-4670, fax 414-257-2466
e-mail: jmoulder@its.mcw.edu
A technical assessment of the scientific literature on EMF and health. Also available in the GAIN area of America OnLine.

The Interference Handbook
Government Printing Office
Publication 004-000-00482-5
GPO Order Desk
202-783-3238
An FCC-produced booklet listing ways to eliminate RFI.

Terminal Shock
by Bob DeMatteo
New Canada Publications
NC Press Limited
Box 4010, Station A
Toronto, Ontario M5H 1H8, Canada
A few years old, but still a useful primer in video-display radiation and other health issues; read it in conjunction with Moulder, cited above.

Microwave News
PO Box 1799, Grand Central Station
New York, NY 10163
212-517-2800
The journal of the microwave industry, with much information on EM fields and health.

VDT News
PO Box 1799, Grand Central Station
New York, NY 10163
212-517-2800
Covers all aspects of video display terminal/computer workstation health, safety, and design issues.

These organizations can provide more information on workplace health hazards, including PC hazards:
National Institute for Occupational Health and Safety (NIOSH)
800-35-NIOSH (800-356-4674)

National Council of Acoustical Consultants
66 Morris Ave., Suite 1A
Springfield, NJ 07081-1409
201-564-5859, fax 201-564-7480
Provides information on sound pollution.

Occupational Safety and Health Administration (OSHA)
200 Constitution Ave., NW
Washington, DC 20210
800-582-1708
This federal organization investigates workplace health and safety.

Handheld gaussmeters are available from:
F.W. Bell, Inc.
407-678-6900

Electro-Magnetic Design
612-888-7473

MEMTEC Corp.
603-893-8080

Real Goods Trading Co.
800-762-7325

Schaefer Applied Technologies
800-366-5500

Walker Scientific
508-852-3674

Widerange Instruments
408-423-1983

These companies market devices that claim to shield you from monitor emissions:
NoRad
1160 E. Sandhill Ave.
Carson, CA 90746
800-262-3260, 310-605-0808

Safe Technologies
1950 Northeast 208 Terrace
Miami, FL 33179
800-638-9121, 305-933-2026, fax 305-933-8858

Nanao's line of Flexscan monitors are TCO and Energy Star compliant.
Nanao USA Corp.
23535 Telo Avenue
Torrance, CA 90505
800-800-5202, 310-325-5202

10

Pollution in the computer industry

CHAPTER 10

AT THE DAWN of the personal-computer age, PC manufacturing was seen as an inherently clean industry. Computer-manufacturing facilities had no smokestacks belching pollutants or pipes spouting waste into nearby streams. Instead, silicon chips, circuit boards, computers, and other electronic devices were made by white-coated workers working in spotlessly clean factories, their ultramodern buildings set in pleasant green parks. Most of these factories were located in Silicon Valley, the area in Santa Clara County, California, that is the world center of the electronics industry. Through the 1960s and '70s, Silicon Valley boomed financially, seemingly proving that technology could produce riches without pain.

That comforting image was destroyed in 1981 when two heavily polluted sites were discovered in the heart of Silicon Valley. Within a short time, more than 100 such sites were found. Silicon Valley, it turns out, is among the most polluted places on earth, contaminated by the sources of its wealth—factories that make the parts that go into PCs and other electronic devices.

Today, the electronics industry, PC manufacturing included, is recognized as one of the world's most dangerous polluters. Making the chips, boards, drives, and other components of PCs requires scores of hazardous and toxic chemicals. In densely populated Silicon Valley, more than 100,000 tons of hazardous waste are produced by electronics manufacturers every year. These chemicals sometimes escape into the surrounding environment, where they can pose a serious hazard to people living nearby. People who work in computer-manufacturing facilities are exposed to even more serious health risks.

Because the pollution risk from PC manufacturing was discovered first in Silicon Valley, that's where most of the research on pollution is now being done and where public awareness of the problem is at its highest. But the same problems exist in other areas of the United States. States with active electronics manufacturing sectors include Arizona, Illinois, Massachusetts, New Jersey, New Mexico, New York, North Carolina, Oregon, and Texas.

Many states are so eager to attract electronics manufacturers that they offer outsized abatements, tax deferments, and other expensive incentives. According to *Voces Unidas*, a newsletter of the South West Organizing Project, the state of New Mexico recently approved an unusual package of incentives to clinch a deal with chipmaker Intel for a new chip fabrication facility (called a "fab" in industry jargon) in Sandoval County. Besides $114 million in work incentives, the company received a $2 million Industrial Revenue Bond, streamlined environmental and construction permits, and a waiver on gross-receipts taxes until the year 2010. Given the fast obsolescence of chip technologies, it is likely that New Mexico will never receive any tax income from Intel before the fab is outdated and closed. Plus, the 8 million gallons of water per day required by the Intel fab puts an additional strain on New Mexico's already strained water system.

While Intel has found a good deal at home, other U.S. manufacturers seeking cheaper labor are moving their facilities overseas to Brazil, Colombia, Honduras, Hong Kong, India, Ireland, Israel, Malaysia, Mexico, Scotland, Singapore, South Korea, and Taiwan. There's also interest in locating PC manufacturing in the business-hungry countries of Eastern Europe, where wages are low and workers are skilled.

Some countries have attempted to get tough with electronics manufacturers. In 1993 Taiwan's Environmental Protection Administration threatened to shut down a chip factory in Kaoshiung, the island's industrial center, after the factory had toxic wastes burned near an elementary school. Hundreds of children became ill from the fumes. Eventually, the case was settled with a fine and a revision of the factory's production practices. But even low-wage, productive countries like Taiwan might be bypassed by electronics firms seeking the lowest possible cost of production. Malaysia, for example, is busily building a chip-manufacturing industry with help from Japanese, Taiwanese, and American firms. Local Malaysian officials are just discovering that the electronics factories they have so eagerly welcomed are creating a health and toxic-waste problem for Malaysia's future. Ultimately, pollution from the manufacture of PCs has global consequences. That makes it everyone's problem.

And the problem isn't getting any smaller. The worldwide chip market increased by 7% in 1992, according to a report by the Semiconductor Industry Association, with most new consumption coming from the United States and the Pacific Rim nations. Chip manufacturers are ramping up operations to meet the increased demand for low-cost PCs.

PCs are not the only products that use computer chips. Embedded chips now appear in just about every consumer product, from microwaves to TVs, automobiles to dishwashers, hearing aids to exercise bikes. New autos contain about 15 different microprocessors and controllers, some of them identical to those used in personal computers, and that number will double by the turn of the century. Worldwide, some 1.7 billion embedded computer chip controllers were shipped in 1993.

In this chapter we'll take a look at how the PC industry pollutes, what manufacturers and environmental organizations are doing about it, and what part you can play in correcting the problem.

Toxic chemicals in PC manufacturing

Arsine, also known as arsenic hydride, is a colorless gas sometimes used in chemical weapons. It's relatively easy to make. You simply drop a hunk of zinc, which is usually laced with arsenic impurities, into sulfuric acid. (Don't try this at home.) One of the most poisonous gases known, arsine, administered in a large enough dose, will attack red blood cells and quickly destroy the central nervous system. The victim will die within minutes unless given an immediate and total blood transfusion. One cylinder of arsine spilled on an urban thruway could, if wind conditions were right, kill hundreds of people in an area of several square blocks.

Where is the nation's largest stockpile of arsine? Not in some secret weapons depot in the desert. It's in densely populated Silicon Valley, where arsine is used as a doping agent in the manufacture of semiconductors—the silicon chips that make every PC work. In fact, arsine is just one of more than 100 toxic substances used in various stages of the manufacture of microchips and printed circuit boards (called PCBs in the electronics industry, not to be confused with a group of chemicals called polychlorinated biphenyls, also abbreviated PCBs, which pose a pollution problem in many U.S. rivers and lakes). Let's take a look at the PC manufacturing process and some of the chemicals used in it.

How toxic chemicals are used to make PCs

The use of toxic chemicals to make PCs begins at the very heart of the computer, with the manufacture of the integrated circuit, also called the semiconductor chip, microchip, or just plain chip. A chip is a small, highly complex package of transistors that acts as part of the "brain" inside the PC.

There are many types of chips. For example, dynamic random-access memory chips (DRAMs) are the standard memory chips that temporarily store computer information. Another chip, the microprocessor, takes information from the DRAMs and performs all the calculations the computer needs to do its work. In addition to these, PCs might contain scores of chips, each designed to do a specialized task. Computer chips are also used in many other electronic devices, from video games to military hardware.

The wafer Every chip begins its life as an ingot of crystalline silicon. The silicon is sliced into wafers that can hold dozens or even hundreds of chips on their surfaces. Chips are then manufactured by adding and subtracting materials to the wafer, cutting the wafer into finished chips, and then protecting the chips by enclosing them in a solid epoxy resin package.

Masking The process used to create chips is somewhat like the lithographic printing process, with the wafer acting as the lithographer's stone and various chemicals acting as the lithographer's ink-resisting wax and acid wash. First, the parts of the wafer that will not contain circuits must be masked. The wafer is sprayed with a light-resistant, acid-resistant masking chemical that's usually dissolved in glycol ether, a solvent that has been identified as a reproductive toxin by the EPA. Next, a negative image of the circuit design of the chip is beamed onto the coated wafer. The wafer then undergoes a developing process that washes away the masking chemical where it wasn't exposed to light. What remains is an acid-resistant mask everywhere but where the chips' circuits will be.

Etching The wafer is then given an acid bath, which etches the parts of its surface that aren't protected by the mask. Most often, the acid used is super-corrosive hydrofluoric acid, which can sear fourth-degree chemical burns down to the bone with only brief contact. Sometimes less-corrosive but still-dangerous sulfuric acid is used. The acid is flushed away with yet another solvent, which can be an acid, a phenol, or glycol ether.

Doping The etching process creates a wafer with channels of naked silicon. These channels will be the chips' circuits. First, however, the channels must be doped, or implanted with other materials to produce certain electrical properties. Doping is done inside a sealed chamber using highly toxic gases formed from elements that improve silicon's electrical conductivity. These gases include arsine, made from arsenic; phosphine, made from phosphorus; and diborane, made from boron. Unfortunately, the high reactivity and unusual electrical properties that make these gases so desirable as dopants are the same ones that make them extremely toxic to human beings.

Metalizing Metalization is the next step. Conductive metals, such as gold, silver, chromium, or aluminum, are laid down in the etched grooves to create the actual circuits that will carry electrons within each chip. Toxic heavy metals such as arsenic, cadmium, lead, and beryllium, and deadly cyanide salts, might also be used in the metalization process.

Testing Now the individual chips are cut from the wafer and tested. As many as half might be defective; these will either be recycled for their metals or just thrown away.

Packaging Tested chips are then packaged in epoxy resins to protect them and make them easier to handle. The resins are mixed with toxic catalyzers like methyl ethyl ketone peroxide. A radioactive gas, Krypton-85, is often employed to test for leaks after each chip has been sealed in its package.

Cleaning The entire process, from wafer to packaged chip, requires extremely clean conditions. Any contaminant, even a tiny speck of dust, will ruin a chip, so chips are frequently cleaned with any of several different volatile solvents to remove grease and particulates. Solvents are used in great quantities all along the chip-making assembly line; these include methyl chloroform, trichloroethylene (TCE), toluene, xylene, benzene, acetone, and even plain old rubbing alcohol. Most of these are known carcinogens (cancer-causing substances).

PCBs & disk drives The finished chips are usually mounted on printed circuit boards, or PCBs. The PCBs usually consist of a plastic base layer equipped with mountings for various chips, and printed metal circuits to carry electrical signals from one chip to another. The main system board of your PC is an example of a PCB.

The manufacturing process used to make PCBs is somewhat similar to that used to make chips. A plastic resin base is masked, etched, metalized, cleaned, and tested. Then chips, resistors, and other electronic parts are soldered to the board. PCBs require even more cleaning than chips, mainly because of the debris left by soldering, assembly, and trimming the board, so PCB manufacturers consume cleaning chemicals in great amounts. Glycol ethers are the preferred solvents. (Large quantities of ozone-depleting chlorofluorocarbons, usually CFC-113, can also be used to clean excess solder from PCBs. See the section on CFCs later in this chapter.)

Manufacturing hard disk drives also requires enormous quantities of cleaning solvents. For example, CFCs are used to flush contaminants from the surfaces of disk-drives (the spinning part of the disk that contains the stored information) before each drive is sealed.

Toxic gas discharges & air pollution

Highly toxic gases are crucial to current chip- and PCB-manufacturing processes. Large volumes of these gases are used in Silicon Valley and other chip-making centers.

In 1982, the release of toxic gas from a Union Carbide chemical plant in Bhopal, India, killed more than 4,000 people. There is the potential for a similar disaster in Silicon Valley and other chip-making centers. So far, there has been no major release of toxic gas in Silicon Valley, but discharges of other, less toxic gases aren't uncommon. In June of 1992, for example, an entire neighborhood in San Jose, California, had to be evacuated because a highly acidic gas leaked from a solvent-supply company. Ten people sustained injuries from the noxious yellow cloud, which covered several blocks.

Air pollution over Silicon Valley can be severe in the summer, when atmospheric inversions keep pollution from dispersing. The EPA estimates that Silicon Valley industries discharge millions of pounds of pollutants every year. The same thing is happening in every other center of the electronics industry.

Water contamination

What happens to the spent process baths, cleaning solvents, and rinsed acids and metals that are left behind after the chip-making process? These chemicals don't stay safely inside the fabs or in underground storage tanks.

San Francisco Bay's largest copper and nickel polluters are almost all electronics manufacturers, according to data published by the City of San Jose in July of 1993. The roster of polluters reads like the exhibitors list for an electronics convention: National Semiconductor, Advanced Printed Circuit Technologies, IBM, Litton Applied Technologies, Intel, Linear Technology, Western Digital Media, Sigma Circuits, Adaptive Circuits, and others.

According to the Silicon Valley Toxics Coalition (SVTC), a grass-roots group that tracks the toxic waste problems of the PC industry, some 200 public and private drinking-water wells in the Valley have been contaminated by more than 134 different chemicals leaking from 150 underground storage tanks. A study by the California Regional Water Quality Control Board found leaks in 85% of the underground storage tanks used by manufacturers.

The result of all this is that, today, the Valley area has the highest density of Federal Superfund sites (29 and counting) of any county in the United States. And the culprits include some of the best-known names in the business: IBM, National Semiconductor, Intel, Hewlett-Packard, and many others.

The most famous and perhaps the worst groundwater contamination site in Silicon Valley was discovered in 1981 near an underground storage tank at the Fairchild Semiconductor plant in south San Jose. Wells adjacent to the tank were found to be contaminated with the cleaning solvent methyl chloroform (1,1,1 trichloroethane). A study by the California Health Department found that the birth-defect rate in the surrounding community was three times the national average. Another notable site of groundwater contamination in the Valley is the Naval Air Station at Moffett Field, where 19 contamination sites were found to contain levels of toxic chemicals thousands of times over California state limits.

One IBM plant in San Jose has been leaking toxic groundwater contaminants for a decade, creating an underground toxic plume five miles long that will take an estimated $100 million to clean up. A Hewlett-Packard facility in Palo Alto is also leaking organic chemicals into the groundwater. Hazardous chemicals, including trichloroethylene and benzene, are threatening sites all over the Valley where water wells are planned for the future.

PCs & the ozone layer

The electronics industry is the second largest user of CFCs, after the refrigeration and air-conditioning industry. And, until recently, PC makers let most of these CFCs escape into the air. The highest volume of atmospheric CFCs ever measured was recorded in 1987 over the IBM disk-drive manufacturing facility in San Jose.

When CFCs are released into the atmosphere, they eventually destroy ozone molecules in the upper atmosphere that shield the earth from the sun's ultraviolet radiation. In early 1992, NASA announced with some alarm that significant depletion of the ozone layer—up to 40%—was anticipated not just in Antarctica, where it had first been discovered a few years earlier, but also in northern areas of the United States, Canada, Russia, and Europe.

If not reversed, the depletion of atmospheric ozone will have serious health consequences. According to estimates by the UN's Environmental Programme, increased ultraviolet-radiation exposure caused by a 10% to 20% reduction in ozone will result in 300,000 cases of skin cancer every year, 1.75 million cases of cataract-induced blindness, and a likely increase in immune-deficiency diseases, including AIDS.

Health problems in the computer industry

People who work in the electronics industry are threatened by an array of health problems. Production workers are routinely exposed to solvents, acids, caustics, heavy metals, plastic films and emulsions, and epoxy resins, as well as the fumes, vapors, and volatile gases they give off. The documented effects of these substances include chemical burns; nerve, kidney, and lung damage; heart disease; hormonal disruption; mental and emotional dysfunction; reproductive problems; and a wide variety of cancers.

Exposure isn't always a simple matter of accidentally handling a hazardous substance or breathing a toxic vapor. In many fabs, toxics pervade every niche of the work environment. Arsenic, for example, can be absorbed by workers who clean out and change the oil for the furnaces and the ion implantation equipment used in doping chips. Even these low-level doses of toxics might have long-term effects.

The high potential for exposure to toxic materials has had an obvious result: The rate of occupational illness for electronics-manufacturing workers is three times that of manufacturing workers in other industries. According to a study by researchers at the Occupational Safety and Health Administration and the University of California at San Francisco, systemic poisoning caused by overexposure to harmful chemicals accounts for almost half of all illnesses among semiconductor industry workers. Joseph LaDou, a researcher at UCSF, has determined that production and maintenance workers suffer 60% of all the injuries and illnesses incurred by workers in the electronics industry, although they make up only 33% of the work force.

A special set of hazards is faced by workers in the so-called "clean rooms" where chips are made. Clean rooms are designed to keep the number of particles in the air to a minimum because a chip can be ruined by contamination with even the tiniest speck. Clean rooms are kept dust-free by air-filtration systems that circulate the same air over and over again. Unfortunately, recirculation also concentrates solvent vapors. That's no great problem for the chips, but it's bad for the chip workers, who can be exposed to harmful concentrations of toxic vapors every working day. Sometimes the level of toxic vapors becomes so acute that the rooms must be evacuated and flushed out. One answer is to use robots, but few companies can afford to completely roboticize their clean-room assembly lines.

Cancer Many electronic-manufacturing processes haven't been in use long enough for oncologists to study their long-term health effects on workers. But there's already an increase in cancer cases on record. One of the best-known examples became public knowledge in 1984, when more than 250 Hispanic female workers at the GTE Lenkurt plant in New Mexico filed occupational disease suits against the company. The women assembled electronic components for GTE telecommunications equipment, using the same solders, solvents, acids, epoxy resins, and other hazardous chemicals used to make microchips and PCBs. They suffered from ovarian, uterine, and pericardial cancers. Many of the plaintiffs died before the case was settled out of court and documents were sealed.

Reproductive hazards Women make up more than 60% of the labor force in the electronics industry. Working on chip- and PCB-assembly lines, women are routinely exposed to small (and sometimes large) amounts of hazardous chemicals, some of which are classified by the EPA as *teratogens*, or reproductive toxins (that is, they cause fetuses to become malformed, resulting in miscarriages, stillbirths, and children born with birth defects).

In 1986, Digital Equipment Corporation discovered that the miscarriage rate among the company's female assembly-line employees was twice that of its female clerical employees. That rate was confirmed by a 1992 Johns Hopkins University study conducted for IBM. The Johns Hopkins researchers found that 10 of 30 pregnant women who worked with two glycol ether solvents, diethylene glycol dimethyl ether and ethylene glycol monethyl ether acetate, had suffered miscarriages. The women in the GTE Lenkurt suit also had high rates of miscarriage, still births, excessive menstrual bleeding, and hysterectomies.

Green initiatives in PC manufacturing

To many PC manufacturers, staying on the cutting edge of technology and beating competitors to market is more important than developing pollution-free production processes or ensuring safe conditions for workers. But that's not true for all of them. Recognizing that poor environmental and health practices are unethical, as well as bad for business, some companies are taking the initiative to clean up their acts.

Reducing toxic waste

The EPA recently began a new program dubbed 33/50, in which electronics manufacturers are being asked to reduce their use of 17 toxic chemicals by 33% by the end of 1992 and 50% by 1995. Many well-known names in computing, including IBM and Hewlett-Packard, are voluntary participants. Hewlett-Packard and Intel have even taken the program a step further and are asking their suppliers to do the same. Intel says that if it has to choose between two suppliers equal in other ways, it will go with the one with the better environmental record. In fact, concern for the environmental impact of products is spreading rapidly among manufacturers, as each seeks a competitive advantage by appearing more environmentally correct than its rivals.

The PC industry is also cooperating to promote waste reduction. IBM and Hewlett-Packard trade information about reducing toxic wastes. The Santa Clara County Manufacturing Group, a Silicon Valley consortium that includes Apple, Intel, Amdahl, Digital Equipment Corporation, and Lockheed, claimed to have reduced its overall chemical emissions by 4.3 million pounds between 1987 and 1991.

Some companies are turning to waste-recycling systems to reduce pollution. Aeroscientific Corp., a PCB manufacturer, recently installed a $1.3 million sludge-reduction system that the company claims has cut its annual toxic sludge production from 50 cubic yards to 3 cubic yards. Other companies have stopped disposing of solvents after a single use in a chemical bath; they now filter and reuse cleaning fluids. And many companies that store liquid waste in underground tanks are installing double-walled tanks to replace leaky single-walled models. Tank replacement is expensive, but it's far cheaper than cleaning up major groundwater contamination.

Reducing CFCs

CFC-based solvent cleaners might be bad for the environment, but they're easy to handle and relatively inexpensive. Until recently, manufacturers have been slow to adopt alternatives. But the industry attitude has changed radically since 1989, when 81 countries agreed to phase out the use of CFCs by the year 2000. That date has since been moved up to 1995. As an additional incentive, federal law now requires components made with ozone-depleting chemicals to be labeled as such.

Computer and electronics manufacturers have realized that the time has come to develop alternative processes that don't use CFCs. And many manufacturers have done so. The largest firms, including IBM, Intel, Compaq, and Apple, have gone a long way toward reducing and even eliminating the use of CFCs in their fabs. For example, in July 1992, Apple Computer announced that it had completely eliminated the use of CFCs to clean electronic assemblies and manufacturing equipment. All Apple factories now use a new assembly technology that can produce high-quality circuit boards without the need for cleaning. Manufacturing operations that require cleaning have been converted to a water-based process. (While the water-based cleaning process is better than the old CFC-based one, it produces waste water contaminated with lead.)

Through the new technology, Apple's worldwide CFC emissions were reduced more than tenfold, from 270,000 pounds in 1990 to less than 2,500 pounds in the first half of 1992. Apple expects to phase out all CFC use by 1994.

IBM, at one time the biggest CFC polluter in Silicon Valley, is also reducing its use of CFCs. Big Blue's south San Jose plant, where the world's highest rate of CFC emissions was recorded in 1987, now emits none at all. IBM cleans its PCBs with soap and water and uses capture-and-expurgation systems to purify the remaining toxins from waste water. Other major manufacturers, including Intel, AT&T, NCR, and Sony, are following suit. Fujitsu is using an ultrasonic water cleaner that it claims is far more efficient than washing in a chemical solvent.

Such no-clean or low-clean processes are not only good for the earth, but they also save manufacturers millions of dollars. Intel claims that it saves up to $4 million per year by not having to buy and dispose of CFCs—money that the company can spend on developing faster, more efficient processors.

The picture isn't all rosy, however. Many of the smaller firms that supply parts, subassemblies, and PCBs to the large manufacturers haven't yet switched to non-CFC processes. CFC use in the electronics industry will likely remain a problem until the turn of the century. But it's one pollution problem that seems to be on its way out.

Improving worker health & safety

Most larger companies train production employees in the proper handling of chemicals and in methods of dealing with spills and other accidents. And they invest in federally mandated safety equipment such as air cleaners for areas in which solvent vapors are present.

But most of them could be doing much more to protect the health of their employees. Lexmark, a company that manufactures printers, has developed an environmental assessment program that evaluates each chemical used in production and selects safer alternatives as they become available. Lexmark recently switched its supplies and motor assembly lines to a natural citrus-based cleaner that's harmless to workers. Apple has a program in which a peer review group made up of environmental, health, and safety professionals visits Apple facilities to check on compliance with health and safety laws and with company policies. IBM has a relatively good occupational-injury rate, in part because nearly every manufacturing process it uses is rigidly controlled by a set of formal, written procedures.

However, the success of company safety policies depends on the willingness of the firm's management to take responsibility for safety. Federal regulation isn't an effective motivation for companies whose executives and managers don't care about safety, and neither are lawsuits brought by workers. Occupational illness and injury lawsuits are usually settled out of court for far less than the cost of building a truly safe PC-manufacturing workplace. Manufacturing facilities in countries that lack strong labor unions or worker-protection laws, such as Malaysia, are rarely safe places to work. And it's to these countries that many PC manufacturers are moving their fabs.

Developing green chips

Reducing pollution in the industry isn't enough, say many observers. The whole chip-making process as it's practiced today is inherently hazardous, and despite the manufacturers' best intentions, there will always be health risks to workers as well as pollutants to discard. The industry needs to develop completely green chips that require no toxic materials in the manufacturing process—nicknamed "all-vegetable chips," because they might use some of the chemical reactions involved in photosynthesis.

The technology to create an all-vegetable chip doesn't yet exist, but developing it would be worthwhile for economic as well as ecological reasons. According to Rand Wilson, coordinator of the Campaign for Responsible Technology, an all-vegetable chip "is in fact the thing that's going to make the U.S. competitive again" in chip manufacturing. By that, Wilson means that eliminating the high cost of using and disposing of toxic pollutants will make chip manufacturing as inexpensive in the United States as it is for chip makers overseas. (See the Green-PC resources section for information on how to contact the Campaign for Responsible Technology.)

Advocates of green-chip technology have turned their attention to Sematech, a consortium of U.S. electronics manufacturers partly funded by the U.S. government. Sematech's mandate from the government is to develop smaller, faster chips that will challenge Japan's dominance in the world chip market. Reasoning that Sematech, which draws half its funds from federal tax dollars, should be held accountable to the needs of workers and communities, the Campaign for Responsible Technology and other groups have been pressing Sematech to broaden its mandate and devote research funds to green-chip development.

Sematech has made some progress in this area. The consortium has already demonstrated techniques for replacing arsine gas with solid arsenic, which is easier, cheaper, and safer to handle, and for purifying and recycling acids used to etch chips. In October 1992, under pressure from CRT and other environmental groups, the U.S. Congress assigned one-tenth of Sematech's annual $100 million budget to the development of a "pollution-preventing, environmentally safe microchip manufacturing process." The authorization bill further requires Sematech to consult with environmental and labor organizations during development. Currently, CRT is trying to convince the consortium's industrial members to devote $10 million to environmental research as well. However, progress in this area has slowed recently as the Clinton Administration relaxes pressure on U.S. computer manufacturers to encourage them to stay in the United States.

The Silicon Principles

One organization that has been working for the last decade to convince the PC industry to clean up its act is the Silicon Valley Toxics Coalition (see the Green-PC resources section for information on how to contact them). In the mid-1980s SVTC identified 29 Superfund toxics sites in Santa Clara County, California; it was one of the first groups to alert the public to the dangers of using CFCs in PC manufacturing. SVTC members also helped draft the nation's first local ordinances for the storage of toxic chemicals and gases, which have become the models for similar state and federal laws.

Antipollution efforts within the PC industry have tended to be reactive rather than proactive. In other words, companies try to fix what's already a problem, but rarely plan for problems that might crop up in the future. This is why the SVTC and its sister organization, the Campaign for Responsible Technology, have drafted a comprehensive set of guidelines, called the Silicon Principles, that PC makers can use in planning ways to reduce their use of chemicals, improve worker health and safety, establish good relations with local communities, and design environmentally responsible products.

The Silicon Principles in full are as follows:

1. Establish a comprehensive toxics-use reduction program.
   - Phase out the use of CFCs and other chlorinated solvents.
   - Phase out all carcinogens, reproductive toxins, and neurotoxins.
   - Phase out the use of acutely toxic gases.
   - Develop Toxics Use Reduction plans, materials, and waste audits, and mass balance materials accounting.
2. Develop health and safety education programs and health monitoring.
   - Develop health and safety training that's sensitive to diversity of work force.
   - Make health monitoring comprehensive and available to public inspection.
   - Establish nondiscriminatory transfers for pregnant production workers.
   - Earmark 5% of all R&D money for environmental, health, and safety programs.
3. Work with local communities to establish "good neighbor agreements."
   - Include emergency planning and worst-case scenario planning, including transportation planning.
   - Provide full disclosure to local communities and regular monitoring, including inspection.

- Establish corporate commitment to hiring, training, and promoting local residents.

❹ Implement a worker-improvement program and economic-impact statements.
- Ensure that workers are involved in process design and workplace governance.
- Assess environmental, social, and economic impacts of new technologies and new facilities.

❺ Support a national R&D policy directed by civilian (not military) needs.
- Support a change in federal R&D funding from the Defense Department to the Department of Commerce.

❻ Establish corporate policies requiring equal standards for subcontractors and suppliers.
- Establish technical assistance and technology transfers to encourage pollution prevention at all stages of production, rather than shift the pollution down the production chain to smaller contractors.
- Hire responsible contractors who engage in responsible environmental and labor policies.

❼ Establish corporate standards that are enforced equally domestically and internationally.
- Establish corporate policies that ensure full compliance worldwide that meets the strictest standards.
- Require all facilities worldwide to make full disclosure of toxic reporting.

❽ Establish a life-cycle approach to all manufacturing, from R&D to final disposal.
- Design new products from a life-cycle perspective.
- Internalize costs of disposal and guarantee return and safe disposal of all used products.

❾ Work closely with local communities and workers to ensure full oversight and participation.
- Commit to open partnership with workers and community to ensure comprehensive participation.

What you can do

Everyone who uses PCs should work to reduce pollution and worker hazards in chip and computer manufacturing. If you work in the industry, you can take direct action by encouraging your company to adopt the Silicon Principles. Living by the Silicon Principles won't be easy for most companies, at least at first. Resources and ingenuity will have to be applied to redesigning production processes and even rethinking the basic design of electronic components. In the long run, however, the effort to reduce pollution is crucial.

Companies that have made serious advances in pollution reduction have found that these advances have yielded savings in materials and development time for new products that more than offset the initial cost of pollution control. The more dedication a company shows to clean manufacturing processes, a high level of worker health, and a working partnership with the surrounding community, the more benefit it will reap down the road.

PC users outside the industry can help, too. Give your support to organizations such as the Silicon Valley Toxics Association, the Campaign for Responsible Technology, and Computer Professionals for Social Responsibility that are working for a clean computer industry. Fax or e-mail the CEOs of computer companies and let them know that you're concerned about this issue. Choose vendors who are working to reduce pollution, and don't buy from vendors who pollute and are doing little about it. Silicon Valley Toxics News, the SVTC newsletter, will keep you informed about the latest developments in the Silicon Valley area, including announcements about which companies have been cited for toxics violations.

Do what you can in your own community. The PC and electronics industry isn't as centralized as it was 20 years ago; chances are good that there's at least one manufacturer or supplier in your area. Work to pass toxic-waste storage and disposal laws that take into account the unique problems of the industry. Convince local manufacturers to allow community monitoring of chemicals in storage.

Choices that make a difference

- ❐ Realize that pollution in the PC industry is everyone's problem.
- ❐ Keep informed about chip manufacturing pollution problems.
- ❐ Buy from companies working to reduce PC pollution.
- ❐ Support organizations working for clean PC manufacturing.
- ❐ Work to pass toxic-waste storage and disposal laws in your community.

Green-PC resources

Two books that report extensively on computer pollution are:
Toxic Work: Women Workers at GTE Lenkurt
by Steve Fox
Temple University Press
Philadelphia, PA 19122
An account of the poisoning of female manufacturing employees of a GTE electronics plant in New Mexico.

The High Cost of High Tech: The Dark Side of the Chip
by Lenny Siegel and John Markoff
Harper and Row
10 E. 53rd St.
New York, NY 10022
An overview of pollution and other hazards in the electronics industry.

These organizations can provide more information on pollution in the computer industry and its effects on workers:
Campaign for Responsible Technology
c/o Rand Wilson
760 N. First St., 2nd Floor
San Jose, CA 95112
408-287-6707
Dedicated to extending democracy into the design and development of new computer technologies.

Computer Professionals for Social Responsibility
P.O. Box 717
Palo Alto, CA 94301
415-322-3778
An industry group working for responsible business practices by computer companies, free access to electronic information, and other issues.

National Environmental Health Association
720 S. Colorado Blvd.
South Tower, Suite 970
Denver, CO 80222
303-756-9090, fax 303-691-9490
Provides information on worker health issues.

Occupational Safety and Health Administration (OSHA)
200 Constitution Ave., NW
Washington, DC 20210
800-582-1708
A federal organization monitoring workplace health and safety.

Silicon Valley Toxics Coalition
760 N. First St., 2nd Floor
San Jose, CA 95112
408-287-6707
SVTC supports antipollution initiatives and green chip development; publishes an informative newsletter, the Silicon Valley Toxics News, and also The Legacy of High Tech Development: The Toxic Lifecycle of Computer Manufacturing, a report by Ted Smith and Phil Woodward.

This organization provides information on industrial solvent recycling and reclamation:
National Association of Chemcial Recyclers
1200 G St, NW, Suite 800
Washington, DC 20005
202-434-8740, fax 202-434-8741

Risk*Assistant is a program for quickly assessing the health risks of exposure to chemicals in the environment. Call for nonprofit pricing:
Risk*Assistant
Thistle Publishing
P.O. Box 1327
Alexandria, VA 22313
703-684-5203
For DOS and Windows

Hazmat Administrator and ChemCheck are two programs that help managers prepare and revise chemical inventories and Hazardous Material Management plans for multiple facilities. Contact:
Gaia Systems
3000 Alpine Rd.
Menlo Park, CA 94028
800-858-7888, fax 415-854-8297
For Macintosh and DOS.

11

Software that saves the earth

CHAPTER 11

IT'S BEEN KNOWN for a long time that getting more PCs into the classroom and providing the tools and training that will help teachers use them creatively are important steps toward improving American education. (See chapter 6 for tips on donating used PCs to schools.)

American educators point with some pride to the fact that more than half of American classrooms have a computer. What they don't point out is that the majority of these computers are seldom used, if they're functional at all, and they're hardly ever integrated into the curriculum. One ancient Apple II for 30 kids, the typical PC-to-student ratio, isn't an asset that classroom teachers can do much with. Most of the time the computer sits on a rolling cart in the corner, ignored.

It doesn't help that much educational software is ineffective, irrelevant, or simply boring. Educational programs aren't the best vehicles for teaching reading, spelling, and math; the personal guidance of a parent or teacher is the best way to teach these basics. However, well-designed software can be just the ticket for conveying the complexities of more sophisticated subjects.

There's a wide and growing selection of educational computer programs that teach environmental concepts. Do such programs have any real value? To the extent that computer programs substitute for the actual experience of organizing a classroom recycling program, or visiting a local landfill, or exploring the ecosystem at the local pond, the answer is "no." But as a supplementary tool for getting students to think both theoretically and analytically about the environment, the answer is "yes." The best environmental software forces students to make hard decisions about environmental problems and explore the consequences on screen, with no harm done. Then they can take what they've learned and apply it to real-world problems.

This chapter discusses two basic kinds of environmental software: educational programs and computer simulations. Educational programs on the environment use multimedia—graphics, sound, text, and interactivity—to explain such abstract concepts as ozone depletion, the greenhouse effect, and tropical deforestation.

Computer simulations use video-game techniques to convey a sense of the actual experience of a complex task such as managing a wildlife preserve or building an entire planetary ecosystem. Simulations can also be used in biology classes to substitute for the dissection of real animals. In the following sections, we'll look at representative programs from each category.

The environmental programs available today are aimed mainly at junior-high and high-school students. Most don't run on school-standard Apple IIs; they require a Macintosh or IBM-compatible PC equipped with color graphics. This could pose a problem for schools, which still might not own IBM-compatible PCs or Macs. If the necessary PC isn't available in your classroom, consider renting one, borrowing one from a local business, or soliciting a donation. Older IBM PCs can be had for very little money, and they're still capable of running most environmental programs. (See chapter 6 for more on finding older PCs.) Only a few PCs are needed per classroom because these programs are best used by groups of students working together. The programs themselves cost less than $100, except for those on CD-ROM, which could cost up to $250 and require a CD-ROM player, too.

Educational & informational software

Educational programs about the environment present information in a way that involves students and captures their attention. Students can explore databases of environmental information, see pictures, hear sounds, and answer questions put to them by the computer. With the help of the computer, students can grasp complex ecological processes that are harder to understand via a traditional textbook and perhaps impossible to observe in real life. These programs often include small role-playing games and simulations to highlight aspects of the environment. Following is a selection of educational programs about the environment, arranged in order of the suggested age of players:

EcoSaurus Environmental programs aimed at younger students and preschoolers are few and far between. One of the best is this program, which presents colorful information about dinosaurs and ecology for young children. Simple ecological principles are taught by engaging cartoons, and the graphics and sounds are good. Ages 4 to 9.

EcoSaurus
First Byte, Inc.
19840 Pioneer Ave.
Torrance, CA 90503
310-793-0610
For DOS

Audubon Adventures Series The two programs in this series provide ecological information, games, and simulations about whales and grizzly bears. They're sponsored by the National Audubon Society. A teacher's guide, lab packs, and companion video are also available. Ages 10 and up.

Audubon Adventures Series: Whales
Audubon Adventures Series: Grizzly Bears
Top Ten Software
40308 Greenwood Way
Oakhurst, CA 93644
209-683-7577
For DOS

Earthquest Explores Ecology Earthquest is a HyperCard-based, interactive, multimedia smorgasbord about the earth and its environment. Games, graphics, animations, simulations, experiments, models, lists, tables, and pop-up quizzes provide just about every imaginable approach to the study of world culture and the environment. The interactive simulations that model animal population, human population, and biome (large ecological system) are especially informative. It's eclectic and cluttered, but there's enough going on in Earthquest Explores Ecology to keep students exploring for a long time. Ages 13 and up.

Earthquest, Inc.
125 University Ave.
Palo Alto, CA 94301
415-321-5838, fax 415-322-3817
For Macintosh

Save the Planet Save the Planet is an interactive database of information on a wide variety of environmental issues, including the theory of global warming, ozone-layer destruction, and the impact of fossil fuels. The emphasis here is on action; there are many "what you can do" lists. With the help of a Write to Washington section, students can call up the addresses of their senators and congressional representative and use a built-in word processor to fire off letters about the environment. The program comes with a companion program, ECOMAP, that describes the effects of civilization on various ecosystems. Two free annual updates are included in the price of the disk. This is a superior teaching tool. Ages 13 and up.

Save the Planet
Save the Planet Shareware
Box 45
Pitkin, CO 81241
303-641-5035
For Macintosh and DOS

Conservation Biology This computerized test provides 200 questions and answers on conservation topics. It's a useful adjunct to university-level courses in the subject. Ages 16 to adult.

Conservation Biology
Chariot Software Group
3659 India St, Suite 100
San Diego, CA 92103
619-298-0202
For Macintosh

The Green Explorer This software is designed to help you set up a green household. Almost 200 information screens and a database of resources tell you everything you could want to know about recycling glass, plastic, and paper; choosing and using green cleaning products; and disposing of household hazardous waste, among other topics. Projects show how to set up a compost pile, create your own recycled paper, and prepare a home energy and water audit. A quiz game tests your environmental know-how. For teen to adult.

The Green Explorer
MicroBase
3923 South McClintock
Suite 402
Tempe, AZ 85282
800-897-3637
For Windows

EME Software

EME Software publishes a whole series of educational simulations on the environment aimed at junior-high to college students. The science content is good, and the experimental, trial-and-error nature of the simulations gives a real feel for what environmental theorists do. These include:

Hothouse Planet Students are introduced to the theory of global warming, its causes, and potential solutions. They can vary key atmospheric factors and study the potential effects on the planet of such processes as the release of industrial gases, the burning of the rain forests, and natural phenomena such as volcanic activity.

Air Pollution This simulation of carbon monoxide pollution in "Pollution City" models the causes, effects, and solutions of this problem. Students can vary CO levels, make worst-cases analyses, and determine safety margins.

Water Pollution The first part of this program introduces students to the subject of water pollution and its effects. Then they can perform experiments on pollution models they design.

Water Budget How to manage a water budget is the subject of this program. Using values from a built-in database of 45 locations worldwide, or from their own data, students can explore the concepts of water recharge, usage, deficit, and surplus.

Our Ozone Crisis NASA/Goddard Institute for Space Studies helped create this program about the changes occurring in the earth's atmosphere. Changes in ozone levels can be analyzed on a global or local level. Students can also set up their own experiments on the effects of volcanic eruptions for comparison.

Home Energy Conservation How to analyze and improve energy usage. Home heating audits and analyses of energy usage patterns and appliance efficiency are among the experiments that students can perform.

EME Corp.
P.O. Box 2805
Danbury, CT 06813-2805
203-798-2050
For DOS, Macintosh, and Apple II.

Environmental computer games & simulations

Environmental computer simulations construct a software model of an environmental process—anything from the life and death of a neighborhood pond to the ecosystem of an entire planet—and then alter the model in response to your input. Scientists use custom simulations to model weather patterns, ocean currents, and other complex processes. On the PC level, simulations are used mainly as the basis for games.

Environmental simulation games can be surprisingly involving and educational, perhaps even more than environmental educational programs. Playing a simulation encourages analytical problem-solving, theorizing about general aspects of the environment, making quick judgments with limited information, and experimentation. Usually there are millions of possible game paths and no one right way to play, though relatively few paths lead to a winning game. If your civilization ends up choking on its own effluvia, you can always start a new game and try a different path. And, of course, simulations are limited in scope to what the game programmers have thought of; the games can't take into account conditions and processes that aren't already programmed in.

Environmental simulations tend to fall into two categories. Role-playing simulations put players into the shoes of an individual who has to solve a local environmental problem. A good example is Decisions, Decisions: The Environment, from Tom Snyder Productions. Get a group of teenage students to play one of these games, and you'll soon hear heated arguments over who's right and what to do next. Planetary simulations, like Balance of the Planet and SimEarth, are complex, rather impersonal games. Hundreds of variables are involved, more than most younger students can grasp. Most of these games are recommended for players aged 13 to adult. Following is a current selection of the best environmental simulations currently available.

Role-playing simulations

EcoAdventures Text, sound, and graphics teach about the ecosystems of tropical rainforests and oceans in an adventure-game format. You're an explorer with an ecological mission to find a rare animal, and at the same time to protect the rainforest or the ocean. After a set time, you're returned to headquarters to answer questions from the press (really, a quiz) about what you learned on your adventure. There's plenty of information on the plants, animals, ecology, and human residents (or visitors) of the ecosystems in question. Ages 11 and up.

EcoAdventures in the Rainforest
EcoAdventures in the Ocean
Chariot Software Group
3659 India St., Suite 100
San Diego, CA 92103
619-298-0202
For Macintosh and DOS

Coral Kingdom This CD-ROM takes students into the heart of a coral reef ecosystem. Students can go on underwater missions to discover means of resource partitioning, adaptations, and energy flow in these fascinating microworlds. There are also color slide shows that are thematically arranged. Ages 12 and up.

Coral Kingdom
Sunburst Communications
800-338-3457
For Macintosh

The Greenhouse Effect This is a CD-ROM compilation presenting text, graphics, charts, animation, and video clips on this controversial topic. Covered are the theoretical causes and effects of global warming, reviews of scientific investigations, information on alternative energy sources, and steps students can take to reduce greenhouse gas emissions. Ages 12 and up.

The Greenhouse Effect
Full Circle Media
25 Valley View Ave.
San Rafael, CA 94901
415-453-9989

Pollution Control You're the head of the Pollution Patrol in a city aptly named Misery. There's trash everywhere, the air is dirty, the water is polluted, and the local lake is full of dead fish. Your task is to find the sources of all this pollution and to clean things up, using everything you know about the environment and about negotiating with local businesses and groups. Ages 12 and up.

Pollution Control
Focus Media
485 S. Broadway, Suite 12
Hicksville, NY 11801
800-645-8989
For Apple II and DOS

Decisions, Decisions: The Environment This is a policy-making simulation in which you play the mayor of a town with problems. You tackle one of the town's environmental crises—dead fish in Snyder Pond. Whose fault is it: Malaco, the town's main employer? Overfishing by local residents? Illegal dumping? You must research and solve the problem before the next election. Decisions, Decisions is a complex, balanced simulation that provides real insight into the political ramifications of environmental action. Separate guides for students and teachers are included. Ages 13 and up.

Decisions, Decisions: The Environment
Tom Snyder Productions
80 Coolidge Hill Rd.
Watertown, MA 02172
800-342-0236
Macintosh, DOS, and Apple II

Sid Meier's Civilization This game allows you to develop a civilization from scratch. You can grow from a tiny village to a mighty culture that conquers the world or settles Alpha Centauri. This complex, time-consuming program is mainly an economic and military simulation, but environmental elements enter into the game as civilizations become more technically advanced. You'll have to move carefully not to drown your civilization in its own waste while you outdevelop your opponents. Ages 15 to adult.

Sid Meier's Civilization
MicroProse Software
180 Lakefront Dr.
Hunt Valley, MD 21030
800-879-PLAY, fax 410-771-1174
For DOS and Amiga

SimEarth, The Living Planet In SimEarth, the best-selling planetary simulation, students design a global ecosystem, create primitive species, and nurture them toward intelligence. Depending on the conditions set up at creation, evolution can take strange paths. Even social insects and dinosaurs can develop high intelligence and build civilizations.

The rules are based on the Gaia Hypothesis theory proposed by James Lovelace and Lynn Margulis, as well as good old Darwinian selection. Players can add spice by messing with greenhouse gases, showering the earth with meteors, or blocking the sun with ash from erupting volcanoes. Intelligent species, once they evolve, can ruin the earth all by themselves. If they survive, they can head out into space to colonize (and maybe wreck) new worlds. A classic simulation game. Ages 13 and up.

Other simulations from Maxis include SimCity, the classic city-planner simulation. Environmental concerns are integrated with economic and social issues, just like in real life, for ages 10 and up. There's also SimAnt, in which you view your backyard from an ant's-eye view. This is an excellent simulation of an alien society in competition with our own. Learn why ants are arguably the most important animals on earth. Ages 10 and up.

SimEarth, The Living Planet
SimCity 2000
SimAnt
Maxis
Two Theatre Square, Suite 230
Orinda, CA 94563-3041
800-336-2947, 510-254-9700, fax 510-253-3736
For Macintosh, DOS, and Amiga

Balance of the Planet More intellectual and abstract than some other simulations, this game asks players to balance the competing demands of development and the environment while attempting to create a utopian civilization. As world environment czar, you have total power to levy taxes, fund environmental research, and develop new technologies in a 50-year race to save the earth from ecological collapse. The game contains many variables and much information and is complex to play. Ages 15 and up.

Balance of the Planet
Chris Crawford Games
408-946-4626
Distributed by:
Software Toolworks
60 Leveroni Court
Novato, CA 94949
800-234-3088

Global Effect Global Effect is a world-building game for two players. The game offers a chance to create and maintain competing civilizations. The object is to help your cities dominate your opponent's and colonize the world by using planetary resources, generating power surpluses, assembling nuclear arsenals and ABM defenses, and managing the impact on the ecosystem. Not for pacifists. Ages 15 and up.

Global Effect
Electronic Arts
1450 Fashion Island Blvd.
San Mateo, CA 94404
415-571-7171, fax 415-570-5137
For DOS and Amiga

Dissection simulations

Hundreds of thousands of frogs, pigs, and other animals are dissected by students in public-school biology classes every year, an experience that turns many away from further study in biology.

PCs can provide a cheaper, cleaner, and more effective alternative. Computer simulations are being used in many biology classrooms in lieu of actual dissections, with considerable success. Without scalpel or forceps, students can still uncover, layer by layer, the inner mysteries of earthworms, bullfrogs, and even human beings without ever having to touch a real animal. Dissection programs provide detailed information on anatomical features that students might not discover for themselves, and the programs can include other instructional aids as well: animations, quizzes, games, and more. The computer allows students to go at their own pace, rather than having to keep pace with the class.

Proponents of hands-on dissection claim that it provides a greater understanding of the complexity of an organism and of comparative anatomy than any other method of instruction. It's true that current programs can't duplicate the biological detail of a living organism, or simulate the three-dimensionality and tactility of real dissection. Advanced students of biology and medicine still have to work with real specimens. The real question is: Do the millions of school children who perform dissections every year need such a detailed experience? Few will be going on to careers in medicine or biology, and the rest will probably retain as much useful information by working with a computer simulation as they would by working on a real animal.

A study by T.L. McCollum in a Cincinnati high school showed that students retain as much or more knowledge from slide shows and biology lectures as they do from actual dissection. Dissection simulation might be one of those cases, like jet-pilot or air-traffic-controller training, where a basic educational experience on computer has some definite advantages over the real thing.

Animal-rights activists promote dissection simulations because they can spare the lives of millions of animals. But simulations also have practical educational, environmental and economic advantages. These include:

Affordability Dissection software costs much less than actual specimens. According to the New England Anti-Vivisection Society, a year of preserved bullfrogs for three classes of 24 students costs up to $356, not including the cost of teaching materials, dissection tools, and disposal. Frog Dissection, a program published by Cross Educational Software, costs just $30 and can be used again and again. With the money saved from not having to purchase animal specimens, a school could purchase a new PC to run the simulation. Even with supplementary videos and three-dimensional plastic models, simulations are less expensive over the long run.

Safer classroom environment Using simulations instead of real animals eliminates the need to use toxic chemicals like isopropyl alcohol and formaldehyde in the classroom, and it keeps them out of the waste stream. Plus, students can't cut themselves or others with electronic scalpels.

Improved biology education Students often acquire a negative view of biology by participating in dissections, and many avoid advanced biology study altogether because they don't want to dissect animals. Several recent studies show that, in many cases, the atmosphere in the classroom during dissections is so chaotic that practically any other method of teaching anatomy is more effective.

Simulations also offer educational opportunities that real dissection can't. For example, most programs allow students to put specimens back together once they've been taken apart, something even the best biology teacher in the world can't do.

Compliance with state regulations Some states, including California and Florida, uphold the rights of students to conscientiously object to performing dissections. Other states are likely to follow. Computer-based alternatives are an inexpensive way to offer these students instruction in anatomy.

Selected simulation programs

Here's a selection of programs that can be used in school or at home to teach anatomy without dissection. As of this writing, there's no inexpensive software that covers the anatomy of rats, rabbits, cats, fetal pigs, and other mammals often used for school dissection, but with the increasing popularity of computer-based dissection, they're likely to appear soon.

Operation Frog Operation Frog allows junior-high biology classes to study a simulated American bullfrog. The program offers step-by-step dissection and reassembly with clear, colorful graphics. The anatomy is simplified. There's one set of muscles and no bones—but plenty of interesting related activities. The DOS and Macintosh versions include animations and digitized photos. Ages 13 and up.

Operation Frog
Scholastic Software
P.O. Box 7502
2931 E. McCarty St.
Jefferson City, MO 65102
800-541-5513
For Macintosh, DOS, and Apple II

Frog Dissection Another bullfrog anatomy tutorial, Frog Dissection offers color graphics, step-by-step dissection, definitions of structures, and many review questions, as well as a teacher's manual. Ages 13 and up.

Frog Dissection
Cross Educational Software
504 E. Kentucky Ave.
Rustom, LA 71270
318-255-8921
For Macintosh, DOS, and Apple II

The Worm The anatomy of the common earthworm is covered in this simulation, which provides color cross-sections with detailed descriptions of every major biological function, including digestion, reproduction, and sensing. Quizzes, teacher's guide, and worksheets are included with the package. Ages 13 and up.

The Worm
Ventura Educational Systems
3440 Brokenhill St.
Newbury Park, CA 91320
800-336-1022, 805-499-1407
For Macintosh, DOS, and Apple II

Bodyworks: An Adventure in Anatomy Bodyworks explains the human body in colorful detail, using accurate graphics and nontechnical descriptions of organ functions. There are many closeups, diagrams, and short text articles, which can be searched through with an online index. This would be a good program to run concurrently with one of the frog dissection programs for comparative anatomy studies. Students are likely to find the insides of their own bodies far more interesting and relevant than those of worms or frogs or even fetal pigs. Ages 13 and up.

Bodyworks: An Adventure in Anatomy
Software Marketing Corp.
9831 S. 51st St., Suite C113
Phoenix, AZ 85044
800-545-6626, 602-893-2400
For DOS

Choices that make a difference

- ❐ Use educational software to teach about the environment.
- ❐ Use software simulations to promote analytical and theoretical thinking about the environment.
- ❐ Spare animals, save money, and make the classroom environment safer with dissection simulation programs.

Green-PC resources

For more information on using software to simulate animal dissection in schools, contact:
New England Anti-Vivisection Society (NEAVS)
Research Modernization and Animal Rights
333 Washington St., Suite 850
Boston, MA 02108
617-523-6020
Publishes a useful handbook, Beyond Dissection.

National Association for Humane and Environmental Education
67 Salem Rd.
East Haddam, CT 06423
203-434-8666
Publishes an information packet called Alternatives to Dissection that includes 14 sample lesson plans.

National Association of Biology Teachers
11250 Roger Bacon Dr., #19
Reston, VA 22090
703-471-1134

Ventura Educational Systems
3440 Brokenhill St.
Newbury Park, CA 91320
800-336-1022, 805-499-1407
Offers a catalog of dissection software and teachers' aids.

12 The environment online

CHAPTER 12

SOLVING environmental problems requires quick access to the right information. Suppose you want to know the long-term health effects of a chemical pollutant found in the stream near your home, or the text of a German ordinance on product recycling, or the progress of a clean-air bill through your state's legislature. All of this information is available—but where? How do you find what you need in the hundreds of environmental journals, thousands of databases, tens of thousands of books, and millions of journals, newsletters, reports, and papers?

Successfully navigating this sea of information takes knowledge, determination, patience, and a little luck. You'll find the task a lot easier if you take advantage of the wide variety of online sources of information on the environment, all of which you can access from your own PC. More information is available online—through information services, bulletin boards, and databases on CD-ROM—than can be found in all but the very largest research libraries. With a PC, a modem, telecommunications software, and a low-cost CD-ROM player, you can tap into vast storehouses of knowledge about the earth—or about any other subject under the sun. Without stirring from your chair, you can search academic library databases, read environmental papers, reports, and bibliographies, exchange information with working environmentalists, and debate the fine points of green computing with people thousands of miles away.

This chapter covers green networks and information services and explains how to access them. It also provides information on environmental databases available on CD-ROM. By no means all possible online or CD-ROM sources are listed here; the ocean of environmental information out there is so immense that it would require a thousand-page reference book just to list everything. But it will be a long time before you exhaust the resources mentioned in this chapter.

Online environmental information

There are literally thousands of online information sources, but not all have information of interest to environmentalists. Some of the most useful sources are listed in this section, broken down by type: bulletin boards, major online services, and online news services.

To use online resources, you first need a modem and telecommunications software. Then you need to master the basic techniques for logging on to (gaining access to) and using online resources. The procedure can be complicated. Read your telecommunications software's documentation thoroughly and practice logging on to a local bulletin board service before you try to do more complex searches. Some major services, like Prodigy and America OnLine, provide custom software that completely automates the log-on process; exploring these services might be the easiest way to get your feet wet in telecommunication and online research.

Bulletin board services

Bulletin board systems, or BBSs, are online services that allow people to call in and exchange information. They're generally run on a nonprofit or low-profit basis by individuals or organizations with information to share. Many PC manufacturers operate free BBSs, where they can post the latest information about their products and communicate with their customers. Other BBSs focus on a particular subject, such as games, or a particular type of computer, such as the Macintosh or the Amiga.

There are hundreds of BBSs in every state in the United States, and many thousands more overseas, but the typical lifetime of a BBS is short. Longevity depends on the self-sacrificing dedication of its system operator (called a sysop) and the unswerving loyalty of its membership. If you have environmental or other information to share, you can set up a BBS yourself with just a PC, a modem, and BBS software, but it takes a lot of unpaid and little-appreciated work to keep it going. Still, the value of BBSs as unregulated, unmediated conduits of information can't be overestimated.

You can use BBSs in several ways. If you have environmental information to share that's of local interest—for example, a new recycling project in your community—you can post a message to local environmental or general-interest BBSs. (See the Green-PC resources section for sources of information on BBSs in the United States.) Or, if you're trying to locate environmental information, you can tap into an existing BBS that has the data you need. One big advantage of using a BBS for research, rather than a major online service, is that online time for a BBS is generally free, other than the cost of the phone call.

There are several specialized BBSs with up-to-date information on air and water pollution, hazardous materials and toxic waste, medical and biological aspects of the environment, downloadable environmental directories, and more. (See later in the chapter for more on the EPA's BBSs.) As of 1993, BBSs with information of general environmental interest included those shown in Table 12-1.

Table 12-1 **BBs of General Environmental Interest**

Name	Modem number
Daily Planet BBS	808-572-4857
Earth Art BBS (GreenNet)	803-552-4389
Earth-Net	516-321-4893
Eco-System BBS	412-244-0675
Enviro BBS	703-524-1837
Greenpeace Environet	415-512-9108
Heartbeat Earth	408-257-2306
MNS Online	518-381-4430
NERC BBS	703-506-1025
Polution Prevention Info. Clearinghouse (EPA)	703-506-1025
Shore BBS	301-476-5098
Vitality Directory BBS	619-634-1912

Online commercial services

Online services like CompuServe and America OnLine offer many of the same services as small BBSs, but on a larger scale. These services include message posting, e-mail, online chats in real-time with other members, libraries of downloadable software, and databases to search. All this comes at a price, usually a monthly fee and per-hour access charges.

Most online services offer conferences on environmental topics (conferences are also called areas, clubs, exchanges, or forums, depending on the service you're discussing). Several of these are described briefly in the following sections. For a service devoted entirely to the environment, see the section on EcoNet.

America OnLine America OnLine (AOL) is especially appealing to Macintosh users because it sports a user interface modeled on the Macintosh operating system and HyperCard. However, the AOL Windows version is also popular, and maybe that's why the service has attracted 600,000 subscribers in just four years. AOL is accessed through a custom software program supplied by the service to all members.

The Environmental Club, AOL's online forum, has ongoing discussions on air and water pollution, recycling and solid waste, and related topics. There's an environmental chat area, downloadable files, and archives of the Environment News Service. (See later in the chapter for more on ENS).

Network Earth, the environmental conference linked to the TBS television show of the same name (see later in the chapter for more), also has an area on AOL. Other news services include the Nuclear Information and Resource Service and the GAIN (Global Action & Information Network) Library.

America OnLine
800-227-6364, ext. 5254 for a free enrollment kit and software
Forum: Lifestyles & Interests/Environmental Club
Keywords: Earth, Environment

BIX The BYTE Information Exchange (BIX for short) is an online service operated by the publisher of *BYTE* magazine. You'll find plenty of detailed technical information on all aspects of computing. There's also an exchange on the environment.

BIX
800-695-4775 for more information
Type JOIN at the prompt, then ENVIRONMENT.

CompuServe CompuServe (CIS) is the biggest commercial service going, with hundreds of thousands of members and a very rich array of services, including useful general-purpose databases such as CENDATA (the Census Bureau Service), Books in Print, and the National Technical Information Service. (You'll be billed a surcharge for access to specialized databases, in addition to CompuServe's usual per-hour charge.)

CompuServe's forums of environmental interest include the Earth Forum, the Outdoor Forum, and the SafetyNet Forum. The Earth Forum hosts discussions of environmental issues and has many downloadable files. The SafetyNet Forum covers such topics as toxic pollution, workplace hazards, and solid-waste management, as well as emergency services and planning. To subscribe to CompuServe, you'll need a membership kit, available at most computer stores and many bookstores. Or call CompuServe at the following number:

CompuServe
800-848-8199 for customer service and enrollment information. Ask for extension 190 and receive a free enrollment kit courtesy of the Earth Forum.

Earth Forum: GO EARTH

SafetyNet: GO SAFETYNET

EcoNet EcoNet is the only major service dedicated solely to the environment, and, as such, is the single most valuable online resource for any environmentalist or researcher. It's part of a worldwide supernetwork operated by the Institute for Global Communications and the Association for Progressive Communications (APC), and it can offer you e-mail access to like-minded people around the world. Other networks of the APC include PeaceNet, ConflictNet, and international partner networks in Australia, Brazil, Canada, England, Germany, Nicaragua, Russia, Sweden, and Uruguay.

EcoNet features some 200 conferences sponsored by many of the world's major environmental organizations. You'll also find environmental information that's available nowhere else online, such as programs to model and solve various kinds of environmental problems. EcoNet's online publications and databases include the Environmental Grantmakers Association's Directory, federal legislative information compiled by the Global Action Network, the Sierra Club National News Report, the National Wildlife Federation's Conservation Directory, and the Greenpeace National Newsletter. Conferences and online "offices" are also maintained by two television news programs on the environment, NBC Nightly News' Assignment Earth and Turner Broadcasting System's Network Earth.

EcoNet has extensive electronic mail connections with other networks around the world. An e-mail message posted to EcoNet will reach almost any environmentalist who has access to a computer network. Table 12-2 is a partial list of the international online systems to which EcoNet members can send mail. You can even contact people who aren't online by sending them a fax or telex directly from EcoNet. For EcoNet membership information, contact:

EcoNet
18 de Boom St.
San Francisco, CA 94107
415-442-0220, fax 415-546-1794

International Online Systems to Which EcoNet Members Can Send Mail — Table 12-2

AppleLink	AT&T Mail
ArpaNet	BITNET
BIX1	Portal
CIGNet	Prairie
ComLink	PsychNet
(Germany)	Red BolNet
CompuServe	(Bolivia)
DASNet	ScienceNet
EasyLink	SF/Moscow
FidoNet	Teleport
GeoNet	(Russia & USA)
GTE Mail	TeleMail
HandsNet	TYMNET/OnTyme
Internet	UNDP
MCI Mail	UNINET
MetalNet	UUCP Mail Net
NASA Mail	The WELL

GEnie The General Electric Network for Information Exchange is a general-interest service much like CompuServe, with conferences, e-mail and messaging services, and downloadable software. Unlike CompuServe, however, no membership kit is needed.

GEnie contains wire reports from France, Germany, Spain, Japan, and China available, as well as the UPI and PR newswire. It also offers a surcharged Reference Center with some online databases of interest to environmentalists, including BIOSIS Previews, COMPENDEX PLUS, Enviroline, and Medline (see later in the chapter for more information on online databases).

GEnie
800-638-8369 for more information on rates and sign-up procedures

The Internet

The Internet is a vast supernetwork that links more than 2,000 smaller networks and their millions of users. Once the network for the Department of Defense Advanced Research Projects Agency, Internet is now the main conduit of information between National Science Foundation supercomputer centers and affiliate networks, which contain information of interest to environmentalists. Library and scientific databases from dozens of academic libraries are also available, as is an extensive "white pages" of scientific researchers around the world.

For environmentalists outside of the university and research center orbit, Internet is also the main e-mail link between such commercial online services as CompuServe, GEnie, and America OnLine. In fact, the easiest way to gain access to the Internet is to subscribe to one of these services. USENET is the loosely organized BBS of the Internet; there are scores of USENET forums (called newsgroups) on the environment.

Accessing the wealth of Internet information requires some telecommunications expertise; I recommend that you purchase one of the many books on the subject (some are listed in the Green-PC resources section) and buy one of the public-domain programs that aid

Internet access. The commercial service Delphi already offers extensive access to Internet information. By the time you read this, most other online commercial services, such as America OnLine, will link to newsgroups of your choice and allow you to upload and download files to various areas of the Internet. For information on Delphi, contact:

Delphi
800-695-4005

INFOTERRA

INFOTERRA is part of the United Nations Environmental Programme's information exchange and referral service. Based in Nairobi, Kenya, INFOTERRA is a decentralized information system operating through a worldwide network of national environmental institutions, such as the U.S. EPA, that are designated as National Focal Points (NFPs).

INFOTERRA's mandate is to provide free or low-cost environmental, technical, and scientific information to individuals and countries worldwide, on everything from control of acid rain in Eastern Europe to the best means of processing ink from banana plants. With the resources of the UN behind it, INFOTERRA can sleuth out information sources that might not be accessible to individuals. It can provide your organization with referrals to government agencies, international organizations, and environmental experts in any UN member nation. For serious international environmental research and project organization, INFOTERRA is an invaluable resource.

INFOTERRA offers several layers of environmental information in electronic form. The organization's primary publication is the International Directory of Sources, an extensive database of environmental information clearinghouses, organizations, and experts. It's available on disk for DOS-based PCs. On request, NFPs or the central office in Nairobi can conduct custom online searches for you through all of the UN's many databases at the cost of access (that is, phone time and any surcharges for access to individual databases). If you're an official of a developing country, the search is free.

Information can be supplied on paper, via fax or modem, or on disk. INFOTERRA also posts information to the many U.N. BBSs and provides e-mail connections with international organizations and governments. In addition, the United Nations Environmental Programme maintains an area on EcoNet.

When you're applying for information to INFOTERRA, be as specific as possible in stating the type of information you want, what it's to be used for, and the format best suited to your needs.

INFOTERRA
U.N. Environmental Programme
DC2-0803 United Nations
New York, NY 10017
212-963-8093

INFOTERRA/USA
U.S. Environmental Protection Agency
Rm. 2904, PM-211A
401 M St., SW
Washington, DC 20460
202-260-5917, fax 202-260-3923

Environmental news online

Most of the newswire services, such as UPI and Reuters, run environmental stories from time to time. But the Environmental News Service (ENS) is the only global news agency devoted exclusively to environmental reporting. Drawing on a worldwide network of journalists, experts, researchers, and organizations, ENS can scoop most other news agencies on environmental topics, and provide more depth as well. It prepares daily independent reports, some of which appear in print but most of which are available only online. ENS is available on America OnLine in the Environmental Club, on EcoNet, or on an individual subscription. For access information, contact:

Environmental News Service
3505 W. 15th Ave.
Vancouver, BC V6R 2Z3, Canada
604-732-4000, fax 604-732-4400

Greenwire

Greenwire prepares a daily summary of global environmental news gleaned from major newspapers and journals, as well as original articles, interviews, and editorial material. The cost is high—beginning at $1,500—but it might be just the resource for larger environmental groups or an institution.

Greenwire
703-237-5130 for information.

Network Earth

Network Earth is a conference that appears on several services, including America OnLine, CompuServe, and EcoNet. It's sponsored by the Turner Broadcasting System (TBS) television program Network Earth, which airs Sunday evenings at 11 P.M. EST. At first, Network Earth was a response line for people who had seen the most recent show, but it now offers many more features. You can tap into libraries of information from environmental organizations, discuss the environment with Network Earth reporters and staff, and participate in Network Earth environmental polls. You can criticize or praise the most recent program, make suggestions, and even convince the producers to cover the activities of your local environmental group or air your own environmental video segments.

The information resources of Network Earth on America OnLine are extensive. Besides the show schedule, program transcripts, staff contact areas, and news summaries, there is an Action Center for e-mailing and faxing your views on crucial and breaking events. There's also a Congressional Scorecard area for keeping tabs on how your representatives vote. The Network Earth resource library features the following subject areas:

- EPA dictionary of environmental terms.
- Environmental reports and backgrounders.
- Reviews of environmental books and periodicals.

- Ecoconsumerism.
- Classroom materials.
- Energy.
- Wastes and toxics.
- Recycling.
- Land use and misuse.
- Biodiversity and habitat preservation.
- Air quality and climate.
- Oceans and aquatic life.

To contact Network Earth, log on to America OnLine, CompuServe, or EcoNet. See how to contact them in the sections on each service.

Online research databases

You can tap into research databases on the environment without going through an online service like CompuServe. The databases that environmentalists are most likely to find valuable are accessible through commercial database publishing services and through the EPA's vast network of online materials.

One representative commercial provider of environmental databases is Dialog Information Services. Dialog contains more than 20 environment-related bibliographies and collections of abstracts, as well as extensive newspaper and magazine indexes. Dialog databases will provide you with more than 61.1 million references to or abstracts of documents relating to the environment. These databases include:

Aquatic Sciences and Fisheries Abstracts This database includes citations from the literature on marine and freshwater environments and aquatic pollution, and it contains 363,000 records from 5,000 sources.

BNA Daily News A collection of daily legal publications on the environment, including BNA Chemical Regulations Daily, BNA California Environment Daily, and BNA Environmental Law Update.

Biosis Previews 1969+ Comprehensive worldwide coverage of topics in the biological and biomedical sciences, including information on the effects of toxics on plants, animals, and people. Contains 7.7 million records.

CA Search 1967+ Contains abstracts from chemical literature, 1967 to the present. It contains more than 10 million records.

CAB Abstracts Agricultural and biological information from the 26 main journals of the Commonwealth Agricultural Bureaux, U.K. Contains 2.9 million records from 8,500 journals in 37 languages.

Compendex*Plus Citations from engineering and technology literature, including material on pollution-control engineering. Contains 2.8 million records from 4,500 journals and reports.

CRIS/USDA Information from the USDA on federal and state research in agriculture, food and nutrition, forestry, and related topics. CRIS/USDA usually presents the full text of project reports. Contains 37,000 project records.

Embase 1974+ Abstracts and citations from the world's biomedical literature. Contains 4.7 million records from 3,500 sources.

Energy Science and Technology Published by the U.S. Department of Energy. Covers wind, solar, geothermal, tidal, and other alternative energy sources, as well as information on nuclear and fossil fuel, conservation, and energy policy. Contains 2.6 million records.

Enviroline Comprehensive coverage of the world's environmental literature. Contains 150,000 abstracts and citations from 5,000 sources.

Environmental Bibliography Citations and abstracts from 300 periodicals in the general field of environmental research. Contains 426,000 records, and is also available on CD-ROM.

Federal News Service The full text of Capitol Hill hearings and testimony, as well as briefings before the EPA and other agencies.

Federal Register This electronic publication of the U.S. government notifies the public of official actions and includes the text of new regulations issued by the EPA, the FDA, and other government agencies.

Geobase Index to literature on geology, geography, ecology, and related topics. Contains 432,000 records.

National Technical Information Service (NTIS) Technical reports and environmental impact statements. Also available on CD-ROM. Contains 1.5 million records.

Oceanic Abstracts Indexes worldwide literature on marine subjects and contains more than 200,000 citations.

Paperchem Database of international technical literature on paper and pulp technology, containing more than 297,000 records.

Pollution Abstracts Surveys the international literature on air, land, and water pollution. There are 175,000 records in this database.

PTS Newsletter Database Contains the full text of articles from more than 500 business and trade newsletters on a very wide range of subjects, including computers and the environment.

Toxline Indexes the literature on the adverse effects of chemicals, drugs, and physical agents on living systems, and contains 1.6 million records from many sources.

For more information on Dialog, contact:
Dialog Information Services, Inc.
3460 Hillview Ave.
P.O. Box 10010
Palo Alto, CA 94303
Call 800-3DIALOG (800-334-2564) or 415-858-3785 for rates and subscription information. Be sure to ask for the current database catalog and price list.

Other database services Other commercial online research services that offer environmental databases include:

BRS (Infopro Technologies)
800-456-7248, 703-442-0900

Chemical Information Systems (CIS)
800-247-8737, 410-442-0900

Data-Star
800-221-7754, 215-687-8440

Mead Data Central
800-346-9759

National Library of Medicine (NLM)
800-334-8480

National Technical Information Service (NTIS)
703-487-4650

NewsNet
800-345-1301, 215-527-8030

Westlaw
800-328-9352

Online pricing Information is the new currency, and database publishers don't give their products away. Extensive online database searching can be very expensive. For example, access to Enviroline through Dialog costs $2 per minute or $120 per hour, according to the current Dialog price list. You'll find that other online database publishers quote similar prices. You can spend a lot of money if you don't have a good idea of what you want to know before you start. Half an hour spent studying each research services' printed instruction manual and catalog of databases will pay for itself on your first search. Even with the high per-hour charges, however, online research is less expensive than the cost in work hours to do the same research in a library, especially if you need information immediately. (An even more cost-effective way to search the world of environmental information is on CD-ROM; see later in the chapter.)

EPA online

The EPA also publishes databases on every aspect of the environment. Most are accessible with an EPA user account or through the National Library of Medicine, the Chemical Information Systems (CIS), the National Technical Information Service (NTIS), or one of the other commercial database services.

Obtaining an EPA user account ID requires some effort; you must contact each program (for example, the Office of Air and Radiation) and find out what databases it currently controls access to, then make a formal request for access. Use Access EPA (see later in the chapter) for initial contact information.

A sampling of EPA databases accessible with an EPA user account include:

Aerometric Information Retrieval System Information on air pollution and industry emissions; also covers wide-area air pollution sources such as forest fires.

Facilities Index Data System (FINDS) 475,000 sites regulated by the EPA, with references to other EPA databases.

Ocean Data Evaluation System Data on marine water quality and other oceanographic information.

Permit Compliance System Data on 65,000 water discharge permits and sites regulated by the National Pollutant Discharge Elimination System.

Records of Decision System (RODS) A case-by-case history of EPA and community actions.

Resource Conservation and Recovery Information System (RCRIS) Facility characteristics and other details for 324,000 hazardous waste sites.

Section Seven Tracking System (SSTS) Tracks information on all registered pesticide-producing establishments.

Access EPA The Access EPA directory is the one-stop source for information on all EPA databases and other information services. It is made available through the Government Printing Office (GPO) and the National Technical Information Service (NTIS). Access EPA, which is updated annually, includes information on documents, dockets, clearinghouses and hotlines, records, databases, models, EPA libraries, and State Libraries.

Access EPA is available online through the EPA Library Online Library System (OLS) and the Government Printing Office (GPO) Federal Bulletin Board System (GPO BBS). An online document describing in more detail the offering in Access EPA, as well as the specific procedures for dialing in to EPA and GPO databases, is available in the library areas of EcoNet, America Online, and many other services. To order Access EPA in its paper form, ask for:
Access EPA
NTIS Number: PB93-170041
EPA Document Number: EPA/220-B-93-008
available from:
National Technical Information Service (NTIS)
5285 Port Royal Road
Springfield, VA 22161
703-487-4650, fax 703-321-8547
Rush Service: 800-553-NTIS

or

GPO Document Number: 055-000-00437-4
U.S. Government Printing Office
710 North Capitol Street, NW
Washington, DC 20402
202-783-3238, fax 202-275-0019

EPA OLS The EPA's OnLine Library Service is available to EPA employees and the public. It contains bibliographic citations from books, EPA and other federal agency technical reports, conference

proceedings, indexes, audiovisual materials, maps, journals, and a variety of other documents. OLS provides summaries of selected titles from many databases, including the National Catalog, the Hazardous Waste Superfund Collection Database, Access 93 (an online version of Access EPA), and more. To contact the Online Library System (OLS), call:
513-569-7183, fax 513-569-7186

A Public Access OLS User Guide is available from:
Public Information Center (PIC)
202-260-7751 or 202-260-2080.

For further information on EPA computing services, including information on obtaining an EPA user ID, contact:
National Computing Center User Support Hotline
800-334-2405

The EPA offers a free, relatively easy-to-use database called COLIS (Computerized On-Line Information System). You can enter using the password "EPA."
EPA COLIS
908-548-4636

For more information on COLIS, including a user's guide, contact:
Roger Hillger or Hugh Masters
908-321-6630.

CD-ROMs on the environment

A single silvery CD-ROM disk can hold 650MB of data, the equivalent of tens of thousands of pages of text or hundreds of color maps, graphs, and photos, all in a convenient package five inches across and a fraction of an inch thick. The major advantage of CD-ROMs is that they can save you many hours of research time. In a hour of access to the right CD-ROM, you can do research that would take three days in an academic library. And because you can usually grab information off the CD-ROM and paste it right into your own computer documents (subject to copyright restrictions), you can dispense with library photocopiers, saving paper, energy, and time. For environmental research that requires frequent access to large, specialized data sets, CD-ROMs are quicker and less expensive than going online, although the information will be less current because few CD-ROM databases are updated more than four times a year.

In short, if you need the world's environmental information at your fingertips, a CD-ROM player is one of the wisest investments you can make. No serious environmental researcher or reporter can afford to ignore the CD-ROM information channel. Luckily, CD-ROM players are now available for as little as $200, and there are increasing numbers of low-cost disks available on the environment.

Some of the following titles are expensive, suitable mainly for academic libraries, environmental organizations, and serious researchers. But others, like PEMD's Discovery Environmental Data CD-ROM, are inexpensive and crammed with more data than you're likely to need. Here are the most useful environmental CD-ROMs currently available:
Acid Rain
Knowledge Access International
2685 Marine Way, Suite 1305
Mountain View, CA 94043
415-969-0606
Price: Free to agencies
Coverage: N/A
Updated: Annually
For DOS
This CD-ROM contains literature and citations on acid rain in United States and Canada.

Aqualine
Cambridge Scientific Abstracts
7200 Wisconsin Ave.
Bethesda, MD 20814
800-843-7751
Price: N/A
Coverage: N/A
Updated: Quarterly

For DOS
Literature and citations on worldwide water, wastewater, and oceanic issues.

Biological Abstracts
SilverPlatter Information, Inc.
100 River Ridge Dr.
Norwood, MA 02062
800-343-0064
Price: $7660
Coverage: 1990–present
Updated: Quarterly
For DOS
BIOSIS abstracts and citations from major life sciences journals.

Climatedata NCDC 15 Minute Precipitation
EarthInfo, Inc.
90 Madison St., Suite 200
Denver, CO 80206
Price: $1095
Coverage: 1971–1988
Updated: N/A
For DOS
Worldwide precipitation records.

Dialog OnDisc: Energy/Environment Disc
Dialog Information Services, Inc.
3460 Hillview Ave.
Palo Alto, CA 94070
800-334-2564, fax 415-858-7069
Price: $2500 annual subscription
Coverage: 1980–present
Updated: Quarterly
For DOS and Macintosh
An extensive bibliography and citations to the world literature on energy and the environment.

Discovery Environmental Data
PEMD Education Group, Ltd.
PO Box 39
Cloverdale, CA 95425
707-894-3668, fax 707-894-5200
Price: $149
Coverage: 1918–91
Updated: Yearly
For DOS and Macintosh
A compilation of worldwide environmental data from a wide range of sources.

Environment/EnergyLine Abstracts Plus
Bowker Electronic Publishing
245 W. 17th St.
New York, NY 10011
800-223-3288
Price: $1295 annual subscription
Coverage: 1991–present
Updated: Quarterly
For DOS and Macintosh
Abstracts from environmental literature.

GAIA/Environmental Resources
Wayzata Technology, Inc.
PO Box 807
Grand Rapids, MN 55744
800-735-7321, fax 218-326-0598
Price: $249
For Macintosh
Picture database, publications databases, and texts on GAIA theory.
Environmental Periodicals Bibliography on CD-ROM (EPB)

NISC
3100 St. Paul St., Suite 6
Baltimore, MD 21218
Price: N/A
Coverage: 1973–present
Updated: Semiannually
For DOS
More than 442,000 citations from the environmental literature.

GeoRef
SilverPlatter Information, Inc.
100 River Ridge Dr.
Norwood, MA 02062
800-343-0064
Price: $2400
Coverage: 1785–present
Updated: Quarterly
For DOS
A bibliography, indexes, and other materials compiled by the American Geological Institute.

Green Energy CD-ROM
Djanogly City Technical College
Sherwood Rise, Nottingham Rd.
Nottingham NG7 7AR, UK
44-602-424422, fax 44-602-424034
Price: N/A
Coverage: 1991
Updated: N/A
For DOS
Data on European renewable energy technologies, some compiled by students; there are versions in six languages.

MEDLINE
SilverPlatter Information, Inc.
100 River Ridge Dr.
Norwood, MA 02062
800-343-0064
Price: $750
Coverage: 1966–present
Updated: N/A
For DOS
Abstracts and citations of medical literature from the U.S. National Library of Medicine.

National Technical Information Service (NTIS)
SilverPlatter Information, Inc.
100 River Ridge Dr.
Norwood, MA 02062
800-343-0064
Price: $2500
Coverage: 1983–present
Updated: Quarterly
For DOS
Abstracts and citations on energy, environment, and other technical subjects from the National Technical Information Service.

Natural Resources Metabase
NISC
3100 St. Paul St., Suite 6
Baltimore, MD 21218
Price: $595 annual subscription
Coverage: 1970–present
Updated: Semiannually
For DOS and Macintosh
U.S. environmental and ecological information.

Think for Yourself CD-ROM
PEMD Education Group, Ltd.
PO Box 39
Cloverdale, CA 95425
707-894-3668, fax 707-894-5200
Price: $149
For Macintosh
A compilation of U.S. environmental, economic, health, and demographic data from a wide range of sources.

World WeatherDisc: Climate Data for the Planet Earth
WeatherDisc Associates, Inc.
4584 N.E. 89th
Seattle, WA 98115
206-524-4314, fax 206-543-0308
Price: $295
Coverage: 1740–present
Updated: Biennially
For DOS
Comparative weather descriptions and climatic data.

Paper journals

In this imperfect world, sometimes you have to get your information on paper. Up-to-date reporting, color graphics, and those all-important advertisements about environmental products and services still appear mainly in print media.

A few of the following environmental journals maintain online services on EcoNet (noted in the descriptions), but most don't publish information online. Nonetheless, they're definitely worth reading, even on paper. (Write to the editors and urge them to publish online versions.) Check them out in your local library or subscribe and pass the used issues on.

Amicus Journal
Natural Resources Defense Council
40 W. 20th St.
New York, NY 10011
212-727-2700
Coverage of national and international environmental policy.

Audubon
National Audubon Society
700 Broadway
New York, NY 10003
212-797-3000
A glossy nature journal with some environmental content.

Buzzworm: The Environmental Journal
Buzzworm, Inc.
2305 Canyon Blvd., Suite 206
Boulder, CO 80302
303-442-1969
Comprehensive coverage of national and international environmental issues.

E: The Environmental Magazine
Earth Action Network, Inc.
28 Knight St.
Norwalk, CT 06851
203-854-5559
A nonprofit independent magazine of the environment. It maintains a conference on EcoNet.

Earth Island Journal
300 Broadway
San Francisco, CA 94133
415-788-3666
Eyewitness econews from around the world.

Garbage: The Practical Journal for the Environment
Old House Journal Corp.
2 Main St.
Gloucester, MA 01930
508-283-3200, 800-274-9909
Garbage features a slick format and irreverent reporting, with an emphasis on recycling and solid waste issues. It maintains a conference on EcoNet.

The Green Business Letter
Tilden Press
1519 Connecticut Ave., NW, Suite 301
Washington, DC 20036
202-332-1700, 800-955-4733
Tips for improving corporate environmental responsibility.

Greenpeace
1436 U St., NW
Washington, DC 20009
202-462-1177
Greenpeace has hard-hitting investigative ecojournalism, though it's much reduced in size and resources from earlier years. It sports a decidedly radical slant.

Sierra
Sierra Club
730 Polk St.
San Francisco, CA 94109
415-776-2211
The mainstream nature/environment journal.

Worldwatch
Worldwatch Institute
1776 Massachusetts Ave., NW
Washington, DC 20036
Covers international environmental issues and global problems.

Choices that make a difference

- ❐ Use paper-free online sources for environmental research and communication.
- ❐ Post information about local, national, and worldwide environmental issues to commercial services and environmental bulletin boards.
- ❐ Join and support online conferences and forums on the environment.
- ❐ Share green-PC tips and techniques online.

Green-PC resources

Networkers and CD-ROM researchers will find these paper publications useful:
CD-ROMs in Print
Edited by Norman Desmarais
Meckler Corp.
11 Ferry Lane
Westport, CT 06880
203-226-6967, 800-635-5537, fax 203-454-5840

EcoLinking
by Don Rittner
Peachpit Press
2414 Sixth St.
Berkeley, CA 94710
510-548-4393, fax 510-548-5991
The definitive book on environmental networking and online resources.

"Information Systems Inventory"
Publication PB 91-172940
"Access EPA: Major EPA Databases"
Publication PB-914151613
available from
National Technical Information Service
703-487-4650
The first lists 500 of the EPA's environmental information systems and databases; the second lists databases accessible with an EPA user account or through the NTIS and other information systems.

The User's Directory of Computer Networks
by Tracy L. LaQuey
Digital Press
1 Burlington Woods
Burlington, MA 01803
800-634-2863

Vulcan Computer Monthly
P.O. Box 55886
Birmingham, AL 35255
800-874-2937
Publishes a state-by-state list of BBSs in the United States. A similar list can be found in:
Computer Shopper Magazine
One Park Ave
11th Floor
New York, NY 10016

Basic Internet information is available in:
The Internet Guide for New Users
by Daniel P. Dern
McGraw-Hill, Inc.
11311 Monterey Ave.
Blue Ridge Summit, PA 17214
800-233-1128

For more information on the Internet and a copy of the NSF's useful Internet Resource Guide, contact:
National Science Foundation Network Service Center
617-873-3400

You'll also want to look at this directory of electronic journals and newsletters on the Internet, including several environmental titles:
Directory of Electronic Journals and Newsletters
by Michael Strangelove
Office of Scientific and Academic Publishing
Association of Research Libraries
1527 New Hampshire Ave., NW
Washington, DC 20036

13

The green-PC consumer

CHAPTER 13

MOST PEOPLE believe that the personal computer industry is controlled by the powerful corporations that produce the hardware and software we all use. But you, the PC user, have the real power in this system. You have the one thing every PC company wants and none of them can live without: your money. If you're a corporate buyer who places orders for hundreds or thousands of systems, you have even more power; PC makers will go far to satisfy your needs. And you have the power to spend your money where it will do the most environmental good, to choose green-PC products and buy from vendors who work to protect the environment.

This chapter will show you how to choose green-PC products and vendors, where and how to shop for maximum environmental benefit, and how to deal with some of the problems caused by PC consumerism.

Green-PC consuming

Being a green-PC consumer starts with an understanding of how you choose what PC products to buy. Most people make PC purchases on the basis of features, brand, and price. To be worth buying, a computer product must meet the following requirements:

- It has to be technically capable of doing the job.
- It has to be priced at or below the market average for similar products.
- It has to be an industry-standard product, carry a trusted brand name, or bear the stamp of approval of an industry publication.
- It has to be new, look good, provide extra power, or be especially easy to use. That is, it has to include an "extra-value" feature.

These are all important considerations for choosing PC products. But there's one other important criterion: the product's impact on the environment. Once you decide to take environmental impact into account, you acquire a whole new set of things to find out about the products you buy. You'll need to follow some or all of these practices:

- Buy from PC companies that espouse green principles and support environmental causes.

- Buy PC products that represent the greenest technology available.
- Buy PC products with minimal and/or environmentally responsible packaging.
- Buy through sales channels, like online shopping, that minimize pollution and waste.
- Stay up to date on the complexities of recycling, packaging, energy, and solid waste issues as they pertain to computing.
- Get together with other consumers and groups to influence manufacturers on green-PC issues.

Of course, making a commitment to green-PC consuming means you have to do a lot more work with each purchase. How far you want to go to be a green-PC consumer is up to you. You might decide that you can't afford to follow every one of these suggestions each time you buy something for your PC. Keep in mind, however, that even a small effort can yield important results. If environmentally responsible companies prosper, other firms will follow their lead.

A green-PC consumer's checklist

Probably the best sources for basic consumer information on PC products can be found in the comparative reviews published in most computer magazines. These reviews are a great help in deciding whether a product has the features or the price you're looking for. But most computer magazines pay little attention to green-PC issues, although that situation is changing. Comparative reviews of computer monitors now invariably include information on electromagnetic emissions and Energy Star compliance (see chapters 4 and 9 for more).

As a green-PC consumer, you'll need to ask some out-of-the-ordinary questions about the products you're buying. Here's a checklist of things to look for when you're buying PC equipment. Ask yourself:

- Do I need a new unit?
- Can I upgrade my current equipment?
- Can I find a solution to my problem in software rather than hardware? (See chapter 2.)

If you do need new hardware, then consider the following general points when planning your purchase. Ask these questions about the manufacturer:

- Does the manufacturer have a reputation for environmental responsibility? (See the following section.)
- Does it offer an environmentally responsible way to recycle or dispose of obsolete equipment? (See the following section and chapter 6.)
- Does it offer online ordering and technical assistance?

Look for these features in all PC hardware:

Green packaging The unit should be packaged in material that's both recycled and recyclable. The packaging should incorporate as little foam as possible and no bleached paper. There's more on PC packaging later in this chapter.

Low or no radio frequency emissions All hardware should have an FCC Class B certification. Check the label of a showroom unit or contact the manufacturer for the FCC certification number. (See chapter 9 for more on rfi.)

Appropriate design Look for units that are compact and efficient in their use of materials. Evaluate your office furniture and spatial arrangements and make sure that you have the appropriate desks, lighting, ventilation, etc., for the unit.

Recyclability Find out if the plastics used to make the equipment are tagged with plastic identification numbers. These numbers make it easy to sort and recycle the parts.

These are green features to look for in a CPU:

Low energy consumption The CPU should display the EPA's Energy Star logo, which indicates that it uses as little electricity as possible (see chapter 4).

Compact design Smaller CPUs use less plastic and other resources than big behemoths with lots of empty space inside.

Here are green features to look for in a monitor:

Conforms to MPR 2 or TCO Make sure the monitor conforms to one of these Swedish standards for low-frequency EM field emissions (see chapter 9).

Clear, glare-free screen & adjustable base Make sure the monitor has an antiglare coating and a tilt-swivel base so you can adjust it for the best ergonomic position (see chapter 8).

Here are green features to look for in a printer:

Long-lasting consumables Ask how long the ribbon, inkjet cartridge, toner cartridge, imaging drum, and other components of the printer will last. Will they have to be frequently replaced, creating additional solid waste (and costing you a bundle)?

Uses plain paper The printer should use plain paper that's easy to recycle—not hard-to-recycle thermal paper.

Low or no ozone emissions The printer should produce no ozone or come with a changeable ozone filter.

Low sound pollution Impact printers should be equipped with internal acoustic shielding (see chapter 9) to keep noise to a minimum.

Buy from environmentally responsible PC companies

When you go shopping for PC products, take into account the environmental reputation of the manufacturer. Does the company use environmentally responsible packaging materials? Does it directly support green causes and organizations? Are green principles part of the company's strategic vision? Is the company a major polluter and, if so, does it have a plan for improvement?

Also, look to see if companies offer programs that encourage the green use and disposal of their products. In Germany, companies have "womb-to-tomb" responsibility for the environmental effects of what they manufacture. In the United States, most companies give little thought to the environmental problems created by their products after the sale.

A few environmentally responsible companies have developed programs to help consumers deal with PC waste. It's worthwhile to ask such questions as: Does your notebook manufacturer offer a battery recycling program? Does your laser manufacturer sponsor a toner-cartridge return program? Does the company provide explicit information on other ways its products can be recycled or reused?

Unfortunately, there's no publication or resource that monitors the environmental policies and actions of the computer industry, and gathering this kind of information for yourself takes time and trouble. Only you can decide if you want to make the effort. The information in the chapter will at least get you started.

Most major PC and peripheral manufacturers now have programs for reducing manufacturing pollution and for complying with the EPA's increasingly stringent requirements for safe disposal of hazardous waste. However, many smaller companies around the world are serious offenders, and they're getting away with it. For more information, you can monitor EcoNet for computer-related pollution and safety problems that make the news, or contact the Silicon Valley Toxics Coalition for information on specific companies. (See chapter 10 for how to contact the SVTC, as well as more information on pollution and safety in PC manufacturing and what companies are doing about it. Chapter 12 has more information on EcoNet.)

Certainly, you'll want to patronize companies that are trying to clean up their manufacturing act. But some computer manufacturers go farther by incorporating green principles into their strategic goals. You'll know a company is committed to environmental issues when it issues a public pro-environment statement of principles. Such companies often support green organizations directly with donations of equipment and grants of cash. (Whether the company is actually complying with its own goals is another matter, but most make the attempt.)

Donation programs can be quite creative. For example, several laser printer manufacturers accept used toner cartridges from owners of their laser printers and make a small donation to environmental organizations for each toner cartridge returned. Hewlett-Packard and Canon donate 50 cents per cartridge to the Nature Conservancy and the National Wildlife Federation. B&B Electronics donates money to a nature organization with each sale of its energy-saving device, Green Keeper (see chapter 4).

As an example of what computer companies can do for the environment, let's look at the environmental policies of three well-known names in personal computing: Apple, IBM, and Microsoft:

Apple Computer Apple considers itself a cutting-edge company, and it has a well-developed environmental program. A 1990 statement of principles signed by former Apple chairman and CEO John Sculley pledged Apple's commitment to assume "a leadership position" in environmental health and safety issues. Among Apple's objectives are:

- To comply with all federal, state, and local environmental regulations in all countries in which Apple does business.
- To adopt a corporate standard for health and environmental protection when laws don't exist or are inadequate.
- To provide safe operations and products.
- To anticipate and deal with future environmental, health, and safety risks.

Like many large organizations, Apple already has an internal recycling program for paper, cardboard, glass, and cans. According to a 1991 statement by David Skinner, head of Apple's internal recycling program, the company is "looking at savings of more than $150,000 a year on waste disposal costs." Apple also has in place two consumer-outreach recycling programs: one for used Macintosh Portable and Powerbook batteries, the other for spent toner cartridges from Apple laser printers. (See chapters 3 and 6 for more about these programs.) To meet the requirements of California's Clean Air Act, Apple is sponsoring programs that foster alternative ways to commute to work, including company-sponsored shuttle buses, telecommuting, ride sharing, and bicycling.

Apple has a well-funded philanthropy program and has been donating PCs to a variety of nonprofit organizations for years. In 1992, the company participated in a program with the Environmental Support Center to donate Macintosh computers to 100 grass-roots environmental organizations. Apple also announced a group of grants called EarthGrants, in which the company donates high-end Macintosh systems to nonprofit groups and universities for environmental research and education. For information on how to contact Apple for grants or other environmental information, see the Green-PC resources section.

IBM International Business Machines, for years a major polluter in the Silicon Valley area (see chapter 10), is also a pioneer in pollution prevention. The company has had a formal environmental program since the late 1960s, incorporating one of the most thorough sets of guidelines on environmental issues by any business anywhere in the world. In fact, IBM has a formal, written policy for nearly every corporate activity.

IBM Corporate Policy 139 on Environmental Affairs, issued in 1990, states in part that "IBM is committed to environmental affairs leadership in all of its business activities. IBM has longstanding corporate policies of providing a safe and healthful workplace and safe products, protecting the environment, and conserving energy and natural resources." Policy 139 further states that IBM's corporate environmental objectives include:

- Being an environmentally responsible neighbor.
- Practicing energy conservation and recycling.
- Using development and manufacturing processes that don't harm the environment.
- Designing products that are safe and energy-efficient and that can be recycled.
- Assisting in the development of technological solutions to global environmental problems.
- Conducting rigorous environmental audits and self-assessments.

A 1992 IBM internal memo added: "IBM feels an obligation to use our resources for the benefit of humanity. Conservation of energy and natural resources is financially as well as socially responsible."

To aid IBM's movement toward environmental responsibility, the company founded the IBM Engineering Center for Environmentally Conscious Products (ECECP) in November 1991. The center works with all IBM companies to enhance new products' environmental attributes and to emphasize the reuse of materials in existing products. ECECP was a key source of expertise in plastics recycling and "design for disassembly" for the designers of the PS/2 E, IBM's first Energy Star computer. (See chapter 4 for more on the PS/2 E and Energy Star.)

IBM also has extensive internal recycling programs. The company is a major consumer of almost every type of material used in making electronics, and its savings from conservation and recycling are similarly large, even in seemingly trivial items. One IBM site has saved one million paper cups per year since it switched to reusable plastic "IBM cups." Overall, the company recycles more than half the wood, metal, paper, glass, and plastics from its worldwide manufacturing sites.

IBM is one of the world's most generous corporate philanthropists. In 1992, the company distributed some $25 million in grants of cash and computing equipment to universities and research institutions studying environmental problems. Two annual environmental action awards are presented by IBM to its own employees: the Environmental Affairs Technical Excellence Award, presented to employees for technical and innovative accomplishments that further the company's environmental objectives; and the IBM Chairman's Environmental Affairs Citation, presented to the two IBM locations that have contributed the most to IBM's environmental, health, and safety programs. To contact IBM for more information, see the address in the Green-PC resources section.

Microsoft Microsoft, primarily a software developer, faces few of the hardware-related pollution issues that bedevil a company like IBM. But Microsoft is one of the world's biggest sellers of floppy disks, and it consumes millions of pounds of paper to manufacture software boxes, books, manuals, registration cards, promotional materials, and anything else that has to do with the business of being the world's biggest software company and one of the biggest publishers of books about computers.

In contrast to IBM, where every action is governed by a published policy, Microsoft is run informally. Corporate management isn't fond of statements or guidelines, so there's no formal corporate policy on the environment. Nor are Microsoft officials on record as expressly supporting environmental initiatives in the PC industry.

However, there are several unofficial initiatives in place. Recycling programs at Microsoft's plants handle plastics and hundreds of tons of paper. Some paper packaging used in Microsoft products is derived from the company's own scrap. The use of foam peanuts in Microsoft packaging was finally ended in August 1992, a decision that was expected to pay for itself within six months. According to a source at the company, Microsoft is considering using recycled paper in its manuals and providing a way for consumers to return used software packaging to Microsoft dealers, but is unlikely to do so unless pressured by consumers.

At Microsoft's main facilities outside Seattle, programmers and office workers recycle 300 tons of paper, plastics, cans, and other materials. Grass clippings from the surrounding lawns are composted, and CFCs from air-conditioning systems are collected and recycled.

Microsoft doesn't have as extensive a philanthropy program as IBM, but it does give to some environmental causes. Recently, the company donated 4,000 copies of Microsoft Works software and 4,000 Microsoft mice to the East-West Educational Development Foundation (see chapter 6). The software was packaged with recycled PCs and distributed to charities in the United States and Eastern Europe. For more information, contact Microsoft at the address in the Green-PC resources section.

Look for green-PC packaging

The kind of packaging a PC vendor uses is a good measure of its commitment to environmental responsibility. Some companies employ the easiest or least expensive packaging solution; others try to use green packaging. Obviously, the greenest product packaging is no packaging at all, but that's not a practical solution for PCs and other fragile electronic equipment, which must be cushioned during transport. Nor can software developers be expected to sell loose disks. Given that PCs, peripherals, and software have to be packaged in some way, the ideal packaging should at least be minimal, reusable, recyclable, degradable, and made from recycled products.

Few kinds of packaging meet all those criteria. In fact, deciding whether a particular packaging technology is or isn't environmentally benign can be difficult. The entire life-cycle effect of a packaging technology must be considered, from the creation of the papers and plastics used in the packaging to the environmental impact of the package's disposal. Often, there's no data to help you make an intelligent choice. The Boston-based Tellus Institute is currently conducting life-cycle studies of packaging in 60 product categories, including electronics. The first results from these studies were made available in 1993 and should go a long way toward helping manufacturers and consumers choose the greenest possible packaging. Meanwhile, we'll all have to make the best decisions we can based on what's currently known.

Many companies are looking for ways to save money on packaging. In a surprising number of cases, this can have environmental benefits, too. Toshiba America Information Systems, for example, which recently redesigned its cardboard boxes for PCs, claims that the old boxes required 60% more cardboard than the new ones. The money Toshiba saved in packaging will be spent on developing more cutting-edge products.

Toshiba also replaced hard-to-recycle polystyrene component trays—the packaging inside a box that holds small parts like cables, disks, spare bulbs, and so on—with easy-to-recycle cardboard trays. IBM and Apple have stopped using boxes made of bleached white paper laminated to a cardboard backing. The bleaching process, studies have shown, releases toxic organo-chlorine compounds into the waste stream. The new unbleached boxes, which are made from recycled materials, cost less to manufacture and are more attractive to environmentally conscious consumers.

Let's face it. There's not too much you can do to reduce the environmental effects of PC packaging before you buy a product. If you shop at a computer store, you might get to see the box before you pay your money, but then again, you might not. If you shop by mail or online, you won't see the package at all until it arrives on your doorstep. In either case, you won't see what packaging is inside the box before you open it. So your best bet is to contact the companies whose products you use. Let them know whether or not you're happy with their packaging, and suggest new green packaging approaches. Many manufacturers maintain discussion areas on the major online services. For more information, see the section on online shopping in this chapter.

Here are some guidelines to follow when you're trying to decide whether packaging is green or not, and what to do with it when the packaging is all yours.

Is the product overpackaged? Some manufacturers seem to have a mania for excessive packaging. It's not uncommon to find software manuals shrink-wrapped inside software boxes that are themselves shrink-wrapped. Contact manufacturers and urge them to reduce the amount of packaging they use.

Is the packaging made of green materials? Look for PC packaging incorporating the following materials:

- Cardboard boxes that are made of recycled, unbleached, unlaminated stock and designed to reduce or eliminate the need for foam packaging. The box should prominently display both recycling symbols: the "may be recycled" symbol (three arrows chasing each other around a triangle) and the "made from recycled materials" symbols (three arrows on a dark circular background).
- Packaging materials that aren't colored red or yellow. Red and yellow inks often contain cadmium, a toxic heavy metal.
- Alternatives to foam peanuts, such as recycled shredded paper, recyclable tissue paper, and molded cardboard.
- Alternatives to polystyrene packaging trays, such as trays made from recycled and recyclable paper or cardboard. However, it is unrealistic at this point to expect heavy hardware like CPUs and laser printers to ship without serious cushioning—and that means foam.
- Biodegradable shrink-wrap and poly bags, or—better yet—no plastic film packaging at all.

Are you recycling & reusing packaging materials? Once the packaging is yours, deal with it responsibly. Keep the box, poly bags, and foam inserts to transport your PC or peripherals. Store software in the original box, if you have room. Recycle what you can't keep. See chapter 6 for further suggestions on green-PC recycling.

Buy through green channels

It's not just what you buy that's important, but also how you buy it. There are three main retail channels through which you can buy PC equipment and software today: computer stores, mail-order catalogs, and online shopping services. From the green-PC point of view, each of these has its advantages and disadvantages, depending on what you're planning to buy. The green-PC consumer chooses the channel that minimizes the environmental costs.

Here are some suggestions for the greenest ways to buy PCs, as well as tips on how to minimize the drawbacks of direct-sales channels.

Try a computer store

You might think that there are no circumstances in which you should get into your car and head to a computer store. What about the waste of gas, exhaust pollution, traffic, and all that? Plus, everything you might want to buy and more can be had from direct retail channels like mail order.

But some components, such as monitors, keyboards, trackballs, and graphics tablets, interact closely with your body. They have to fit you and the way you work. All the written descriptions and photos in the world won't tell you what you need to know about them—how a keyboard feels, or whether you like the overall color cast of a monitor. You really have to try them before you buy them, and you can only do that in a store. So before you pick up the phone and call a mail-order vendor, pick up the phone and call your local computer store. See if they can set you up with a test-drive of the hardware you're interested in. If you want to buy it, then bargain with them until the price is close to what mail-order firms charge.

What about the money-back guarantees of mail-order vendors? Why can't you just order a monitor or a keyboard by phone and then return it if it doesn't work out? Ecologically, that's a lousy practice. You'll have shipped the product twice, with all the pollution that entails, and still have nothing to show for it. And returning the product is likely to cost you money; you'll be paying shipping both ways and probably a restocking fee, too.

Use mail order

Mail ordering (which really should be called phone ordering, since most of it is done by phone, although the catalog comes by mail) is quickly becoming the main channel of PC commerce. According to the research firm Dataquest, Inc., the number of PCs sold by mail and phone order doubled between 1991 and 1992. Today, hundreds of computer companies offer thousands of products to anyone who can dial a toll-free call and provide a credit-card number. Millions of PCs and peripherals and tens of millions of software packages are shipped to mail-order customers every year.

On the whole, mail order is better for the environment than everyone hopping in their cars and heading off to the local computer store or down the highway to the mall. Any time telecommunications replaces travel, the environment benefits.

But the benefits are lessened considerably by the extra volume of cardboard boxes, bubble-pack, packing slips, packing tape, stick-on plastic envelopes, and foam loose-fill peanuts that have to be used. Remember, mail-order firms box their wares, which are already in manufacturer's packaging, with yet another layer of packaging. Much of this extra packaging is due to shipper regulations that require double layers of packing material to avoid damage to electronic products in transit. The rest is due to wasteful practices by mail-order companies that overpackage products with ecologically unsound materials like foam peanuts and unrecycled cardboard. And, of course, there are the millions of paper catalogs mailed out each season by mail-order firms, consuming huge amounts of paper and ink.

Of the larger mail-order companies, PC Connection/MacConnection appears to have the most highly developed pro-environment policy. The PC Connection and MacConnection catalogs are printed on recycled paper, and the company uses cardboard boxes with high recycled-material content. Instead of foam peanuts, it uses a biodegradable packing tissue made at two local mills from PC Connection's own waste paper, which is nearly 100% postconsumer waste. In addition, the company recycles nearly all its own office paper and has renovated existing structures for office space rather than building new ones. It even has an environmental research specialist on staff.

PC Connection/MacConnection has found that a reputation for environmental responsibility is a valuable marketing advantage. In a 1990 interview, the company's cofounder, Pat Gallup, described how PC Connection/MacConnection responded to the hundreds of complaints it had received from customers about the foam peanuts the company formerly used. "This is a way to show our customers that we're listening to them," she said. "Our competitors will have to respond by adopting similar shipping methods." (To contact PC Connection/MacConnection, see the Green-PC resource section.)

The case of PC Connection/MacConnection shows that mail-order firms are sensitive to customer suggestions, so if you don't like the way the company you buy from packs its wares, complain about it. Send faxes and use the vendor's toll-free order number to make your views known.

Stop duplicate catalog mailings Once you start buying computer products online or by mail, as suggested above, your name and address will become very valuable. Vendors will eagerly sell information about you to firms that compile mailing lists for direct-mail marketers—resulting in a rapid increase of the amount of computer-related junk mail in your mailbox. If you've been purchasing PC equipment by mail for a year or so, chances are that hardly a day goes by without a piece of PC-related junk mail appearing in your mailbox. Do you want that stuff added to all the other junk mail you deal with? According to *E Magazine*, each U.S. consumer receives 17 trees worth of unwanted mail a year, which adds 2 million tons of waste paper to landfills and incinerators.

Often, you'll receive more than one copy of a mail-order catalog; some less-than-intelligent mailing-label printing programs don't scan for duplicate addresses or names. Call the cataloger's toll-free number and let the operator know you're getting duplicates. Or pass on the extra catalog to a friend.

Get off mailing lists Some mail-order firms give you the opportunity to remove your name from their mailing lists, but most don't bother, figuring you don't care or don't mind having to deal with hundreds of extra mailings per year. You could call each offending cataloger or direct mailer, asking to be taken off its list. This will take you hours, maybe days, and it probably won't work because any direct mailer who actually takes you off its list might simply buy a new list with your name on it at some future point.

Or you can write to the Direct Marketing Association's Mail Preference Service (MPS). Write a letter containing your name, address and any additional names at that address that you want removed from junk mailing lists and send it to:

Mail Preference Service
Direct Marketing Association
P.O. Box 9008
Farmingdale, NY 11735-9008

You will notice a decrease in your junk mail beginning about three months after your name is entered into the MPS system. However, you can't request deletion from specific lists through MPS. If there are any companies that you do want to get mail from, contact them directly and let them know that you want to be kept on their "in-house" list only. That way, you'll continue to receive the mailings you want, but your name will not be released to other direct marketers.

Order online Mail order, while better than store hopping, isn't the greenest way to shop. Online computer shopping via a commercial online information service provides all the environmental advantages of mail order, with the additional plus that no paper mail-order catalog is required. In fact, quite a few of the same companies that run mail-order businesses also offer online ordering.

Online vendors set up their "stores" in special areas provided by CompuServe and other online services. Once you navigate to the service's shopping area, you have access to each vendor's online catalog and ordering system. You can find detailed descriptions, vital statistics, and prices for thousands of products, far more than can be included in most paper catalogs. By using e-mail, you can get instant advice on products from the vendor or the manufacturer without having to deal with salespeople. And once you've placed an order, you get instant confirmation that it has been received and is being processed.

There are two drawbacks to online PC shopping. One is that so far only a small fraction of all PC manufacturers, developers, and vendors offer online ordering. The other is that for some services there's a surcharge of up to $22.80 an hour, making it an expensive way to shop for small purchases. As more people shop online, however, shopping surcharges will likely be dropped altogether, just as PC mail-order companies now offer free catalogs and toll-free order numbers.

CompuServe Electronic Mall CompuServe's Electronic Mall, the world's largest online shopping service, is free of connect-time charges, making it a relatively inexpensive way to shop. You can order direct from such major mail-order catalogs as PC Warehouse/MacWarehouse and PC Zone/Mac Zone, as well as from companies, such as Computer Express, that operate only online. In all, the CompuServe Mall includes about 30 vendors. Call 800-848-8199 for CompuServe customer service and information on how to enroll. If you're already logged on to CompuServe, type GO MALL at the prompt.

Other online shopping sources America OnLine, GEnie, and Prodigy also offer online shopping, though their "virtual malls" aren't yet as extensive as CompuServe's. America OnLine's shopping service is free for the first two hours, then costs 10 cents a minute. Call America OnLine at 800-827-6364, ext. 5883, for an enrollment kit. If you're already logged on to the service, go to the Travel and Shopping department. GEnie's shopping service is free evenings and weekends. Call 800-638-9636 for sign-up information. Prodigy's shopping service is also free. Contact Prodigy at 800-776-3449.

ZiffNet offers a Buyers' Market, Buyers' Digests, Demos Showcase, and other shopping services—but for a price of up to $22.80 an hour. Call 800-666-0330 for a free sign-on kit, or type GO ZIFFNET if you're on CompuServe. ZiffNet is also on the Prodigy online service. Contact Prodigy at 800-776-3449, or jump ZIFFNET if you're already logged on.

Shop by CD-ROM Buying software can be a wasteful and frustrating process. Chances are you've bought one or more programs that didn't work as advertised or didn't suit the way you work. No matter how unhappy you are, however, you can't return software once it's been opened, and there's generally no guarantee for the quality of a software product beyond replacing bad disks. Because most PC users have had this experience at least once in their computing lives, the problem of "bad-fitting" software results in millions of junked boxes, manuals, registration cards, cardboard inserts, disks, and shrink-wrap, plus the waste of the resources used to manufacture and distribute the package.

To address the problem, many commercial developers offer demonstration versions that let you try out program features for free. Unfortunately, it's hard to find all the demos you'd like to see, and it's expensive to download them from online services or order them from developers. And you still have to buy the overpackaged versions at a store or by mail.

To the rescue come CD-ROM collections of software that make application shopping easier, quicker, and far less wasteful. Several companies, including manufacturers like IBM and Apple, distributors like Ingram and Merisel, and developers such as Time-Warner Interactive, now offer CD-ROMs encoded with the full versions of many popular software programs in an encrypted form. Interactive demo versions of each program are included. After trying the demos, if you decide to purchase a program, you call a toll-free number and "buy" a password that unlocks the program of your choice and lets you download it from the CD-ROM.

The green advantages of such a system are obvious. Since all the software, including documentation, is on a CD, there are no boxes, paper manuals, or shrink-wrap. (All the packaging and documentation for 80 programs, a typical number included in one of these CDs, makes a pile 20 feet high and weighs about 150 pounds.) There's no shipping, either, a big savings in gas and air pollution. And buying by disk is convenient. The customer can have any piece of software immediately, just by making a phone call.

Where do you get one of these CDs? One or more is bundled with nearly every new CD-ROM drive. Publishers are also giving them away as promotional items, packaging them with other software, and selling them direct, usually for less than $10.

Contact manufacturers online

Hundreds of PC companies, especially software developers, maintain e-mail addresses and forums on the major online services. Send e-mail directly to the manufacturer's technical assistance department, and you'll get quicker responses to your complaints, questions, and suggestions than if you sent a letter or try to call by phone. To give you an idea of the extent of online developer resources, here's a list of more than 100 companies maintaining folders on America OnLine (a Macintosh-oriented service):

Aatrix Software
Access Software
Activision
Advanced Gravis
Affinity Microsystems
Aladdin Systems
Aldus Corp.
Altsys Corp.
Alysis Software
Applied Engineering
Argosy Software
Ariel Publishing
Articulate Systems
Asymetrix Corp.
Baseline
BLOC Development
BioScan
Bowers Development
Broderbund
Byte Works
Caere Corp.
CE Software
Claris Corp.
Computer Peripherals
CoStar
DacEasy
Davidson and Associates
Dayna Communications
Dell Computer Corp.
Digital Research
Digital Vision
Direct Software
Dove Computer Corp.
DUBL-Click Software
Electric Image
Emigre Fonts
Farallon
Fifth Generation
FontBank
Gateway 2000
GCC Technologies
General Magic
GeoWorks
Global Village Communications
Graphisoft
Gryphon Software
Inline Design
Infocom
Iomega
Kent*Marsh
Kiwi Software
Koala
Language Systems
Leading Edge
Letraset
LucasArts
Macromedia
Maxis
Micro Dynamics

Micrografx
MicroMat Computer Systems
Micron Technology
MicroProse Software
Microseeds Publishing
Microsoft
Mirror Technologies
New Era Software Group
Now Software
Object Factory
Olduvai Software
ON Technology
Origin Systems
Personal Computer Peripherals Company
Pixar
Portfolio
Power Up!
ProVUE Development
Quark
Radius
Reactor
Salient
Shiva Corp.
Sierra On-Line
Softek Design
Softsync
Software Publishing Corp.
Spectrum Holobyte
Specular International
Strata
Strategic Simulations
SuperMac
Symantec
TechnologyWorks
TGS Systems
T/Maker
Unlimited Adventures
Virtus
The Voyager Co.
Westwood Studios
WordPerfect
Working Software
Zedcor

Use the power of many

The coordinated actions of PC user groups, professional associations, and environmental organizations can effectively steer PC manufacturers and developers toward environmental responsibility. The movers and shakers of the computer industry might not be interested in what you as an individual consumer have to say about green computing, but 100 or 1,000 voices are more likely to be heard, especially if it's clear that your group is buying products only from environmentally responsible vendors.

Let PC companies know your group's opinion on their actions and their products, and tell them that, as a group, you'll make purchasing decisions with the environment in mind. Your group might be more effective if you target a narrow range of green computing issues, such as getting companies to reduce manufacturing pollution or encouraging them to use environmentally responsible packaging. Be sure to provide concrete suggestions for ecologically sound alternatives.

Post messages on companies' BBSs and online forums or mount a fax-modem campaign until you get a response. Even better, coordinate your actions via e-mail with other groups on environmental issues of common interest. Chapter 12 lists the environmental areas of major online services, where you'll find like-minded PC users.

Choices that make a difference

- ❒ Evaluate the environmental responsiveness of vendors before you buy.
- ❒ Buy PC products with designs and packaging that are minimal, recyclable, and made from recycled products.
- ❒ Buy through green sales channels like mail and online ordering.
- ❒ Reduce PC-related junk mail.
- ❒ Let companies know your opinion of their actions and products.
- ❒ Organize into consumer groups for greater green influence.

Green-PC resources

To find out more about the environmental programs of Apple, IBM, and Microsoft, contact:
Apple Clean Earth Campaign
Apple Customer Assistance Center
800-776-2333, and 416-477-5800 in Canada
Community Affairs Department
Apple Computer, Inc.
20525 Mariani Ave.
Cupertino, CA 95014
(408) 974-1109
Apple EarthGrants
408-974-7825

IBM Corp.
Old Orchard Rd.
Armonk, NY 10504
914-765-1900

Microsoft Corp.
One Microsoft Way
Redmond, WA 98052
206-882-8080, fax 206-883-8101

The following mail-order firms carry green-PC products and have incorporated green principles into their business goals:
Earth Care Paper
Ukiah, CA 95482
800-347-0070

PC Connection/MacConnection
8 Mill St.
Marlow, NH 03456
800-800-5555 (PC Connection) and 800-800-2222 (MacConnection)

Real Goods Trading Company
966 Mazzoni St.
Ukiah, CA 95482
800-762-7325

Contact the Direct Marketing Association to have your name removed from mailing lists:
Mail Preferences Service
Direct Marketing Association
11 W. 42nd St.
P.O. Box 3861
New York, NY 10163

Journals aimed directly at the ecoconsumer include:
The Boycott Monthly
Center for Economic Democracy
P.O. Box 64
Olympia, WA 98507
Tells which groups are boycotting which products, and why.

Green MarketAlert
MarketAlert Publications
345 Wood Creek Rd.
Bethlehem, CT 06751
203-266-7209
Tracks the impact of green consumerism on business; covers marketing, advertising, government regulation, and more.

14

The green-PC advocate

CHAPTER 14

BEING a green-PC consumer, as described in the previous chapter, can be part of a larger endeavor on behalf of the environment. You can join the growing number of people who use their PCs as instruments of environmental advocacy. An advocate, according to *Webster's Third International Dictionary*, is someone who "argues for, defends, maintains, or recommends a cause or proposal." Today, PCs have become vital to the work of advocates in all fields, including the environment.

The unparalleled data-processing ability of PCs makes advocacy on behalf of the environment more effective. PCs enable one person to do the work of many, and enable small advocacy groups to do the work of large organizations. Using the power of computer networks, green-PC advocates can easily coordinate their efforts to tackle environmental problems around the world.

How can you use your PC to further environmental causes? The first step is to choose an environmental group and become active in it. Here are some ways you can help them become more effective, especially if you join a local or grass-roots group that relies on volunteer effort:

- Use your computer skills to help computerize your green organization, if it hasn't been computerized already, and make sure members are informed about green computing issues and solutions.
- Create a lean, responsive organization by linking distant coworkers with electronic mail.
- Go online to research information, publish your own reports, and make contact with other environmental advocates.
- Use online services and fax modems to lobby corporate and government officials about environmental issues.

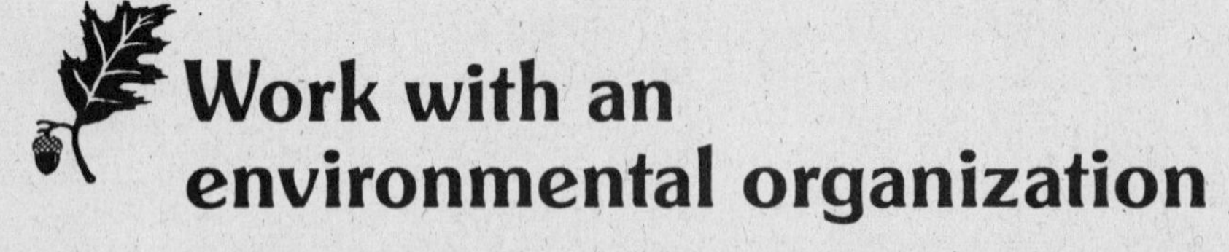

Work with an environmental organization

Your energy and computing skills can be an important part of finding solutions to the environmental problems of your town, state, country, and world. But no matter how committed you are, there's a limit to what you can accomplish on your own. If you don't already support an environmental organization, find one that interests you and get on board. Don't just send money. Give your time.

You might want to start by joining a group in your own community. You'll find local groups by reading the local papers and looking for notices on school and library bulletin boards. Working with a small group that's actively solving local environmental problems will give you hands-on experience that can be hard to get with a larger group. Your computer expertise will be welcomed and could make a big difference to a small group with limited computer know-how and few technical resources.

On the other hand, larger, established groups have more to offer. Many have volunteer and internship programs that might appeal to you. You can also work within the organization to make sure it's alert to green computing issues, such as energy conservation and paperlite computing (see chapters 3, 4, and 5 for more).

Selected green organizations

Following is a list of some of the better-known environmental organizations in the United States. Most can be contacted online via EcoNet, the only online information service dedicated exclusively to the environment. (For more on EcoNet, see chapter 12.) Organizations maintaining "offices" on EcoNet and other online services are specified.

Note that there's currently no grass-roots environmental organization dedicated to green computing. Perhaps you'll want to start one.

Acid Rain Foundation
1410 Varsity Dr.
Raleigh, NC 27606
919-828-9443
Focuses on global atmospheric issues, especially acid rain.

Alliance to Save Energy
1725 K St., NW, Suite 509
Washington, DC 20006
202-857-0666
Promotes fossil-fuel conservation, home-energy conservation, cogeneration, and other energy conservation measures.

Citizens Clearinghouse for Hazardous Waste, Inc.
Center for Environmental Justice
Rowell Court
P.O. Box 6806
Falls Church, VA 22040
703-237-2249
Up-to-date information on hazardous waste products, sites, and cleanup efforts can be obtained from this group, which also has an active litigation program.

Clean Water Action
1320 18th St., NW
Washington, DC 20036
202-457-1286, fax 202-457-0287
Works for clean and safe water, pollution control, and conservation of groundwater, wetlands, and coastal waters.

Conservation International
1015 18th St., NW, Suite 1000
Washington, DC 20036
202-429-5660, fax 202-887-5188
The aim of Conservation International is to conserve ecologies worldwide. It sponsors programs in 21 countries and offers many volunteer opportunities.

Earth Island Institute
300 Broadway, Suite 28
San Francisco, CA 94133
415-788-3666, fax 415-788-7324
Publishes *Earth Island Journal* and offers international programs to preserve and restore the global environment. It maintains an EcoNet office.

EarthTrust
2500 Pali Hwy.
Honolulu, HI 96817
MCI Mail user name: earthtrust
EarthTrust, an international organization linked by e-mail, focuses on international wildlife protection, with a particular concern for marine mammals.

Energy Conservation Coalition
1525 New Hampshire Ave., NW
Washington, DC 20036
202-745-4873
Promotes energy conservation at home and in business.

Environmental Action Coalition
625 Broadway
New York, NY 10012
212-677-1601
and
1525 New Hampshire Ave., NW
Washington, DC 20036
202-745-4870
A coalition of groups working for environmental change. It attracts committed activists and also has many volunteer opportunities. EAL maintains an EcoNet office.

Environmental Defense Fund
257 Park Ave. South
New York, NY 10010
212-505-2100
and
1616 P St., NW, Suite 150
Washington, DC 20036
202-387-3500
Concentrates on developing economically viable methods of environmental protection. This group maintains an EcoNet office.

Environmental Support Center
1825 Connecticut Ave., NW, Suite 220
Washington, DC 20009
202-328-7813, fax 202-265-9419

The goal of the Environmental Support Center is to promote the regional and grass-roots programs of other environmental organizations; it pays for technical assistance and helps with planning and fund-raising. With Apple Computer, this group has donated computer equipment to small environmental groups.

Friends of the Earth
218 D St., SE
Washington, DC 20003
202-544-2600
FOE advocates global conservation and protection. It has effective lobbyists in Washington and the state capitals, mounts many national and international projects, and offers volunteer and internship programs.

Global Action & Information Network (GAIN)
575 Soquel Ave.
Santa Cruz, CA 95062
408-457-0130, fax 408-457-0133
A clearinghouse and network service for people taking action for sustainable development and environmental protection. Maintains an extensive list of files on AmericaOnLine.

Greenpeace USA
1436 U St., NW
Washington, DC 20009
202-462-1177
and
4649 Sunnyvale Ave., N.
Seattle, WA 98103
206-632-4326
Greenpeace is a direct-action environmentalist organization. Members have mounted highly visible, sometimes risky campaigns against nuclear-bomb production, the slaughter of marine mammals, and other causes. The organization provides extensive volunteer opportunities. Greenpeace runs its own bulletin board service, called EnviroNet (415-861-6503) and also maintains an office on EcoNet.

League of Conservation Voters
1707 L St., NW, Suite 550
Washington, DC 20036
202-785-8683, fax 202-835-0491
This voter group publishes information about the environmental records and actions of politicians. It maintains an office on EcoNet.

National Audubon Society
700 Broadway
New York, NY 10003
212-797-3000
and
645 Pennsylvania Ave., SE
Washington, DC 20003
202-547-9009
A mainstream conservation, wildlife, and environmental group. It publishes *Audubon* magazine and maintains an office on EcoNet.

National Resources Defense Council
40 W. 20th St.
New York, NY 10011
212-727-2700
Offers programs for research, education, and legal action on behalf of the environment, as well as legal and academic internships. It maintains an office on EcoNet.

National Wildlife Federation
1400 16th St., NW
Washington, DC 20036
202-797-6800, fax 202-797-6646
The goal of the NWF is to preserve habitats and species of wildlife. This group maintains an office on EcoNet.

The Nature Conservancy
1815 N. Lynn St.
Arlington, VA 22209
703-841-5300, 800-628-6860 for volunteer information
This well-funded and highly effective group purchases undeveloped lands and preserves them from development. It maintains an office on EcoNet.

Rainforest Action Network
450 Sansome St., Suite 700
San Francisco, CA 94111-3315
415-398-4404
The Rainforest Action Network works to preserve and protect the rain forests. Many volunteer and internship positions are available worldwide. Maintains an office on EcoNet.

Sierra Club
730 Polk St.
San Francisco, CA 94009
415-776-2211
A mainstream environmental and wildlands preservation organization. It publishes *Sierra* magazine and offers extensive volunteer opportunities. Maintains an office on EcoNet.

Student Conservation Association
P.O. Box 550
Charlestown, NH 03603
603-543-1700, fax 603-543-1828
Offers education for student volunteers in national parks, wildlife refuges, and other conservation areas. There are two major volunteer programs with 1,500 openings yearly.

Union of Concerned Scientists
26 Church St.
Cambridge, MA 02238
617-547-5552, fax 617-864-9405
Focuses on advanced technology issues, especially arms control and energy. Internships are available.

The Wilderness Society
900 17th St., NW
Washington, DC 20006
202-833-2300
Protects wildlife and ensures the conservation of federal lands. It maintains an office on EcoNet.

World Resources Institute
1709 New York Ave., NW, Suite 700
Washington, DC 20006
202-638-6300, fax 202-638-0036
Assists organizations in developing environmental policy.

Computerize your green organization

Most local and grass-roots environmental organizations are either undercomputerized or uncomputerized. Without PCs, members waste precious work hours and spend money that would be better put directly into environmental action. If you belong to such a group, you can use your PC savvy to computerize it and increase its effectiveness.

Getting the equipment

The first thing to do is to get PCs for each active member of the group. Everyone needs a PC to join the electronic mail network you'll create next (see the following section, Networking by e-mail). Equipping everyone with a PC doesn't have to be expensive; in fact, it can cost almost nothing. Most of your work can be accomplished with a used AT-class PC, a monochrome monitor, and a 2400-baud modem. A simple setup like that can be purchased for $200 to $300. You might be able to get donations of outdated PCs from computer user groups or businesses in your community, especially if you're working on a local environmental problem. (Chapter 6 has more information on buying and finding donors of used PCs.)

Grants

Several computer manufacturers have grant programs that can supply you with all the computing power you need. Apple Computer, for example, recently distributed Macintoshes to 100 grass-roots environmental groups. Some grant programs are aimed at organizations that require higher-tech computers to do desktop publishing, pollution modeling, satellite image analysis, weather studies, or other calculation-intensive work. Contact the public-affairs offices of large PC companies for information. (There's more about the grants programs of Apple and IBM in chapter 11.)

Software

Finding the right software is less of a problem. Your local user group has a collection of inexpensive application programs, including word processors, personal databases, and telecommunications programs. Many of these programs are shareware; that means if you decide to use them you send a modest fee, usually $25 or less, to the developer. Low-cost software is also available from every commercial online service and from many bulletin board services as well.

Networking by e-mail

Once your organization is computerized, you'll find new ways to make it more efficient, more responsive, and more connected with the environmental movement. The online networks carry a seemingly inexhaustible quantity of environmental information; there are dozens of online services and scores of online databases that you can use for research. Literally thousands of public and private electronic messages are exchanged between environmentalists every day. (See chapter 12 for more on online environmental resources.)

The first step toward plugging into the global network of environmental information is probably the hardest. Members who have made a definite commitment of time and energy should be linked together by e-mail (electronic messages exchanged via modem to and from "mailboxes" on an e-mail service). E-mail makes it possible for every member to send and receive messages, documents, press releases, and so on to every other group member. The instantaneous nature of e-mail means that you can receive a message or read a news item online and immediately respond. (E-mail is discussed in more detail in chapter 5.)

Making online contact

Electronic mail is offered by CompuServe, Prodigy, America OnLine, and other commercial online information services. The exact method of signing on and sending e-mail differs from service to service. (See chapter 12 for a list of online services and phone numbers where you can contact them for information.) Many environmentalists and environmental groups prefer to use the extensive e-mail capabilities and international directory of environmentalists that can be found on EcoNet. Members use EcoNet as a resource not just for gathering information, but also for making contact and developing working relationships with other environmentalists. According to EcoNet member W.J. "Rocky" Rohwedder, EcoNet is, "Not simply a data bank of information; it's a data bank of people." EcoNet has become a vital unifying force for the environmental movement as a whole.

Decentralizing

An environmental organization linked by e-mail reaps other benefits, too. As large environmental organizations have discovered, maintaining a central office in Washington or New York is incredibly expensive, consuming money that could otherwise be doing good for the environment. A networked organization can often do without a central office in a high-cost urban area. Instead, it can operate out of a multitude of online "offices" whose physical location is unimportant. Don White, the director of Earthtrust, a networked environmental group of volunteers who keep in touch with the main office in Honolulu via MCI Mail, believes that electronic mail has enabled his small organization to accomplish goals during the last two years that rival the achievements of organizations with 20 times Earthtrust's annual budget.

Quick response

As noted previously, e-mail also enables environmental organizations to respond quickly to ecological crises that are happening thousands of miles away. Your group can monitor the bulletin-board sections of online services for the latest postings. When news of a crisis is posted, you can quickly contact other members of your group by e-mail. Each member can respond with e-mail, letters, and faxes to the people dealing directly with the crisis. At the same time, your group can coordinate actions with other groups online around the world. In that way, local efforts can be combined into a national or international response to breaking events.

This is exactly what happened after the Exxon Valdez oil spill in 1989. Local Alaskans posted eyewitness reports of the spill on EcoNet and other online services. The reports were seen by environmental groups across the United States who were able to start mobilizing before the news media had picked up the story. These online reports were among the most important initial sources of information for the media as well, and undoubtedly helped them give this remote event a sense of immediacy for the American public.

Fax advocacy

Not every organization, journalist, agency, or official can be contacted online or by electronic mail. But nearly all of them have fax machines. That's why the fax has become the communications channel of choice for most advocacy groups. You can use your computer for fax advocacy, too. Equip your computer with a fax modem, and you can fax reports, press releases, newsletters, scanned photos, and other material from your PC directly to anyone with a fax machine.

Faxing is not as green as communicating by modem—see the discussion of faxing versus electronic mail in chapter 5—but it does offer many advantages over ordinary mail and phone contact. These include:

Convenience Faxing with a fax modem is easy—just switch on the fax modem, open the fax utility from within your word processor or other application, and send your message. You can dash off a letter or news release without leaving your PC or bothering with paper, envelopes, and stamps. If the line is busy, most fax modems will keep dialing until the connection is made.

Speed A fax transmission is nearly instantaneous. That all-important edge in speed can make the difference when you're lobbying your legislator on an imminent environmental vote or issuing a statement on a breaking event.

Cost A fax modem transmission is less expensive than a letter. A one-ounce first-class letter requires about 40 cents for stamp, a single piece of letter-sized paper, and an envelope, while a one-page transmission to anywhere in the United States costs about 15 cents. Most fax modems can send a document to many numbers at once, saving the cost of multiple mailings. After about 300 faxes, your organization will have paid off the fax modem, which can cost as little as $80.

Successful faxing

Not everyone wants to be faxed. Every advocacy group and individual activist under the sun has a fax machine and is using it to badger corporate and governmental officials. Some offices can't handle the load, and in self-defense ignore all but the most important faxes. Your fax might go directly to the circular file—a very ungreen situation.

If you're in doubt as to whether your fax will get through, here are a few steps you can take to increase your faxing success:

- Try calling by phone first to check courteously on the recipient's willingness to be faxed.
- Make sure you're sending it to the right person.
- Send the fax just before the recipient's office opens. You won't tie up the recipient's fax machine when office workers want to use it, and your fax will be sitting on top of the pile of faxes that came in overnight.
- Use an eye-catching fax design and make your text interesting to read. Interesting documents don't land in the trash as quickly. Use a large, clear typeface to spare your recipient's eyes.

- If your message is urgent, make sure it says so in big bold letters. Everyone else's fax will be urgent, too, but if yours isn't, it's likely to be lost in the shuffle.
- Follow up with a phone call to make sure the fax was received, then call again a day or two later to make sure it was read.

The environmental downside of faxing

Flooding the phone lines with faxes means that additional paper will be consumed by the many groups and officials who still use standard fax machines. And thermal fax paper isn't recyclable. Minimize the unnecessary use of fax paper by:

- Creating compact documents that use the minimum number of pages.
- Carefully proofreading documents before sending, to catch errors that might require a second transmission.
- Sending a main report only once and following up with one-page updates.
- Targeting your faxes carefully rather than broadcasting them widely.
- Using online contact whenever possible.

Also, make sure that your fax modem can receive as well as send paperless faxes, so that you don't waste paper at your end. Chapter 5 has more information on using a fax modem and minimizing paper use when faxing.

Choices that make a difference

- ❒ Work with local and national environmental organizations.
- ❒ Help computerize your green organization.
- ❒ Establish a communications network for your organization.
- ❒ Publish messages and information about environmental causes on online services.
- ❒ Network with other groups to increase your effectiveness.

Green-PC resources

Want to join a computer user group? Computer Shopper lists many in the United States.
Computer Shopper
One Park Ave.
11th Floor
New York, NY 10016

The U.S. Environmental Protection Agency not only offers an immense amount of green information free to individuals and organizations, but it's the only public agency that's doing something to promote green computing. Contact the EPA at:
Environmental Protection Agency
Public Information Center
401 M St., SW, PM-211B, S.E. Basement
Washington, DC 20460
202-382-2080, 202-382-4700, 202-475-7751

For information on international environmental issues and programs, call or write:
U.N. Environmental Programme
DC2-0803 United Nations
New York, NY 10017
212-963-8093

Books and journals that will aid green-PC advocates in their efforts include:
The Environmental Address Book
by Michael Levine
Putnam Publishing Group
200 Madison Ave.
New York, NY 10016
212-951-8510
Contains the names, addresses, and phone numbers of more than 2,000 people and organizations helping or harming the earth.

Environmental Grantmaking Foundations 1992
Environmental Data Research Institute (EDRI)
797 Elmwood Ave.
Rochester, NY 14620
800-724-1857, 716-473-3090, fax 716-473-0968
Tells who's giving money to environmental causes, who's getting it, and how the money is spent. The EDRI also maintains an extensive computer database of environmental grants.

Environmental Telephone Directory
Government Institutes, Inc.
4 Research Place, #200
Rockville, MD 20850
301-921-2323
Lists the names, numbers, and addresses of people and programs of interest to environmentalists.

Gale Environmental Sourcebook:
A Guide to Organizations, Agencies, and Publications
Gale Research Publishing
835 Penobscot Bldg.
Detroit, MI 48226-4094
800/877-GALE
Print and nonprint information sources on a wide variety of environmental topics.

The Nature Directory: A Guide to Environmental Organizations
by Susan D. Lanier-Graham
Walker and Company
720 Fifth Ave.
New York, NY 10019
212-265-3632

The U.S. Congress Handbook
U.S. Congress Handbook
Box 566
McLean, VA 22101
Gives the addresses, phone, and fax numbers for the Washington offices of senators and congressional representatives.

Your Resource Guide to Environmental Organizations
Edited by John Sereditch
Smiling Dolphins Press
4 Segura
Irvine, CA 92715
714-733-1065
150 environmental organizations, with contact information.

One Person's Impact
P.O. Box 751
Westborough, MA 01581
508-366-0146
This newsletter provides up-to-date action alerts and networking information.

These organizations will give you leadership training and help you find a job in a green organization:

Environmental Careers Organization, Inc.
286 Congress St.
Boston, MA 02210
617-426-4375

Institute for Conservation Leadership
2000 P St., NW, Suite 413
Washington, DC 20036
202-466-3330, fax 202-659-3897

Write Your Congressman! is a combination word processor, mailmerge program, and up-to-date database of U.S. senators, representatives, and their staffs. This is a good tool for small grass-roots organizations lobbying on national issues.
Write Your Congressman!
Contact Software International
1840 Hutton Dr., Suite 200
Carrollton, TX 75006
214-919-9500

Afterword

There are plenty of things you can do to minimize the damage PCs do to the environment. However, even the simple ones require you to make an effort of some kind, an expenditure of time or money or simple willpower. You can discipline yourself to turn off the monitor every night, or you can be easy on yourself and leave it running. You can take time to refill your laser printer's toner cartridge, or you can toss it in the trash can and be done with it. You can take the time to learn something about fax modems, or you can pick up more fax paper at the stationery store.

Considering all the demands that life places on every one of us, do we really need to bother with yet another set of problems? Can't we give ourselves a break and let the garbage and pollution experts worry about this one?

The choice is up to you. The decision to take responsibility for anything in this world, including green computing, rests entirely with each individual. There's no police force or IRS to make sure you're acting to conserve the environment. You have to decide for yourself that it's worth it.

Some people see dozens of documentaries about toxic waste and clear-cut forests and don't think twice about them. Other people become so anguished about ecological problems that they lose their perspective and look for a drastic solution.

Most of us are between these two poles. We recognize that the environment is threatened and want to help. But our capacity for action is limited because our resources of time, energy, and money are limited. We can quickly become overwhelmed by the enormity of a problem (and some environmental problems are enormously complex), or we can get confused by contradictory views among specialists. We can tolerate a certain degree of change in our lives, but there's a point beyond which we're unwilling to go.

If you have a genuine desire to make a difference when it comes to environmental damage from PCs, start at the beginning. Don't try to change all your computing routines overnight; it won't work. Take one thing at a time. If wasting paper bothers you the most, then start there. Give yourself some time to adjust to a new way of doing things. Then whenever you feel ready, evaluate your routines again. See if there's a new green-PC goal—saving energy, recycling batteries—that attracts you and toward which you can work. If you feel you can, move toward green-PC consumerism and then green-PC advocacy. Every effort in the right direction makes a difference.

Index

Index

Q

R

T

U

V

About the author

Steven Anzovin is a partner in the firm Anzovin & Podell of Amherst, Massachusetts, specializing in book project management, book and magazine writing and illustration, copywriting, computer graphics, multimedia programming, database design, and educational materials for the el-hi market. Since 1985 he has written or edited more than 20 books for Prentice-Hall, Compute H.W. Wilson, Facts on File, and others. His monthly column for *Compute!* magazine, "PathWays," formed the basis for the original edition of *The Green PC* (Windcrest, 1993). He holds an M.F.A. in Graphic and Video Arts from the Pratt Institute (New York) and is an Apple Certified Developer.

Other Bestsellers of Related Interest

Stacker®: An Illustrated Tutorial, 2nd Edition
—Dan Gookin
Covers all the new features of Stacker® for Windows and DOS, Version 3.0. A complete user's guide to the disk-doubling data compression software from STAC Electronics.
ISBN 0-8306-4487-3 $19.95 Paper

Stacker® for OS/2® & DOS: An Illustrated Tutorial
—Lisa Heller
Everything the manual doesn't tell you about how to install, customize, use, and troubleshoot Stacker 3.0-3.1. Also reveals instant solutions to eight of the most common problems reported to the Stac OS/2 support staff.
ISBN 0-07-027986-1 $19.95 Hard

Paperless Publishing
—Colin Haynes
This timely book is the only complete guide to electronic publishing, telling writers how to create, publish, and market their work online. Disk contains DOS-and Windows-compatible software.
ISBN 0-07-911895-X $27.95 Paper

Modems Made Easy
—David Hakala
Here it is-a first-time modem-user's guide to making modems work, including valuable information on installation, operation, and the growing world of online services and bulletin boards.
ISBN 0-07-881962-8 $16.95 Paper

The Essential Internet Information Guide
—Jason Manger
Everything users need to access and make the most of the services currently available on the Internet.
ISBN 0-07-707905-1 $27.95 Paper

The Internet Yellow Pages
—Harley Hahn and Rick Stout
Hobbyists, professionals, university users-The Internet Yellow Pages has something for everyone. The comprehensive listing of resources covers well over 100 categories.
ISBN 0-07-882023-5 $27.95 Paper

The Internet Complete Reference
—Harley Hahn and Rick Stout
This is the most complete guide to the world's largest international computer network. Includes a vast catalog of over 750 free Internet resources and information on how to get one month's free access on the Internet.
ISBN 0-07-881980-6 $29.95 Paper